THE
FEMININE
FACE OF GOD

THE FEMININE FACE OF GOD

The Unfolding of the Sacred

in Women

SHERRY RUTH ANDERSON
AND PATRICIA HOPKINS

 BANTAM BOOKS

New York Toronto London Sydney Auckland

THE FEMININE FACE OF GOD
A Bantam Book
PUBLISHING HISTORY
Bantam hardcover edition published October 1991
Bantam trade paperback edition/August 1992

Published simultaneously in the United States and Canada

Bantam Books are published by Bantam Books, a division of Bantam
Doubleday Dell Publishing Group, Inc. Its trademark, consisting of the
words "Bantam Books" and the portrayal of a rooster, is Registered in
U.S. Patent and Trademark Office and in other countries. Marca Re-
gistrada. Bantam Books, 666 Fifth Avenue, New York, New York 10103.

PRINTED IN THE UNITED STATES OF AMERICA

To my grandmother, Hannah Schell, who first
showed me the feminine face of God.

Patricia Hopkins

With gratitude to those who have gone before me,
Frances Shotz Anderson and Milton Anderson;
with blessings to those who will come after,
Margot Jane Rochester and Daphne Rochester-Goring,
and Nicholas, Catherine, and Jacob Anderson;
I dedicate this book.

Sherry Ruth Anderson

Acknowledgments

 Support for the writing of this book came from many sources and in many forms. First among these are the women whose stories form the basis of this book. For their gifts of frank and deep reflection on the experiences of a lifetime, and for their willingness to entrust us with these experiences, we are deeply grateful.

We are also indebted to those individuals and institutions who took a leap of faith and provided financial support for researching and writing this book: Anne-Marie Caple, Carol Davis, Sally DeFelice, Patricia Gibbs, Paul Green, the Institute of Noetic Sciences, Louis Just, Mary McCollum, the L. J. and Mary C. Skaggs Foundation, Phoebe V. Valentine, and Genevieve Vaughan. A special thanks is due Marsha Morrison, who not only brought our dreams and visions down to earth with her first check, but helped us contact others who were interested in funding this project. We also want to thank Gayle Lipsyte and Larry Spiro of the Melia Foundation, a nonprofit corporation that served as fiscal agent for this project.

For special services and support we wish to acknowledge Judy Bartels and Pauline Proschan, whose counsel in the beginning stages of this project was invaluable; Pauline Tesler for advising us on legal matters; and Dorothy Porter, Mary Ford, and Rob Lewis for letting us use their homes as writing sanctuaries. And for their ongoing encouragement, prayers, and humor we are grateful to our friends and sisters in the Tuesday-evening prayer group.

*   *   *

During the five years it took us to research and write this book there were also specific individuals for each of us whose friendship, interest, and belief in what we were doing renewed and sustained our efforts. In that category I am especially grateful to my sister, Earlene M. Sneller, Sandra Lewis, Toni Triest, Frances Vaughan, and Judith Skutch Whitson. Last, no list of acknowledgements would be complete for me without a posthumous thank you to William N. Thetford, whose integrity, simplicity, and humor continue to inform my life.

Patricia Hopkins

I especially want to acknowledge my friend and colleague, Joan McIntyre, for helping find the Shekhinah and for cocreating The Feminine Face of God workshops in 1984. Howard and Carol Anderson, Milton and Frances Anderson, Rick Anderson, and Arlene and George Hecht provided loving help when there seemed to be no place to stand. Oshienushisama and our friends at Sukyo Mahikari blessed us with their prayers. I remember with gratitude my friend Premal Gold whose avid interest in this work inspired and encouraged me. Finally, I thank my beloved husband, Paul Ray, for his courageous heart.

Sherry Ruth Anderson

Contents

Foreword
Jean Shinoda Bolen, M.D.

 The Feminine Face of God is as significant as Betty Friedan's The Feminine Mystique and Carol Gilligan's In a Different Voice were in articulating a growing edge of conscious awareness in women. The Feminine Face of God does for women's spirituality what these two books did for women's roles and women's ethics. I believe it may have an even deeper impact on individual women who, as a result of reading it, will be profoundly changed and quietly empowered to live authentic lives. This is a book that invites women to define for themselves what is sacred, to find an indwelling source of spiritual sustenance in themselves, in communion with others, and with the divine as they know It/Him/Her. The feminine face of God is an aspect of divinity and an approach to the sacred that is not exclusively of women, but women will naturally lead the way because women's receptivity, commitment to relationships, and biological experience provide greater opportunities for this kind of revelation.

Friedan's book spoke to us of how women were defined as inferior by social stereotypes and psychological theory, and were expected to live through others and not have an identity of their own. Women who had until then accepted male expert opinions on who they were, and inequality as the way things always would be, broke their individual silences to talk with one another. Consciousness-raising led to the women's movement, and our world changed. Gilligan's book described how women made ethical choices, and rather than being inferior to men in their ethical decisions as male experts had determined, differed from men in what guided them. In *The Feminine Face of God*, Sherry Anderson and Patricia Hopkins provide us with a perspective on the sacred dimension in women's lives, which differs from patriarchal theology. It begins as the women's movement began, with women telling the truth about their lives.

Ever since I wrote *Goddesses in Everywoman* as a psychology of women, and found it unexpectedly becoming a text on women's spirituality because women found that a sacred dimension enters everyday life when outer life is an expression of inner archetypal life, I've witnessed a pervasive, quiet, grass-roots evolution in women's spiritual lives that *The Feminine Face of God* documents and delves into. By themselves, and in groups, women are exploring the spiritual dimension of their lives, praying, meditating, creating ritual, and paying attention to their dreams, symbols, and metaphors. And for all those who are doing so, I have the impression that countless others yearn to, and will read this book hungrily taking in the experiences of women like them as nourishment and encouragement.

The authors were interested in what constitutes spiritual maturity, or as one woman said, "I already know I am a child of God. The question is, how can I be an adult of God?" They sought out women across North America from various spiritual paths, interviewed these women in depth, and quote them liberally. There are some common threads. Each woman decided to stop looking to authority figures outside herself for the truth, and to trust that what she experienced as sacred was indeed sacred. Every one found the necessity for solitude, and came to trust an inner source of wisdom. None found it easy, and most found it difficult to both maintain a spiritual path and be in a long-term relationship with a man. The authors raise some intriguing questions, including, "Is there a relationship between women saying, 'I don't know how to pray,' and 'I don't know what it means to be a woman?'"

For all that, this is a fascinating book to read. I think that it will be for many women a book that can function as "a resonator" in their lives, which the authors describe as "a friend or sister or companion so true to her own inner reality, that she inspires them to be faithful to theirs." Only instead of the support of one resonator, in this book we find many companions, sister pilgrims on the spiritual path called ordinary life, who by their example and words give us the strength and courage to remain true to our own deep purpose.

Chapter 1

THE QUESTION THAT WOULDN'T GO AWAY

 Shekhinah. Shekhinah. The word simply popped into my mind like an uninvited guest and wouldn't go away. At times it seemed to disappear, but then it would come again, quietly, this strange word—*Shekhinah*. It seemed to be waiting patiently for me to pay attention to it. After hearing it in my mind for three days I tried saying it out loud. "Shekhinah." It had an interesting sound. And when I said it, I felt a soft tug somewhere deep inside.

I began to ask my friends if they knew what it meant. It sounded as if it could be Hebrew, but although I knew some Hebrew, it was not familiar to me. When my husband and friends were unable to help, I tried the library in our small town but found no answer there either. Shekhinah. Shekhinah. It was becoming more insistent now, demanding my attention.

Still puzzling over what it could mean, I was sitting in my bedroom one morning when my friend Joan hurried through the door. She strode across the room and thrust a book into my hands.

"Let's try this," she said. I glanced down at the blue cover on which the word *Kabbalah* was written, and turned to the index. Running my finger quickly down the S column, I read, "Shekhinah: the feminine face of God."

The words sent shock waves rippling down my spine and goose flesh bristling on my bare arms because I realized at once that the Shekhinah was not an uninvited guest at all. She had been announced to me with great ceremony in a powerful dream a full month earlier.

In the dream, I happily soar high above the clouds on a great golden dragon until I wonder, "Is this all there is?" The dragon immediately descends to earth, alighting at the side of a jewellike temple on a large body of water. I want to enter the temple, but I'm afraid to go in alone. I turn back to the dragon, hoping it will come and protect me. But this temple is human-sized and the dragon will not fit through the door.

I begin to climb the stairs to the entrance anyway, and now I see a ferocious temple guardian with bulging eyes looming menacingly in the doorway. Black dogs snarl on either side of him. With uncharacteristic bravery I continue walking, and as I stride through the door the guardian and his dogs evaporate as if made of fog.

Once I'm inside the doorway, an old man with long robes and a white beard emerges from an inner hallway to greet me. Without actually speaking, he lets me know that his name is Melchizedek. He is wearing a handsome dagger with a handle of turquoise and jade, and as soon as I notice this he presents me with a matching dagger, indicating that I am to wear it on my right side. Then he motions me ahead of him. It is clear that he expects me to lead the way.

I step into a long hallway with a high ceiling and red tiles on the floor. Walking slowly, we eventually come to a pair of polished wooden doors at the end of the corridor. I open them silently and lead the way into a large, empty room. A plain wooden stage is set against the far wall. At the back of the stage is a built-in cabinet. I approach the cabinet and pull open the doors.

I am dumbfounded by what I see. Rolled onto finely carved wooden poles is the most sacred object in Judaism, the Torah. I learned as a child that the Torah contains the five books of Moses written on parchment by an Orthodox scribe, and that if even one letter has been written incorrectly, the Torah cannot be used. I have never actually seen a Torah close up or held one, since these privileges were permitted only to men when I was growing up. But now I lift this Torah carefully out of its cabinet and cradle it to me tenderly as if it were a baby.

Then I notice something unusual. Instead of a mantle of velvet covering the scrolls, or a simple ribbon holding them closed, the Torah has been sealed shut by a dark round blot of red wax. I look at Melchizedek. "This is a very special Torah," he says. Pulling out his dagger, he breaks the seal and rolls open the scrolls. They are absolutely blank. "The Torah is empty," he says, "because what you need to know now is not written in any book. You already contain that knowledge. It is to be unfolded from within you."

"What is this Torah for?" I ask.

My question seems to set in motion the next sequence of events. Without speaking Melchizedek lifts the Torah and lightly places it inside my body, from my shoulders to my knees. I accept this gratefully, feeling my body as a sacred vessel.

At once, a great commotion breaks out behind us. Spinning around, I see that the room is now filled with long-bearded patriarchs wearing black coats and trousers. They're holding hands, laughing, singing and dancing jubilantly around the room. They pull me into their celebration. As I dance I seem to see Moses, King David and King Solomon, and Abraham, Isaac, and Jacob. They, too, are dressed in black coats and trousers, dancing with such heartfelt abandonment that I catch their joy and am filled with it. Ecstatically we whirl round and round the room, laughing.

Finally the dancing stops and I ask, "What is this all about?" Melchizedek answers, "We are celebrating because you, a woman, have consented to accept full spiritual responsibility in your life. This is your initiation as one who will serve the planet."

As I wonder what this means, he continues, "And you are not

the only one. Many, many women are coming forward now to lead the way."

"But who will be our teachers?" I protest.

"You will be teachers for each other. You will come together in circles and speak your truth to each other. The time has come for women to accept their spiritual responsibility for our planet."

"Will you help us?" I ask the assembled patriarchs.

"We are your brothers," they answer, and with that the entire room is flooded with an energy of indescribable kindness. I am absolutely confident in this moment that they *are* our brothers. I feel their love without any question. They say then, "We have initiated you and we give you our wholehearted blessings. But we no longer know the way. Our ways do not work anymore. You women must find a new way."

PAT'S VOICE: JOINING FORCES

Sherry had this dream in 1984, shortly before she and her husband, Paul, moved to the San Francisco Bay Area where the two of us met. Four months later we began our collaborative work—writing this book; it is, as the dream suggests, about the unfolding of the sacred in women's lives.

We began this work because we share a deep conviction that something new is emerging in female psyches today. The voice of the deep feminine is beginning to speak clearly and firmly to many women. And it is by sharing our inner truths, our sacred truths, with each other that a "new way," an untraditional perspective about what it means to live an embodied spirituality in the world today, is beginning to take form.

The Feminine Face of God is an attempt to articulate and give shape to this new way. For the past four years we have interviewed women across North America from a wide spectrum of spiritual paths, searching for the common threads in their stories. During the conception, research, and writing of this book our own spiritual maturing was somehow intrinsically linked to what we were discovering from these women. Throughout this time we repeatedly found ourselves facing a seemingly impossible challenge: to give birth and be midwives at the same time. And right from the beginning we knew that this precarious balancing act could be maintained only if we were willing to work in partnership.

We first met in the summer of 1985 through Women's Quest, a loosely organized network of women in the San Francisco Bay Area who came together in small groups in each other's homes to explore and share their spiritual lives. Almost instantly we recognized that we had a great deal in common. Both of us were in our forties and had been seriously committed to our spiritual paths for a number of years. Coincidentally, each of us had been married for fifteen years before getting divorced and we had both helped in the raising of children, although neither of us had children of our own. Also, as we soon discovered, each of us was currently experiencing a hiatus in our lives, having independently decided several months earlier to live off our savings, spend a part of each day in meditation, and wait for inner guidance about what we were to do next. Although these similarities gave us a sense of kinship, they stood out in sharp relief against our very different backgrounds and professions.

Sherry is a Jewish easterner who became a serious student of Buddhism in her middle thirties. Before moving to California she chaired the Department of Psychological Research at the University of Toronto's Clarke Institute of Psychiatry while simultaneously serving as the head dharma teacher at the Ontario Zen Center. Along with her academic responsibilities she produced and hosted a popular radio talk show that focused on psychological and spiritual issues.

By contrast, I am a native midwesterner and grew up in a household that was a mixture of Protestantism and Catholicism. As an adult, however, I have never been formally affiliated with any religion. Professionally I administered a nonprofit organization in the Bay Area before starting my own consulting business. The year before Sherry and I met, I co-authored *Good-bye to Guilt* with Gerald Jampolsky and William Thetford.[1] The book was based on principles from A Course in Miracles,[2] a set of spiritual teachings we had been practicing together for several years.

Sherry and I discovered these things about each other within a few weeks of our first meeting. And we found out something else as well: Each of us was feeling that a whole new kind of spiritual awareness was awakening inside us. Although it was still too embryonic to describe with any clarity, we had no doubts about its reality. Nor did we think it conferred "specialness" on us. Conversations with other women friends and the proliferation of books on women's spirituality confirmed that there were many women in whom this awareness was growing.

The theme of a "new way" in Sherry's dream was our constant topic of conversation as we hiked several times a week in the Marin foothills north of the Golden Gate Bridge. However, its meaning remained as shrouded in fog as the hills we were climbing. Briskly making our way up and down, we challenged and argued and pressed each other to be willing at least to pose the questions for which we had no answers. What does it mean to accept spiritual responsibility in our lives? How can we be still enough or clear enough or compassionate enough to let the deep truth emerge? Is there a "new way"? If so, how do we go about finding it?

We were beginning to feel that the meaning and purpose of our lives demanded that we search for the answers to these questions. Before we met we had each read Carol Gilligan's provocative *In a Different Voice*,[3] a study on moral development in women published in 1982. Now, as we talked, this pioneering work gave impetus to the questions already flooding our minds. Before Gilligan's research, the best-known studies in moral development had concluded that women's moral reasoning is underdeveloped compared to men's, a belief subscribed to earlier by Freud and Piaget.

Central to Gilligan's work is the fact that the widely reported "low levels" of moral development for women reflected scores based on standards derived from the study of males. What her research suggests, however, is that in situations requiring moral decisions, women use different values from those used by men. Men use "principle," or abstract rules of justice to decide whether an action is right or wrong, whereas women consistently use relationship and personal responsibility as their primary reference points in making moral decisions.

It seemed to us that this significant difference might also affect the way women experience the sacred in their lives. After all, we reasoned, throughout history women have learned about spiritual realization from men. Male guides and male interpreters—priests, rabbis, ministers, Zen masters, yogis, and countless other male teachers have defined what spirituality is and how it is to be developed and experienced in our lives. In almost all accounts of the sacred, both language and story have been the expressions of men conveyed in male imagery.

This led us to consider something else: the power of language as a tool not only for expressing but for teaching spiritual principles. Author and theologian Carol Christ has observed that stories shape experience, and experience shapes stories,[4] or to put it another way, the stories we tell and are told mold our perceptions of reality. For many and varied reasons, women's experiences have remained unspoken. Even in those rare instances when women of great eloquence such as Hildegard of Bingen, Saint Teresa of Avila, and the poets Mirabai and Rabia have written about their encounters with the divine, we cannot easily separate their descriptions from the patriarchal ideologies they represent.

One day toward the end of summer as we were contemplating all this, we suddenly came to a disquieting realization. Despite our many years of spiritual practice and extensive reading in various traditions, we knew almost nothing about how women develop spiritually. In addition, we were immediately and acutely aware of something else: We cannot learn how women develop spiritually from men. The responsibility for describing this process is ours, as women.

For many of the reasons just discussed it became clear to us that women on spiritual paths today must look beyond models of the past for inspiration. Stories of heroic women from Biblical times, wise women from ancient Tibet, and idealized saints are no longer adequate. What we need are stories from spiritually mature women in our time and culture who are demonstrating the sacred in today's world. We need to hear from women we can relate to, women like ourselves who fall in love, raise children, run businesses, speak from pulpits, commute on freeways, work for peace, and go through divorces. We need to hear directly from these women about the unfolding of the sacred in their lives in their own words, in the language of their own hearts.

Convinced of this need, we made a bold-spirited—later we would say insane—commitment to research and write a book about women's spiritual unfolding. The only thing we were sure about was the title: we would call it *The Feminine Face of God.*

Two weeks later we were on our way to a cabin in the northern California redwoods, a place remote enough for us to concentrate fully on writing the first draft of the proposal for the book. We were filled with a nervous energy. After all, the project we had just committed ourselves to was a mine field of unknowns. Furthermore, we scarcely knew each other; our friendship was less than three months old.

As Sherry climbed into the front seat of my car, the back piled high with books, typewriter, sleeping bags, clothes, and food, she turned to me and asked the one question we hadn't even stopped to consider as we were forging ahead with our plans. "What if we find out we don't like each other?" she said with an earnestness bordering on the comical. I burst into laughter.

"Don't worry," I replied confidently. "I can put up with anything for five days, and that's all we have to be concerned about right now." Little did I know then that it would take the next four years to answer that question.

Once we had arrived at our cabin and settled in a bit, we stared at each other. "Now what?" we asked. Then, because we hadn't the faintest notion of how to answer that question, we walked outside and sat down opposite each other under the protective branches of a large oak tree. And there we did something we were to do almost every day for the next several years of our collaboration: We closed our eyes, sat in silence, and waited.

After a few moments, when we felt peaceful and in harmony with each other and our surroundings, Sherry asked the question that was on both our minds. "What is needed now?" And out of the silence came an answer with such calm and wisdom that we felt it was a voicing of the deep purpose that had brought us together. "Writing the proposal will not be hard work." I spoke the words as I was hearing them, and we were cautioned against forcing ourselves. Whenever we started to feel anxious and pressured to produce, we were to stop and go for a walk in the redwoods or along the river. If we were willing to do this, what was needed would come to us.

We discovered that this kind of communion was easy, and from the beginning it became an integral part of our process. We had not called upon the sacred by a particular name, but with open, trusting hearts. And perhaps equally important, we expected an answer. In the months that followed we found that this loving, knowing consciousness was present not only when the two of us sat together but later as well, during the few moments we would sit in silence with each of the women before beginning our interview.

> You have set sail on another ocean
> without star or compass
> going where the argument leads
> Shattering the certainties of centuries.
>
> — Janet Kalven
> *Respectable Outlaw*

The "new way." We could not get this phrase out of our minds. It kept coming up like a familiar refrain every time we thought about what we wanted to propose. If women are to pioneer a new way of embodying spirit in the world today, one thing seems certain: we must listen to the deep source of wisdom within ourselves and tell the truth about our lives and what we are learning. This means questioning everything we have been taught or taken for granted that is not validated by our own experience. Simply by asking one key question, *Is this true for me?* about each "truth" we hear, we challenge ourselves to become what we truly are.

As Simone de Beauvoir observed, we must prefer to fathom rather than flatter ourselves. And to fathom ourselves we need not only the courage to follow wherever the questions lead us, but the willingness to let go of the certainty of thousands of years of traditional teachings to enter the unknown territory of our own experience. During those five days in the northern California wilderness we realized that we had to come to terms with a question that would not go away. We had to ask, What is the face of God that can be revealed through women?

We proposed to look for the answers to this question by studying the life stories of thirty women across North America who were recognized in their communities as sources of spiritual inspiration. By the time this project was completed, however, we had actually met and interviewed more than a hundred such women.

Two considerations were of primary importance to us. One was that women who were relatively unknown, acknowledged perhaps only in a neighborhood or region, would be represented in our study as well as women who have received public recognition for their spiritual contributions. The second was that our sample should reflect a broad spectrum of paths—women who had lived in cloisters, medicine women and rabbis and ministers, mothers, artists, teachers, and community workers.

Apart from these requirements there would be only one restriction: We wanted each woman we interviewed to have found her own direct relationship with the divine or the real. The key word here is *relationship*. For this reason we decided not to interview women who served as official spokespersons for any particular religion. Rather, we would make a determined effort to find those women whom we felt had plumbed the depths of their own lives and were trying to bring together and live out their own personal, spiritual relationship with the divine. We would solicit recommendations from as many sources as we had access to—personal, professional, and institutional—and once we had assembled a file of names we would sit together in silence and ask for help in drawing up a final list of women to be interviewed.

From the beginning we knew we would not be doing research in the usual sense of testing experimental hypotheses. We did not know enough even to formulate hypotheses. Nor did we plan to use the data we gathered from a relatively small number of life stories to make generalizations about all women. But we knew we needed to begin to raise the questions that were in not only our hearts, but the hearts of many other women as well. If there is a new way, we thought, helping to uncover it might well be the most important women's work we would ever do.

SHERRY'S VOICE: COMING TO EARTH AND GETTING STARTED

Early one morning toward the end of February in 1986, six months after we had sat under the oak tree and begun our proposal, we were sitting again, this time in Pat's living room. One of the worst winter storms of the season was raging outside. Pat's apartment, resting on pilings over the bay, seemed barely equal to the huge waves whooshing in cascades over the deck railings. And we, too, were beginning to feel under seige. Both of us had been living on our savings, which had rapidly diminished while we were writing the research proposal. Now that it was ready to be submitted, we wondered whether we could find anyone willing to fund such a venture.

Pat was particularly edgy. Ending a relationship and moving out of an apartment she had shared with her partner, concerned about how she was going to earn a living, she was hurriedly putting things in boxes. I arrived in the midst of this last-minute packing, bringing a friend from Seattle who had promised to evaluate our proposal. We perched ourselves amid the growing towers of cartons, drinking coffee, eating danishes, and chatting. Finally, in a barely controlled voice Pat said, "Well, thank you both so much for dropping by, but I really must finish this. The movers will be here by noon."

My friend looked a little hurt and surprised. "But don't you want to know what I think about your proposal?" she asked.

Didn't we want to know? Since she was well acquainted with the philanthropic world and had promised to suggest possible funding sources if she felt our proposal had merit, we were *dying* to know what she thought. However, she had said nothing about the proposal in the two days she had been visiting us. Assuming the worst and wanting to avoid any awkwardness, we had decided not to bring the matter up.

"Yes!" we answered simultaneously.

"I loved it," she said. "I'm prepared to give you ten thousand dollars to get started, and I'll help you raise the balance."

In that moment, something changed dramatically. It was as if a beautiful but ephemeral vision we had been carrying was suddenly brought into form, just as the golden dragon in my dream had finally stopped flying around in the sky and come down to earth. Someone not only believed in our vision but was willing to support it financially. Our project took on an entirely new reality.

For the next year and a half we traveled across the United States and Canada talking with women about the unfolding of the sacred in their lives. Our intention was to spend approximately two days interviewing each woman, and most of the time this is what we did. However, one interview continued for four days, and in a couple of interviews we scheduled follow-up visits. Rarely did we spend less than two days with an individual.

In the weeks preceding our first interview we put a great deal of thought and effort into formulating a questionnaire that would cover attitudes and beliefs about the divine in an individual's life from childhood through the present. Specific questions addressed early spiritual experiences, dreams and inner-knowing, interpersonal relationships, losses and crises, prayer and meditation, the betrayal of vows or deep promises to God or oneself, nature, the body and sexuality, spiritual teachers and advisers. Since both of us felt it was important that responses to these questions be as spontaneous as possible, we did not show the questionnaire to the women either before or during the interview.

What we did at the beginning of each interview, however, was to ask each woman to take fifteen minutes or so to focus on the way in which her life had developed and to distinguish, if she could, four or five periods that she considered turning points in her spiritual unfolding. These might be specific experiences that led her to look for deeper meaning, choices or commitments that she had made, or initiations—both formal and informal—that she had gone through.

Although we had carefully prepared the questionnaire as a "probe," something quite unpredictable and remarkable occurred once we actually got underway. Most of the women, without any probing or prompting, answered all our questions in the course of telling us their life stories. Rarely did we use the questionnaire except as a checklist at the end of each session.

By the time we had completed about half of the interviews one thing was clear: The women we spoke with had a deep desire to tell us what was meaningful and sacred in their lives. The warmth with which we were received and the openness and trust with which each woman related her story made us keenly aware that opportunities for this kind of sharing are virtually nonexistent. Even in the cloistered walls of a psychotherapist's office the dialogue usually focuses on what has gone wrong with one's life, rather than on the deep purpose moving through it.

Time and again we heard these kinds of comments from the women we interviewed:

"I'd like to be interviewed like this for the rest of my life. It's a process that has brought up so much, tapped into so many old memories, that it helps me feel connected to the roots of my life."

"It feels like taking a *mikvah*, a bath of purification. It's a letting go, a freeing process. After you tell the story, you can let it rest."

"I've never had this kind of extended, intimate conversation about my spiritual life before, and I can feel how important and healing this time together has been for me. Telling my story has made me aware that even the parts of my life that are painful to recall and that I'm not especially proud of have been necessary for my spiritual growth."

The discovery that what we were doing was unique, that it *is* unusual for people to talk deeply with each other about what informs and gives meaning to their lives, disturbed us. But if it was disheartening to recognize that as a society we place no importance on sacred sharing in our daily interactions, something else inspired us. The willing spirit with which the women entrusted us with their stories, and the tears which often testified more eloquently than their words to the deep truths they were communicating, told us that we were engaging in a powerfully transformative process. We were "hearing each other into speech," as author and theologian Nelle Morton describes it.[5] For until we can speak our truth and know that we have been heard, we don't wholly know it ourselves. And each time a woman told us her story there was a growing awareness that she, and we, were beginning to find our voices.

As the interviews progressed, we felt as if we were carrying the women's stories inside us all the time. During this period someone asked Pat if she felt lonely now that she was living by herself. "Lonely?" she asked in an incredulous voice. "How could I possibly be lonely? I'm living with over a hundred women twenty-four hours a day in a studio apartment!"

We tape-recorded all our interviews. Once they were complete, we had a staggering three thousand pages of transcripts and a mélange of memories. It was then that we sat down for the first time and read the transcripts, checking them against the tapes. We were amazed to discover that we had not the slightest problem remembering what was said, how it was said, the setting in which the interview took place, and exactly how each woman had looked as we were talking with her. As soon as we heard a voice, and sometimes just by reading a transcript, we seemed to be in the presence of the woman herself. In most of the stories in this book we have used the real names of the woman we interviewed. In a few cases, we have chosen to protect a woman's identity by using a pseudonymous first name.

Once we got started, we read and reread the transcripts searching for clues that might reveal a pattern. *Was* there anything in common about the many ways in which the sacred unfolds in women's lives? Could we find a model, a metaphor, or an image that would serve as a container for the many different processes of spiritual maturing the women had described to us?

"Don't mention those words in my presence," Pat warned me one day.

"What words?"

"Any of them!" she retorted. "Development. Maturity. Spirituality. We don't know what they mean. We don't even know what *we* mean when we use them. How can we talk about 'spiritual maturity' when we don't have any idea what it is?"

Nevertheless, she continued to make notes. And I—hell-bent on finding the "regularities and commonalities in the data" from all my years as a research psychologist—made charts and diagrams. Our frustration intensified as the weeks sped past.

Then gradually something changed. We began to feel ourselves taking root in the lives we were studying. When that happened, we knew it would be unthinkable to use any model or metaphor of spiritual development that was not alive and growing. No ladders, pyramids, wheels, or spheres, we said to each other. And no snakes or butterflies or roses or rainbows either. If we're going to describe women's spiritual unfolding, we need something as organic and complex as the women themselves. Something with cycles and parts that are interdependent. Something that is living. Something, we said, like a garden.

The garden metaphor had a powerful resonance. Gardens can be entered in a thousand ways and at any time. You can enter in childhood from the door of your home and continue to cultivate your garden through the whole of your life. Or the door can slam shut in adolescence, leaving you lost and searching for what T. S. Eliot calls "the unknown, remembered gate."[6] You can enter through a gate that is wide or narrow or so overgrown with ivy and weeds that you have to search carefully for the opening. You may not find your garden until adulthood or old age or the moment of death. Or you may not find it at all.

The garden metaphor felt like a splendid antidote to the usual hierarchical models of spiritual development we have inherited from patriarchal traditions. If we used a hierarchy of any kind—a pyramid or ladder or anything to be climbed—we knew we would be tempted to evaluate one woman as better or more evolved than another. But who could argue that a garden of daisies and hollyhocks was more developed than a garden of artichokes and asparagus? Who could claim that a garden with a great variety of flowers was more inclusive and therefore more highly evolved than one that contained only roses? All gardens, of course, must be cultivated if they are to grow, but each one comes to maturity in its own time, in its own way.

OUR VOICES: GUIDEPOSTS TO THE NEW WAY

This book is not about the ideals of enlightenment or perfection. It is about process, the many and varied ways in which women grow spiritually. And perhaps the greatest gift of this coming to maturity is the potential it offers for recognizing, reclaiming, and valuing our feminine nature. This entails, as we shall see, healing the wounds between human beings and other forms of life, especially the imperiled life of our earth. Over and over like a litany, the women we spoke with told us how intimately connected their own cycles are to those of the earth and how fundamental this bond, this sense of relationship, is to their sense of the sacred.

"To a woman, spirituality, or a life of the Spirit, implies relationship in its very essence," Irene Claremont de Castillejo wrote in her book *Knowing Woman*.[7] And for a woman relationship includes so much: "relationship to God in those intangible, fleeting moments when she is aware of a presence, whether it be in the sudden impact of a white cherry tree in blossom, or the rhythmical furrows of a plowed field; whether it be in a moment of unforgettable union with another human being or alone in the stillness of her own silence. Wherever it may happen there is for her always re-lationship. But the word 'spiritual' is not, I think, generally used in this sense."

Relationship that does not separate and divide but connects and brings together spirit and flesh, human beings and other forms of life, God and matter, is precisely what women described to us as the heart of the spiritual in their lives. However, our ability to connect and blend with others, a quality essential for making and sustaining relationships, also makes us sensitive and susceptible to the needs and wants of others.

And in attempting to respond to these needs we can easily become alienated from our own deepest truths, as Jungian analyst Marion Woodman reminded us: "One of the problems women have today," Marion told us, "is that they're not willing to find the river in their own life and surrender to its current. They're not willing to spend time, because they feel they are being selfish. They grow up trying to please other people and they rarely ask themselves, Who am I? Rarely. And then life starts to feel meaningless because they live in terms of pleasing, rather than in terms of *being* who they are."

Why do we as women find it so difficult to trust the truth of our own experience? Is it because we have been so thoroughly condi-tioned by thousands of years of patriarchal traditions? This certainly seems to be the case for one candid midwesterner who told us, "I've been identified with patriarchal values for so long now that whenever something deep within me begins to ask questions, I feel guilty and disloyal. Then I scramble around trying to make my feelings and beliefs all fit together somehow. It's very hard to put into words, but something uniquely feminine in me is asking to be expressed and I don't know how to let it come out."

"Why do we need to lean on any authority in observing what is actually happening?" Toni Packer, an esteemed teacher of med-itation, demands of people who work with her at the Springwater Center in New York. "Isn't it our anxiety, our constant search for escapes . . . our unresolved fears and cravings for psychological and spiritual refuge [that] bring all authorities into existence?"

Toni's words suggest another reason why it is so difficult for women to trust their own truth and why it has taken us so long to begin our search for spiritual authenticity: We might have to let go of certain "authoritative truths" which, even if we cannot make them fit with our experience, have nevertheless given us a sense of security.

"We women in particular often walk with uncertain steps, as if on quicksand, depending for direction on the feelings or wisdom of others," a plain-spoken Canadian told us. As she implies, letting go of the wisdom of others can bring us face-to-face with emotions we have struggled against feeling for most of our lives: helplessness, rage, and despair. And not just these buried emotions come to meet us, but also the fear of isolation that can arise when we leave spiritual communities that may have been dearer than our own families. Finally, maybe we remember in some hidden part of ourselves the thousands of women who over four centuries were tortured and burned alive for daring to say and practice what they knew.

What we have learned over the past four years is that stripping away the layers of encultured patriarchal values and beliefs is a profoundly disruptive process. One reason for this is that when we let go of authoritative truths that have made us feel secure in the past, what arises in their place is great uncertainty. A more subtle and ironic reason is that in order to operate with any effectiveness in our culture, we have had to immerse ourselves in the values of our male-dominated society. And now that we are becoming empowered socially, politically, and economically, the challenge is to maintain and continue these hard-won gains without becoming pseudo-men in the process.

Yet for all the risks, it is precisely this disruptive, disturbing process of stripping away the old unexamined values that was central to the spiritual unfolding of virtually every woman we spoke with. Sometimes willingly and sometimes resisting stubbornly, the women experienced long-hidden emotions, confronted their fears of isolation, and faced the personal and collective pain of self-betrayal to look with clear eyes into their lives.

Once accepted, this challenge led each woman to cultivate what already had roots in her own sacred garden. She began to listen to the deep sources of wisdom within herself and to share what she was learning with others. Perhaps most importantly, each woman decided to stop looking to authority figures outside herself for the truth, and to trust that what she experienced as sacred was indeed sacred.

At the outset of our research, we read an article about a sisterhood in Portland, Maine, called "The Feminist Spiritual Community," a community we would later visit when we conducted our East Coast interviews. Like sparks returning to a central flame, one hundred and fifty women—Quakers and Presbyterians and Catholics and goddess worshippers and others—gather regularly to support each other and to explore and celebrate a spirituality that flows out of their direct experience.

We were intrigued. Moreover, as we told other women about this community, they responded with an impassioned curiosity. It was as if some kind of expectation were being met, as if the women were murmuring to themselves, "Yes, of course. I always knew there must be a place like that."

As we puzzled over this response, we began to recall fragments from conversations in which women spoke of their yearning for a spiritual refuge, a place where they could come together to pray, heal, bless and be blessed, to celebrate the sacred mysteries.

A young rabbi told us, "Throughout Jewish history there have been sacred places for men to study, called *yeshivot* from the words *to sit*. But we women don't need a place to sit, like dead weights! We need a *rikudya*, a place to dance the energy of the holiness in ourselves and to bring through our bodies the sacred feminine Torah."

At a Buddhist conference one woman challenged her sisters: "Being westerners, we need to create community in the context of our own culture. How can we do that?" Several voices answered,

"We need to set aside special places for ourselves." "We need a grieving room for those who are mourning." "And we'll want a place of solace where we can hold and comfort each other."

Frequently it was not a sacred gathering place that was longed for but a circle, a council, a society of women which had formed in some ancient time and continued into the present age, carrying an unbroken female lineage.

One woman told us about a circle of grandmothers who had come to her while she was on a retreat in the desert. "It was a time of great uncertainty in my life, and I prayed and listened more deeply than I ever had before. On the third day, I lit a small fire and began to dance following the rhythm of my heartbeat. As I did this, I felt I was being encircled by a ring of ancient, brown-skinned women who were blessing me. They were blessing my breasts and womb and legs and belly, and praising my strength and beauty and courage. As my eyes filled with tears of gratitude, they told me that I should not weep because this was my birthright as a woman. 'At one time every young woman was blessed in this way,' they said, 'so no one could be pulled off her knowing by a man. The young ones knew they were whole and connected to everything that lived because we elders sat in witness for them, just as we're doing for you today.'"

The longing for wholeness is evident. In all of these stories, dreams, and visions, and in the intense interest in the Feminist Spiritual Community in Portland, there is the express desire to gather together what has been fragmented and lost.

But why this longing for *women's* circles, for *feminine* gathering places? Is there something about women meeting with women that can bring us to our sacred truths by lending us courage, inspiring hope, and blessing us with laughter in a way that women meeting with men cannot?

Carol Collopy, a spiritual guide and teacher, suggests that the unique gift of women's gatherings today is related to the newness of what we are doing. "I think women's spirituality at this time is like the life you find teeming in tidal pools in the shallows of oceans.

Once that life takes hold, the sea anemones and the tiny crustaceans, the starfish and the plankton, find their own food and their own means of protection. They can sustain their own lives. But in the beginning life in the pools is fragile and must be protected from curious intruders. I believe this is how it is for us right now. We're just developing, just finding our way, and we need deep, quiet, safe places in which to do this."

Carol's image made a profound impression on us. However, we did not fully comprehend what she meant until we were putting the finishing touches on this book. Then within a few days of each other, we each had a disturbing dream.

Sherry's Dream: "I am in a garden, watching a luminous white bird on the topmost branch of an apple tree. Suddenly I notice two thugs dressed in heavy shoes and dark suits clumsily trying to climb the tree. They are after the bird and they call out to her. To my alarm she leaves the safety of her perch and moves toward them. When she is within reach, the first man thumps her hard on the head, stunning her. I watch appalled and helpless, but I am unable to act on her behalf."

Pat's Dream: "I'm on the ground floor of a house, grooming a tiny white dog that has been neglected. Once he is bathed and brushed, I hold him in the palm of my hand and climb to the top floor of the house to show him off to my women's prayer group, which is gathering there. But as soon as we focus our attention on the dog, it is transformed into a white female dove.

"Just then I look up and see the face of a ferocious man peering in at us through a door that has been left ajar. I recognize him as the father of a childhood friend who was feared for his cruelty to his children and dogs. The other women have not yet seen him, but I am terrified because I know he has seen the delicate bird I am holding and wants to destroy her. Covering the bird with both my hands I bolt out the door and past the menacing man as I shout to the women, 'We can't let him kill the bird. Are you coming with me or not?' as I run down the stairs."

We shared these dreams with the members of our small women's prayer group that meets twice a month. After a few moments one of our friends asked quietly, "What's the matter with your birds? Why didn't they simply fly away?"

"Mine was too young and fragile," Pat replied.

"And mine was too innocent to know that it ought to," Sherry continued. "They need to mature before they will be able to protect themselves."

"It is the one who knows the value of a thing who must protect it," our friend replied soberly. "You can't leave the protection to the goodwill of those who may be unconscious or actually dangerous. And you can't leave it to the one who is totally trusting either. There needs to be a discerning adult who will not only recognize how sacred the bird is, but who will be willing to defend it against danger."

Another woman added eagerly, "You see, this is exactly why I need this group. Because you help me to recognize the value of my own experience of the sacred. Without you, I'd ride roughshod over it, ignoring my own feelings and intuitions whenever they don't fit with what the priests or lamas or holy books say."

She sighed and then looked at each of us in turn. "I've been so ready to abandon the white bird in my own garden to any one of a number of religious authorities who assert themselves. But not anymore. Because you are all with me, even when we're apart. I pray for you in the mornings, and I remember how much each of you tries to be true to yourself. I take refuge in you. You help me find the courage to be faithful to what's emerging through my own life."

From this discussion and from our dreams, we sensed how precious small women's circles are at this time when we are just beginning to trust the truth of our experience. Like the white birds, like life in the tide pools, our faith and discernment are still developing. And like the men in our dreams, who reflect the inner males in our own psyches, we need to learn how to release our own grasping at the sacred. We need to acknowledge the fierce primitive within us and transform it if the new life that is emerging is to be protected and nurtured. But we don't have to go through these changes alone. In fact, the dreams suggest that without our women friends we may be too stunned or hypnotized by our inner patriarchal attitudes to tell the difference between what we can trust and what is dangerous to us.

A circle of women can provide a container for emergence in a way that a woman alone or even a one-to-one relationship cannot. Intimate relationships and even friendships can break or at least be greatly strained by life changes. But from the combined wisdom and energy of a small group of women who are committed to "hearing each other into speech," continuity and trust can develop that can be relied on over the long term. And, witnessing each person's direct knowing of her truth, we can be empowered to live our own.

In the chapters that follow we will bring you the stories of women whose experiences reveal some of the many routes to spiritual maturing, women who might be your sisters or daughters or mothers or friends. They are not intended as leaders, in the sense of guides, who go first and determine the correct path for others to follow. But they offer their stories to you as companions, as sisters. They walk beside you and confide in you as beloved friends. It is our wish, and theirs, that they show you how wide the path is, how varied its experiences, how challenging, and how great a privilege to walk upon.

Chapter 2
CHILDHOOD: SEEDBED OF THE SACRED

> Our birth is but a sleep and a forgetting:
> The Soul that rises with us, our life's Star,
> Hath had elsewhere its setting,
> And cometh from afar:
> Not in entire forgetfulness,
> And not in utter nakedness,
> But trailing clouds of glory do we come
> From God, who is our home. . . .
>
> — William Wordsworth
> *Intimations of Immortality*

 While we may disagree with poets and mystics about whether or not we come into this life "trailing clouds of glory," one thing is certain: Deep in our human psyches many of us have a sense of connection that goes far beyond our conscious definition of the word *home*. The serenity reflected on the face of a newborn, the transparency of this tiny being who seems to have not yet quite arrived here, evokes in many of us the ultimate question, Where *do* we come from, really? So profound is this longing for our essential self that even when we are feeling alienated and estranged, our so-called negative feelings point toward the reality our soul knows as home.

As we listened to the women we interviewed for this book describe their childhoods, the poetic observation that it is "not in entire forgetfulness and not in utter nakedness" that we come into this life began to have the ring of an empirical truth. Most of the women we spoke with told us that it was in childhood that they had had their first encounter with the divine. And in most cases they described it as a direct connection with something inside themselves that they knew to be absolutely real—no matter what their parents or peers might say to the contrary.

How and when this initial connection—or recollection—occurred, whether it was felt in the body as an infusion of energy or light, or took the form of a dialogue with angels, the ability to see auras, or an experience in nature, depended on a multitude of factors as various as the women themselves. As we shall see, parental support for this encounter certainly had an effect on the early stages of each woman's spiritual development. However, even when no reinforcement was offered, or when the child was subjected to ridicule or punishment for what she had experienced, this first direct connection with the divine was acknowledged by most of the women as the "seedbed" for the unfolding of the sacred in their lives.

For Bernadette Roberts, a former Carmelite nun we first became acquainted with through her two autobiographical books *The Experience of No-Self* and *The Path to No-Self*, this connection was so significant that she still refers to it as "the day I was born."

"I was five years old," Bernadette told us, "when the following event took place. I was on my way to play with some kids when suddenly I experienced a powerful infusion from within—like the blowing up of a balloon. It was the infusion of an unknown power, energy or presence.

"At that age my mind could not comprehend what had happened, so the first thing I did was to check and see if I had suddenly grown bigger, taller, or what. When I saw no physical change I became frightened and thought 'I'm gonna bust!' Whatever this power was, I thought it might take over and put an end to me, not physically—this never occurred to me—but more like being squeezed out or becoming extinct.

"Then suddenly the expansion stopped and the mysterious power exploded into joy—as if the power had burst into laughter. I remember running and leaping to the front of the house to meet five little boys who were my playmates and saying to them, 'I feel the energy of ten men in me.' I tried to tell them what happened and asked if anything like that had ever happened to them, but they just stood there motionless looking at me like statues. I remember feeling so full of life and then I realized they didn't get any of it. I thought, 'I've got to put some life in them,' so I immediately got a game of cops and robbers going."

Bernadette not only interrogated her playmates, she began a door-to-door survey of the adults in her neighborhood, asking if any of them had ever had an experience of this kind. The results were disappointing. "They acted as if they didn't know what I was talking about," she told us. "I was sure they did, but that somehow they had forgotten about it in the process of becoming a grown-up.

"From that moment on I was aware of a continuing presence inside me, a presence I called my 'interior friend,'" Bernadette said. It was not a relationship she took lightly, although in the beginning she could not resist checking up on her friend by asking "Are you there?" After one such inquiry she received such an unequivocal response—a sudden burst of power and presence—that she never asked again. "I knew then this wasn't a game," she told us quietly. "It wasn't child's play. This was a mystery and it was very awesome."

The abiding presence of an "interior friend" was not the only mystery in Bernadette's life, however. Brought up in a family of enthusiastic sailors on the California coast Bernadette developed an early passion for the sea. "I was captivated by it as a little child," she told us. "The power of those waves, the continuous movement— I thought it was all just marvelous. I could feel the mystery in it and I loved it. Somehow I knew that the mystery that was in the sea was in me too. And yet, little children don't think about the divine. They just experience it. They just know it."

Indeed, it took some time for Bernadette to make the connection between the mystery in the sea and her "interior friend." But one day when she was alone on the beach something became clear to her.

"Suddenly this whole thing, this presence that was inside me, leaped out and stood in front of me," she continued. "Although there really are no words to describe it, it was as if something said, 'This is me. This mystery is me. And this is love. This is your life. This is it.' All at once, what was inside me and what was outside me came together in that experience. Now that struck me as mysterious and wonderful. I remember running down the beach saying, 'I love you.' Just running and saying over and over, 'I love you, I love the sea, I love this thing in me. I love all of it.' And that scene often comes back to me even now, that wild scene of running down the beach. It was simply magnificent. Even when I collapsed, that energy was still present. It was inexhaustible. You could spend your physical energy, but I knew this other energy could never be depleted."

We asked Bernadette if she had any thoughts about what those early experiences meant. After reflecting for a few moments she replied, "It seems to me that in different phases of life we experience the divine differently. It depends, frankly, on how developed our consciousness is. Our consciousness is always moving and changing, and so our experiences of the divine are also always moving and changing. To expect that you come to a point where you can say, 'This is it,' is not the way it works. You may come to that point, but it certainly isn't the end of the divine."

While most of the women we spoke with were able to recall in vivid detail at least one time in their childhood when they felt a direct experience of the sacred, rarely did this awareness continue uninterrupted through adolescence and adulthood. And when it did, as was true for Bernadette and a few other women whose stories we tell in this chapter, the woman had nearly always been brought up in a home in which one or both parents were deeply committed to spiritual values.

When a context of spiritual support and understanding was not provided, however, something quite different occurred in the woman's unfolding process. For one thing, she learned to keep quiet about her encounters with the sacred if sharing them meant disapproval, ridicule, or, as it did in some few cases, punishment.

As one woman explained, "When we look into our childhood we often find destiny there. The child has a vision and our parents or society try to stamp it out; so the child has to go underground." Or as another woman told us, "I knew very early that the nature of reality was different from the story anybody had given me, but my mother had a scathing attitude toward religion and religious people, and my father was really afraid of spiritual things, so I learned to suppress my mystical streak." For those women whose early experiences were not nurtured or reinforced by their parents, it was often years, or even decades, before some life crisis reawakened their childhood connection with the divine and led them through the "unknown remembered gate" into their sacred garden.

GOING UNDERGROUND

"I used to talk to angels all the time," Marion Woodman, a Jungian analyst and author of several well-known books on feminine psychology, told us as we sat in her Toronto office one gray November day discussing her childhood. "I began hearing them when I was three years old."

"What kind of things did they tell you?" we asked.

"They told me how flowers grew and about all the things that went on out in the garden, and about relationships. I would sit by the kitchen window while my mother was ironing and relate to her what the angels were saying to me. Since she was not used to talking with angels she thought she had a crazy child on her hands. She saw insanity in it, and that was terrifying to her.

"However, it was different with my father," Marion continued. "You see he was a Scotsman who had been brought up in a culture which accepted nature spirits. So even though he was a minister, he had no problem at all with my angels. He accepted them.

"I can remember going visiting with my parents and having them caution me before we went into someone's house, 'Now, Marion, you keep your mouth shut when we go in there. You just keep quiet,' because I could walk into a situation and know right away what was going on. Like many children, I was very intuitive. I would say things like, 'You know, somebody has been fighting here.' Or I would look at our hostess and say, 'You don't like your husband very much, do you?' And then there would be this horrible silence.

As soon as we'd leave my father would take me aside and say, 'Marion, it's not that I don't want you to speak, but you say things that are simply not acceptable in society. It's all right for you to tell me these things, but you must not say them to other people.'

"Sometimes my father would take me with him when he went to call on his parishioners. In those days almost every house had a parlor, and that was where I would wait while he ministered in another room. One day after I had been in the parlor for what seemed like a very long time, I grew impatient and wandered into the room where my father sat talking with a very sad-looking woman. 'The angels told me that your little girl died,' I said to her. 'Her name was Lily and she came to talk to me while I was in the parlor.' The woman became very distraught and started to cry. All of this was absolutely true, you see, and I tried to console her by explaining that she shouldn't be crying because Lily and I had had a lovely time together, but it didn't seem to help. After hearing about several incidents like this, my mother finally swatted me one day and told me that I was never to speak of angels again. Never.

"I remember my reaction distinctly. Poor mother, I thought, she can't talk to angels so I will never tell her about them again, but that won't make me stop talking to them. I can remember feeling sorry for her because I knew what she was missing. My angels were my life." Then after pausing for a moment she added, "You know, we are beginning to believe children now when they tell us they've been abused, but we still find it difficult to believe them when they tell us they hear angels."

"Did a time come when you no longer spoke with them?"

"Yes, it happened when I was around twelve years old, and I think it was largely a result of the experiences I had in public school," Marion replied. "You see, my life had been committed to people who could teach me things, like my father who had already taught me a lot at home. So I was very excited about going to school. I thought going to school would be like going to heaven. But right from the start it was awful. Part of it was because I was two years younger than everyone else and therefore less coordinated than they.

But the other thing was that neither my teachers nor my classmates ever seemed to understand what I was talking about, and that was very painful to me.

"Gradually I began to lose contact with myself, and by the time I reached puberty I thought I must really be strange. That's when the break came. I never lost touch with the inner voices—I wrote about them in my diary—but I no longer called them angels. And when I went into high school I became a scholar and worked very hard. By that time I had developed close friendships and been elected to lead several societies, but I never shared with anyone what was in my heart. I continued to write in my diary, but I was completely split." For Marion, it would be almost three decades before that split would be healed through an event we describe in a later chapter.

"Until I was ten I was very close to my great-grandmother," Rosalyn Bruyere, the respected healer and founder of the Healing Light Center Church in Glendale, California, told us as we sat around a table in a room adjoining her office. "I loved Nana and she returned my love by favoring me with special treats and privileges. I guess you could say I was her pet. Although she claimed to be antireligious, I realize now that Nana was very spiritual and that she possessed several spiritual gifts. One of these was the ability to see auras around plants, a talent the family didn't like to talk much about. They called it 'Nana's curse.'

"I remember going out in the backyard with her when I was very young and having her show me these auras. She used the auras to tell whether it was safe to take a cutting from a plant or not. If the aura was growing larger, it was all right, but if it was getting smaller, we would leave the plant alone because, as Nana explained, 'We don't want to damage or offend a plant that is in the down part of its cycle.' This all seemed quite natural, and once she pointed the auras out to me, I could see them too.

"Then when I was seven Nana's husband, Nicky, died suddenly of a massive coronary. They were very, very close and after his death Nana was inconsolable. She was so depressed that her doctor put her on tranquilizers, and when those didn't help he referred her to another doctor—a psychiatrist. After Nana confided that she had been having conversations with Nicky, and also with her deceased mother, he prescribed even more drugs for her. Eventually she was put in a sanatorium and given electric shock treatments. After that Nana didn't see auras or hear voices anymore."

The loss of these abilities in her beloved mentor had a profound effect on Rosalyn. "It was after all this happened that I made a decision to keep quiet about what I saw and not tell anybody so they wouldn't lock me up and give me shock treatments too. What is interesting about that decision in retrospect is that shortly afterward I developed a pronounced astigmatism and had to start wearing glasses.

"I was educated in Northern California during the sixties, the space-race era when the emphasis was on making scientists out of everyone. In high school I focused on math and science and by the time I entered college I was not the least bit interested in anything spiritual. Things of that nature just never entered my mind."

When Rosalyn was in her mid-twenties, however, something happened that radically altered her scientific perspective on life. She was living in Hollywood at the time with her film-technician husband and their two young sons. "It started with the boys who were a little over two and three at the time," she explained. "They began to talk about something they called 'fuzz' that floated around. At first I didn't pay much attention to them, but then one day I saw it too. 'Oh no,' I thought. 'I've been with small children so long my mind has turned to mush, and now I'm going crazy!'

"For several months I tried to deny the whole business, but then Easter came, and there was a big family gathering at my aunt's house. At about four that afternoon my mother, who had to work the swing-shift in a factory, started to leave. As she went out the door, one of the boys said, 'Look, Mom. Grandma has orange fuzz around her tummy.' I looked, and sure enough I saw the fuzz, but I had absolutely no idea what it meant.

"The next morning my aunt called to tell me my mother had been taken to the hospital during the night with a bleeding ulcer.

When the boys and I arrived at the hospital I expected to see the orange fuzz again. But by then the bleeding had been stopped, and there was a kind of sickly blue light around her body instead.

"In our neighborhood at that time there were a lot of people in show business, and one of them, an aging Shakespearean actor, was a close friend of ours. When we returned from the hospital that day I told him what I had seen around my mother's body. I'll never forget his response. 'First of all, my dear, you must stop calling it fuzz,' he said to me in his splendid British accent. 'What you are describing is called an aura, and it's highly unlikely that you could see it unless you've recently received a bump on your head.'

"At last I had a word for what I'd been seeing, and that gave me something to go on. A few days later I went to the Los Angeles Public Library and looked up everything I could find with *aura* in it, maybe eighty or ninety references written by swamis, Tibetans, Native Americans and God knows who. I did a lot of reading, and what I learned was that no two people seemed to agree about what it was, what it was made of, how it worked, or what the colors meant."

For the next year and a half Rosalyn worked with a Spiritualist teacher and after that with Dr. Valerie Hunt of UCLA and Emily Conrad of Continuum, researching and fine-tuning her ability to read auras for diagnostic purposes. In the meantime she founded her own school of healing arts where she has been training others in spiritual healing for more than ten years now. "Once I started seeing auras again I no longer had to wear glasses," she told us. And then she added, "In fact, my vision is wonderful now—it's twenty-twenty."

For Rosalyn Bruyere the Biblical quote ". . . and a little child shall lead them" resonates in a particularly personal way. "I would have to say that my serious spiritual development began when my boys started seeing auras," she told us. "I think they were used as divine agents to get my attention. But I know that the groundwork for it was laid much earlier, during my own childhood days when Nana and I spent those hours together in her garden."

•   •   •

CHILDREN OF NATURE/CHILDREN OF GOD

When I was a child I would go out and find a
place to put little stones around in a circle. I would
put some flowers in the center and this was my
sanctuary. Sometimes I would take small objects I
found that were special to me and keep them there.
I never told anyone about those places. At first the
consciousness was just this presence and a kind of
knowing. Then the spirituality got very centered in
Christianity.

— Vijali Hamilton
Artist

When we are children everything in our environment vibrates with
aliveness. Plants and trees, insects and animals, pebbles and rocks,
sky and sea have something to say to us, and we are not self-conscious
about talking to them in return. In some elemental way we seem
to know that to connect is to respond, and as children we respond
to everything. Whether we are walking barefoot on cool grass,
smelling the earth's fragrance as we lie on our belly tracking an
insect, or catching raindrops on our tongue during a summer shower,
we know that we are intimately related to the natural world and
that there is mystery at the heart of this intimacy.

For all of these reasons it is not surprising that many of the
women we interviewed first connected with the divine through
nature. For Twylah Nitsch, a Seneca elder who lives on the land
of her ancestors in upstate New York, this connection took place
at a very early age and was consistently reinforced in the context
of her Native American tradition.

"I wasn't old enough to go to school yet," Twylah, a vigorous woman in her early seventies told us, "so I must have been under five when I spent one whole summer digging a hole with a large spoon in the side of a bank near our house. I had to dig and dig because the ground was so full of roots and my goal was to make a hole big enough to sit in—like in a cave. And that took a lot of hard work. Digging through all those roots was tough.

"What I remember most about that experience is something my grandmother said: 'When you take the dirt out, make sure you have a place for it,' she cautioned me, 'because the dirt is used to being in that particular place, and it is at home there. Don't take anything that is part of something and just scatter it around. Remember you are disturbing the home of the worms and insects. You are moving them out of the place where they have been living, and you need to make sure that they are happy about where you are taking them.' So I would scoop the dirt into a little basket I had and take it around to various spots. 'Is this where you would like to be?' I'd ask. And if the answer was yes, I would leave it. Otherwise, I'd pick up my basket, go to another spot, and ask again.

"When I had finally made the hole deep enough to sit in I would crawl in there and listen. I could hear the earth talking. I could hear the worms and the insects and other living sounds. They were my friends. And so were the stones. I had a little apron and I would gather the stones up in it, take them to my grandfather, and drop them on the ground in front of him. My grandfather was a medicine man and he would read them for me. The stones spoke to me. They still do. That summer was one of my first experiences of connecting with the sacred, and I remember it very well."

"There's not a single picture of me as a child smiling," Choqosh Auh-Ho-Ho, a Chumash Indian storyteller told us as we were having lunch with her and her daughter in their small home on the Monterey peninsula. "I was so desperately, heart-wrenchingly unhappy that I used to sit in my closet with the door closed and beg God to take me away. I didn't want to be part of this world."

Choqosh was six years old then. She remembers the day the bomb was dropped on Hiroshima and Nagasaki and "something happened to the air all around Los Angeles." You were only three then, we say. How could you remember that? "Oh, but I do," she says growing very sober. "Something happened in the air that day that I could feel and I knew that nothing would ever be the same again. To this day each time I hear the name Nagasaki or Hiroshima I feel such terrible pain in my body. I weep and cannot speak until it passes."

Choqosh's father left when she was one year old. She has no memory of that, but she does recall that "my mother carried great bitterness." She remembers being locked out of her home when she was in her early teens and feeling terribly alone. "I kept trying to figure out how there could be a God when life seemed so excruciatingly unfair," she tells us. When we ask who actually raised her, she says flatly, "Me." Floods of memories pour out then, sad, engulfing memories of fear and confusion that float up to the surface of her mind.

Suddenly something changes. She grins and challenges us: "You really want to know who raised me? It was a peppertree at the end of our block, that's who raised me. A peppertree with a short trunk that came up like this," she says, scooping her arms out grandly from her midsection. "It had a great nest inside that was like a womb. Its branches swept out in different directions, and they went all the way down like a weeping willow. You could sit in that womblike space and look out at the world without the world seeing you. And if nobody was watching, you could sleep in there. I felt safe and loved and protected in that tree. It was my link with God/creation—with what was stable and real. Years later I returned to pay my respects to that Mother Tree. It had been removed without a trace."

Trees, there was something about trees. Over and over we heard stories about trees as companions, comforters, confidantes, and best friends in our discussions with the women about their childhoods. One of our favorites was told to us by a friend in her fifties who for a number of years helped direct a center for children and adults with life-threatening illnesses. We asked her to write about it in her own words so that we could include it here.

"Even now, nearly forty years later, I remember that black cherry tree as one remembers a best friend. This is as close as I can come to telling you what it meant to me as a young girl growing up in the Middle West. Our relationship was not abstract or conceptual; the tree was never a metaphor or symbol for me of something else. I simply loved the tree.

"It stood all by itself at the top of a grassy knoll in our large backyard. In the spring its branches were a cascading fountain of pinkish white flowers, their delicate petals a stunning contrast to the rough, black bark of its trunk and branches. As a child I spent many afternoons lying beneath those branches looking up through the layers of gauzy white blossoms to the sky above and feeling the warm earth against my back. I loved those afternoons alone with my tree, its fragrant beauty, the hum of bees filtering out the sounds of the outside world, the quiet joy I felt inside that spoke of something beyond my understanding.

"In the heat of summer its fruit appeared. Shining clusters of plump, blackish red cherries covered the tree from top to bottom, more beautiful than the ornaments of any Christmas tree I'd ever seen. They were the sweetest, most delectable cherries I've ever put in my mouth, and I ate a lot of them. I wondered at this miracle that happened every year. How did my tree change flowers into cherries? How did that happen? This question was unfathomable in my child's mind, and I loved the mystery of it.

"As strange as it may sound, it was in the fall and winter that I felt closest to my tree. Her spring beauty and summer fruit filled me with delight, but when the days began to grow cool and the leaves turned from darkest green to yellow, I could feel something deep and marvelously intimate begin to take place between us. And as fall turned to winter this feeling of intimacy grew. With no bees humming among the blossoms, no birds fluttering from limb to limb, no leaves and cherries decorating her branches, my tree seemed to reveal herself to me in her purest form—in her very essence. And when I embraced her and pressed my ear against her trunk, I could hear the silence that united us. And I knew that was sacred.

"One day in mid-October of my fourteenth year our relationship was brutally severed. I came home from school that day to find only a short, black stump where my beautiful tree had always been. I remember staring down in a daze at the beads of sap forming slowly on the freshly cut surface. For a moment I thought I was going to be sick. It was as if I had stumbled unexpectedly on an amputated limb of someone I loved. For several seconds I couldn't move. And then the tears came, releasing me from my paralysis.

"Although I knew my family had sold the parcel of land on which the tree stood, what I did not know was that the new owners were going to cut it down in order to build a new house. Also, I had never told my family how much the tree meant to me. I always felt my feelings about it were too private, too tender, to share, so there was no way my parents could have known how important and precious the tree was to me.

"In fact, I've never told anyone about that tree until now. I've probably always felt guilty about not speaking up about my feelings to my father or grandfather who may have been able to intercede. I also feel sad that I didn't acknowledge or thank the tree for all it gave me before it was too late. Maybe that's why I'm being given a chance to do that now. I hope so. Perhaps it's time to say what I've known in my heart all these years: that tree was a sacred presence in my life, and it taught me more about God and love than I ever learned in all the years I went to Sunday school."

For the most part, the stories in this chapter have been about a single event or experience in a woman's childhood which served as her first opening to the divine. For some few women, like Bernadette Roberts and Twylah Nitsch, this opening acted as a reference point for the continuous unfolding of the sacred throughout their lives. The importance of parental and family support in these cases was made very clear to us by Twylah Nitsch at the beginning of our interview with her:

"I was taught that our space is sacred and we are responsible for what happens in it," she told us. "We have a place that we are born into and parents who taught us the principles that we use in carrying out our mission in life. I learned from my grandfather that I had a place where I tied my rope, and no matter who pulled on it or tried to separate me from it, I could always get back to my center. Everyone has a rope, but most people's ropes are dangling because they have no place to tie them."

"Does this mean your rope is tied to something inside you?" we asked.

"Yes," Twylah replied, "but in my tradition it's also tied to the place where you were born."

"So," we persisted, "how does that work if you travel a lot or have to move away from your birthplace?"

"It means that you take your sacred space with you," Twylah answered. "If that feeling of security has been developed from the beginning and built up over a period of years, you can take it with you anywhere you go. Each of us carries our sacred space within us, and our challenge is to live from it throughout our life's journey, throughout our earth walk."

For other women, like Marion Woodman and Rosalyn Bruyere, whose initial experiences with the divine were not always nurtured and valued, the connection with the sacred went underground and did not reemerge until many years later when some life circumstance brought it into conscious awareness. For "Sweet Alice" Harris, however, coming to know the sacred was neither a continuous unfolding nor a case of going underground. Rather it was a kind of compressed evolutionary process which took place in a three- to four-year span between childhood and adolescence and completely transformed her life.

SWEET ALICE'S STORY

It was a warm day in late June when Alice Harris, a tall, robust woman in her early fifties whose wide smile radiates a cheerful serenity, welcomed us into a corner of the reception area that serves as her office at Parents of Watts (POW) in Los Angeles. Seven years before "Sweet Alice," as she is called by nearly everyone, had witnessed from her living-room window an incident of gang warfare between blacks and Hispanics. As she watched clouds of black smoke from a flaming car engulf her neighborhood, she heard herself say, "This has gone too far. Somebody is going to have to do something." And the minute she said "somebody," she told us, "I knew that 'somebody' was me."

Six months later this mother of nine who has been a community worker for more than thirty years founded POW. Today the non-profit organization offers more than a dozen counseling, educational, and employment programs to both teenagers and adults who struggle to live in one of the most infamous ghettoes in America. "Every program we started was because someone came to us with a need," Alice explained.

However, it was not the impressive list of achievements that inspired us most about Alice Harris. It was the warm and open-hearted way in which she received all who came to see her. During the day we spent in her office at POW, the battered folding chair beside her desk was rarely without an occupant. A constant stream of people paraded in and out. Some needed food or housing, others sought counseling or an encouraging word, which was almost always accompanied by a hug. Still others asked only that she pray with them. No one was turned away, and yet there was never the sense of anyone being hurried or given less time than he or she needed in order to be fully heard.

After observing this intimate process for several hours, it became obvious to us that everyone who came through the door was not only welcome but embraced by Alice as a cherished member of her extended family. As we watched the respect and kindness she offered each person—the parent who was a child abuser, an addicted teen-ager, a confused street person, a homeless mother and her baby, the school administrator on the telephone—we asked, "How do you do it? How can you see so clearly what is going on with people and still not judge them, but let each person know that you are on the side of their deepest and best hope for themselves? How do you manage to be so honest and so loving?"

"First of all, I don't do it," she answered quickly. "I'm just a vessel that God works through. I got my degree in knowing from God a long time ago, and because I allow Him to do the work, it happens. The key to it is giving. Don't store up anything. Whatever He puts in the vessel, give it away, keep it going."

"'Degree in knowing from God?'" we asked. "What do you mean by that?"

"Well, it came from something that happened to me in my early teens," she explained, "a time of trial and testing. And once I got through it I knew something in me had changed forever.

"Even as a little girl," she began, "I was known as the 'missionary' in my community. The reason I got this name is that I would sit out in the backyard all day long singing and praying. I don't remember when I started praying for people, but I've been doing it all my life, and I know if I pray for someone, something happens. Nevertheless I used to get angry when my mother would come get me out of the backyard and make me go with her to pray for someone in the neighborhood who was sick."

Although Alice's mother recognized the value of her daughter's prayers, her playmates did not. She often felt lonely and left out by her peers, she told us. Those who had enough courage to answer honestly when she asked why they hadn't included her in some activity would say, "No one wants to bother with you because all you're going to do is pray anyway," or "Some of the kids are afraid of you so they don't want you to come along with us." Comments like these intensified her feelings of being different from other children. "I used to worry a lot about this," she told us, "and especially about what I did that made them afraid to be with me.

"By the time I reached adolescence, however, I had finally become good friends with a girl my age, and that made me very happy. One night I told my mother I was going to a Bible study class with my friend, but we didn't go there. Instead we slipped out and went to a dance for teenagers. My friend had a boyfriend and he had brought another boy with him to the dance. I liked his friend, I guess. The next time I saw him we ended up having sex. I was only thirteen years old at the time.

"The next month I didn't get my period. Then I had to confess to my mother that it wasn't Bible study classes we had been going to, and she just started jumping all over the house saying, 'Oh, my God. Oh, my God.' It wasn't long before the word got around the community and then a lot of people began to say, 'You see, she wasn't as good as everybody thought.' I really brought shame on my family at that time. But I was determined to get back into the fold of having people trust me, even if I had no idea how to go about doing that."

Although Alice felt she had let her family down by her behavior, we were curious to know if she felt shame or disappointment in herself. "I don't think I was really old enough to know if I was disappointed in myself or not. I was hurt because of the way my family and the community were treating me, but I didn't know that much about God then. Keep in mind that although I had been praying and singing for people since I was a young child, I really didn't know why. It was just that I had always done those things.

"During the last month that I was carrying the baby, however, I really began to feel the terrible loneliness and the hurt. I was seeking love from people, and it started to sink in that I had done something wrong, but I still didn't know what to do to correct it."

"Wasn't there anyone you could turn to for help or comfort?" Pat asked.

It was then that Alice told us about a family who lived above their flat, a family the community had "shut out and left alone" because of the unusual way in which they worshipped. Feeling the pain of her own rejection, she reached out to them and, "in return, ended up getting what I most needed," she told us.

"They took me with them to their Bible study classes, and that's when the changes began to take place," she explained. "It was just like picking up the tools I needed. At my own church we got preaching—we learned how to treat our neighbors right and do right, but there was never any explanation about *why* we should do these things. I never understood the *why* of it. But one of the first pieces of scripture I read in the Bible class was this verse from Proverbs: 'Lean not on your own understanding, but in all your ways acknowledge God and He will direct your path.' And those words opened up something for me. I started to see the community in a different way. I stopped looking at people as if they hated me, and I didn't feel any hate for them. I had made a mistake and they just didn't understand it, and neither did I. And since I didn't have that understanding I tried to remember what I had read in Proverbs and let God direct my path.

"But it was a Jewish lady I went to work for as a nursemaid after my own baby was born who helped me realize I wasn't bad like my family and community had thought. She helped me to see that God's forgiveness is beyond our understanding and that I had to forgive myself and live from that. She told me she saw something in my smile that was good, and one day she asked me a simple question: 'Alice,' she said, 'what do you want to be when you get older?'

"I couldn't answer her. I couldn't say a word. You see, until that moment it had never occurred to me that I could be anything. That night I told my mother what had transpired between us and she got furious. She was convinced I'd done something to displease my employer and that her question about what I wanted to be was her way of letting me know she was planning to fire me. I knew my mother would throw me out of the house if I lost my job, and the prospect of this upset me so much that I couldn't quit crying for the next two days.

"Of course the Jewish lady noticed my misery and pressed me to tell her what was wrong. When I finally worked up enough courage to tell her, she looked stunned. 'Why, I have no intention of firing you, Alice,' she said. 'It's just that I think you're too good for this job. There's something in you that can do much better than this.'

"But I can't," I protested. "Mama says I'm finished." Then looking me straight in the face she said, 'You might think you're finished, but I'm not finished with you!' And with that she went to work. Within a few days she helped me get enrolled in a cosmetology course. She even drove me to class on my lunch hour and picked me up afterward so I could continue to earn money working for her while I went to school. I had nearly completed my training before my mother even knew about it.

"I wasn't bad. But looking back on it now, I know this experience was something I had to go through. Bearing that hurt made me realize that I didn't want anybody else to have to go through that kind of loneliness and pain. Now I can recognize and feel it when I'm with someone. I can look at that person and have compassion because I wore those shoes. If I had never worn them, it would have been much different, I am sure. It's like a male doctor in the delivery room. About a minute before the baby comes he pats you on the back and says, 'Mother, I know just how you feel.' Then a woman doctor comes in and says, 'Now I'm going to help you deliver this baby. I've had three of my own and I know how you feel,' and you *know* she knows. There's a lot of difference between those two doctors.

"It's one thing to believe, and another thing to know. I don't need to believe if I know. And if you believe strong enough and hard enough, knowing comes and takes its place. So I can look at the folks who come into the Center and say, 'I know how you feel,' and they can believe me. I have the degree in knowing that God gave me a long time ago and the title that goes with it, Servant for the People, and that's all I want to be. I don't want to be anything else."

A fundamental characteristic in the lives of many of the women we interviewed for this book was the ability to use times of trial and adversity as an opportunity for spiritual awakening and deepening. And as it had for Alice, the pattern often began in childhood.

One woman in her middle forties, for example, whose childhood had been filled with violence, betrayal, and abandonment told us that at the age of six she "made a deal with God. I said, 'O.K., look, let's do it this way. If I have to be here, I'll stay on one condition, and that is that I break this chain of misery in my family.

I'll try and do the best I can, but when I get old and am about to die please don't let me look back and see unhappy children. I don't want to leave behind unhappy children who will have more unhappy children. Please let that chain be broken with me."

Another woman whose childhood had been far from idyllic said to us, "We can not be responsible for more than we know, more than we happen to be at any given moment in any situation. At the time we did our best, and our parents—well, I really believe they did their best too. There is a way to look on everything that lets it be another step toward the sacred."

Although we live in an age when there seems to be a psychological explanation for everything, something much deeper than psychological cause and effect is reflected by these attitudes. Many of the women we interviewed who experienced cruelty and deprivation in childhood were like dormant bulbs that survive in a harsh environment and grow stronger and more beautiful in the process. After all, that is why their stories appear in this book. They are the successful survivors, the women who have become sources of spiritual inspiration to others.

Although childhood was a time of great receptivity to the divine for these women, it was also a time of great vulnerability. If there is a common message in all of their stories, it is the need for honoring the purity and openness of a child's mind. Perhaps someday, as the Swiss psychoanalyst Alice Miller writes, we will come to "regard our children not as creatures to manipulate or to change but rather as messengers from a world we once deeply knew but which we have long since forgotten who can reveal to us more about the true secrets of life, and also our own lives, than our parents were ever able to."[1]

Chapter 3
LEAVING HOME

The familiar life horizon has been outgrown:
the old concepts, ideals, and emotional
patterns no longer fit; the time for the
passing of a threshold is at hand.

— Joseph Campbell
The Hero with a Thousand Faces

 At the end of childhood, we are called to move out of immaturity into responsibility. If we do not make this passage, if we attach ourselves to our childhood home as a mollusk does to a sea rock, we do not mature. This much is obvious. But what is not so obvious is what *home* means to each of us, when we need to leave it, and how.

How do we find the courage to let go of what feels sure and safe and comfortable so that a new possibility can unfold? And how do we do this not just once, at the end of childhood, but many times throughout a lifetime, whenever old certainties need to be released, or perhaps abandoned entirely, so that we can take that enormous step across the threshold of our old home?

In religious traditions founded and taught by men, the answers to these questions have generally been radical and unequivocal: home-leaving has entailed a severance from whomever and whatever has been held dear. The mythologist Joseph Campbell recounts how, in virtually every culture, destiny summons the hero and transfers "his spiritual center of gravity" from his family and homeland to an unknown territory. A distant land, a forest, a kingdom underground, a place beneath the waves or above the sky—the fateful region is always some distant place. And whether the seeker sets forth willingly, is carried, or wanders off by accident, the initial step in patriarchal traditions almost always means severing old bonds in order to enter the new territory.

Sacred literature is filled with such images and stories of home-leaving. In perhaps the most universally told story, the home-leaver is exiled from Paradise: "So the Lord God banished him [Adam] from the Garden of Eden," we are told. "He drove the man out, and stationed east of the Garden of Eden the cherubim and the fiery ever-turning sword."[1] In another familiar account the ancient Hebrews left their homes in Egypt because it was a place of bondage, and they wandered in the desert for forty years, lost and lamenting, until everyone who could remember slavery had died. In Buddhist mythology, Prince Siddhartha left his wife and child in the middle of the night to begin his spiritual quest, and after he became the Buddha he addressed his monks with the resounding call, "O ye nobly born, ye home-leavers." And in the Christian tradition as well, Jesus instructed his followers to leave their homes and families and "cleave only unto me."

Not only are we taught that our forefathers had to sever their relationships in order to begin their spiritual journeys, but it is intimated that the deepest mystical questing requires this step. Eastern and western monastic traditions embrace this perspective enthusiastically: "Full of hindrances is household life, a path for the dust of passion," the Buddha explains in the Sammanaphala Suttana.[2] And the value of this severance is acknowledged in non-monastic traditions as well. "Abraham our father left the certainty of the womb . . . for the wilderness," Rabbi Lawrence Kushner affirms, invoking the memory of generation after generation of Jews who left their homes. "Setting out, leaving everything behind. The social milieu. The preconceptions. The narrowed field of vision.

The language. No longer expecting relationships, memories, words, to mean what they used to mean. To be, in a word, open."[3]

Exiles from the garden. Strangers in a strange land. In every age our spiritual forefathers have left home because they believed that to come to God you had to be stripped of allegiance to tribe or homeland, of the love of parents and wives and children, of the responsibilities and privileges of daily life. Like shamans in hunting and gathering societies who take young men through severe rites of passage, our ancestors believed that until you are stripped bare, you cannot open to the innermost reality.

Our fathers believed this, and perhaps it was true for them. But what about our mothers? What of all the generations of our mothers who did not leave home to wander in the wilderness, but who remained to raise children and plant gardens and cook meals? Were they less open to the sacred? And, to raise a more urgent question, what about us? What about those of us who love our parents and husbands and children, who have responsibilities in the daily world, who *make* homes rather than leave them? To open to our innermost being, do we, too, need to leave home?

When we began our interviews, we honestly had no idea whether or not home-leaving would be a part of women's spiritual unfolding. After all, we thought, aren't women and children the "homes" that men traditionally leave? Nuns, of course, who leave their personal relationships and family life for a religious calling are an exception. But what about spiritual women who do not live the life of a monastic? When there are no institutional requirements, we wondered, do women leave behind what has been dear to them in order to open to the divine?

It was just at this point in our questioning that the whole matter of home-leaving took on a relevance that we could never have predicted. It happened so quickly it was as if a blast of wind had rushed down from the mountains and fanned a small bonfire into a conflagration.

We had left family, friends, and ringing telephones behind to take advantage of a friend's vacant beach cottage on a rugged stretch of the northern California coast to write. Weeks of discussion about what it means to leave home and many readings and rereadings of the transcripts had preceded our departure. Having done our home-work, we felt well prepared for the task at hand. We thought we knew who we were and what we were capable of and whom we could depend on. But within two weeks, our careful preparations and glowing self-confidence were reduced to ashes when we each had to face personal crises that transformed our objective, detached analysis of home-leaving into searing, soul-searching questions.

In the days that followed, we learned a couple of truths about home-leaving. It doesn't necessarily mean that *you* leave anything; sometimes someone leaves you. Nor does it necessarily mean that anyone actually goes anywhere, because after all is said and done, what is left—or lost—is not a relationship or a place or even a context. What is left is a consciousness that once felt secure, had categories to fit things into, and knew who it was, where it was going, and why. And what replaces this sureness is "not knowing." And openness. And something unspeakably, and sometimes almost unbearably, new.

One other thing we learned is that we needed to look beyond the familiar stories and teachings about home-leaving we had learned from men. Questions emerging from our own experiences crowded our minds. Once again we went back through the stories of the women we had interviewed to try and find some answers.

DO WOMEN LEAVE HOME?

"Mystery doesn't mean only some grand, ecstatic thing," one woman told us as she was leaving the spiritual community in which she had lived for many years. "It means stumbling around in the darkness, terrified that nothing will be there if you don't call on God in the old way. Once I knew what my life was consecrated to and what my direction was. Now I don't know, and I don't even know where to look."

Another woman, in the midst of leaving her secure position as a tenured professor at an eastern university, confided, "Again and again I dream that I am walking barefoot, or naked, on a stony path I've never traveled before. I know I have left my old home behind, but I don't know how to find my new home."

"Memories are coming up for me these days from my early childhood," a midwesterner in her early fifties told us. "I'm beginning to realize how conditioned I've been to regard men as sources of spiritual authority in the world. I remember how even as a young girl I used to 'translate' nouns and pronouns in hymns and prayers in order to feel related to God. Now I do it automatically and unconsciously whenever I read any spiritual texts....My sense of self-betrayal is profound. I have spent a lifetime acquiring expertise in a spiritual language that is not my native tongue, and now something in me is violently protesting, 'No more. No more.'"

Perhaps the one decision we do *not* have to make about home-leaving is when to do it. Home-leaving happens. Dreams come. Memories present themselves. As sure as birth contractions come to separate us from the safety of the womb, some hidden timing stirs us, bringing a sense of readiness for the new. We wake up one morning to find that we are no longer able to squeeze into our old identity. What used to feel secure and comforting now feels life-denying, and suddenly we know it is time to leave home.

Every woman we interviewed reached this threshold at least once in her life where, as Joseph Campbell expressed it, "the old concepts, ideals and emotional meanings no longer fit," and each one chose to cross it. In this respect, one of our questions was answered: Modern women, like the heroes of eastern and western religious traditions, leave home.

But having said this, we must quickly add that the women we spoke with rarely left home in the same way as spiritual heroes of the past. For the most part they did not sever their relationships with those they loved. Even more remarkably, they did not usually leave home to quest for the sacred, as did virtually every male spiritual seeker from the Buddha to the knights of the Holy Grail. On the contrary, the women we talked with made their connection with the sacred before they ever left home.

One Christian woman expressed this to us in a calm, no-nonsense tone of voice: "We don't need to go off to any place special to find our connection to God, and we don't need the church to give it to us. We each have our own connection directly. We may need to leave home for other things—for independence, for breaking through or breaking away from social roles, for learning how to trust ourselves—but we don't need to do it for our connection."

It took us a very long time to recognize the truth of this statement because it didn't fit our expectations. We thought that women, like men, would find it necessary to sever relationships and go through austere kinds of testing before trusting the reality unfolding through their lives. Moreover, we clung to this conviction for several months because a few of the women we interviewed actually did undergo this kind of separation.

"There was a death at the center of my life," a former school-teacher told us. "On the outside, everything was perfect—perfect marriage, perfect job, perfect home—but on the inside my intuition and vision had been cut off. At a certain point I realized I had become so blended with my husband that I had no idea who I was or what I cared about. I realized that I was never going to know if I stayed in my home where I was too safe and secure. That whole cocoon just had to burst!"

And burst it did, as this formerly solicitous wife abruptly left home for an exotic land she knew only vaguely from novels. She nearly died there, she told us, but when she returned to her home and husband she was "wide open with nothing to lose, with a completely new reality within myself." She describes her experience in the classical home-leaving imagery of one who has been stripped bare and tested: "I know from that experience that if you don't try yourself to your absolute utmost, you have no idea of your spiritual depths. You don't know who you are. Not that you have to journey around the world, but somehow you have to get free of the seductive nest. When you throw yourself into a situation where you have *not* got what it takes, then you have to open up to God."

But although some women left home in this way, most did not.

Artist and author Meinrad Craighead, for example, left home twice: once to enter the monastery and once to leave it. But she writes that "God the Mother came to me when I was a child. . . . Through half a lifetime of Catholic liturgies . . . we lived at my inmost center. This natural religious instinct for my Mothergod gave me a profound sense of security and stability. She was the sure ground I grew in, the groundsill of my spirituality."[4]

Not all women, of course, feel this "natural religious instinct" in childhood. Many are adults or even elderly before they develop a sense of allowing, or trusting, their essential nature. But whether this openness came early or late in the lives of the women we interviewed, rarely did it depend on leaving home. Rather, home-leaving seems to have been an auxiliary process, something that helped widen or deepen a channel already running through the woman's life. For most of the women we interviewed, home-leaving served to increase permeability to the divine in a life that had already opened to it.

WHY WOMEN LEAVE HOME

Why, if not to quest for the sacred, would a woman need to leave home at all?

"After you've hit the most profound center, then you have to *spend* this life. To expend it!" the contemplative Bernadette Roberts announced to us, explaining why she decided to leave the Carmelite cloister. "You need to live out the whole human experience."

"Why?" we asked. "What were you looking for?"

"I wasn't looking for ecstasy because I had that. In a way, leaving was the greatest sacrifice I ever made because the sisters were so dear to my heart. But I was looking for the challenges of being. I wanted to see how this new state of consciousness worked in the world, how it would work if I was in a pickle or cornered or trapped. I wanted to test it, so out I went. But in one sense you never leave the cloister. When union with God has been attained and you go out into the world, you simply take the cloister with you. In other words, when you have permanent awareness of God, come hell or high water your cloister is always with you."

Sarah Leah Grafstein is another woman who needed to test her spiritual authenticity by leaving home. After being raised in an orthodox Jewish home and spending a decade in serious religious study, she began in her middle thirties to challenge the certainties of her spiritual life. "Who would you be if you were totally isolated from the Jewish community?" she would ask herself. "How observant do you need to be? How much does your connection with God come from within, and how much does it depend on other Jews? How honest are you being with your Jewish trip in the first place? You've got to find out!"

After a full year of these questions Sarah Leah felt compelled to leave her friends and community to live in solitude. Through the next two years of virtual isolation, she told us, "I was ready to give up many times. But whenever I got really desperate, I would reach a whole new level of prayer. In the absence of my familiar spiritual touchstones, teachers came to me in dreams and visions, showing me new forms of practice and prayer. Rituals that were fresh and full of meaning sprang up from my meditations in the woods. And I discovered that I was, after all, really very Jewish."

Indeed she was. A few months after our interview, Sarah Leah telephoned to say that she had decided to become a rabbi. She has since been ordained and is practicing her ministry in Arizona.

Not all women, however, leave home voluntarily, as Bernadette and Sarah Leah did. For some, a profound rejection, an addiction, a serious illness, or a devastating loss breaks into the familiar security of daily life and catapults them into unfathomed depths of their being.

In mythology, there are many examples of such descents.[5] Young Persephone was innocently gathering flowers with her friends when she was abducted by Hades and carried off to the underworld. The Sumerian queen of heaven and earth, Inanna, descended to the netherworld to visit her sister, but instead of a warm welcome she was forced to give over her symbols of queenly power, murdered and left to rot.

Through such terrible descents, these archetypal goddesses die to the innocence and assumed security of the young and healthy who feel impervious to suffering. Having died, they can be reborn. In time, both Persephone and Inanna return to the living, bringing with them the gift of their journeys to the dark realms—a knowledge of vulnerability, of the shadowy parts of themselves and the uncontrollable mystery of death.

So it is today with women who leave home through a descent process. Whatever place of authority they hold in the world, whatever beauty they may have been admired for, whatever knowledge they may have acquired in the uncharted regions of the "underworld," all become useless. Even those who have been spiritual teachers with a following of devoted students revert to rank beginners during the period of their descent.

"In order to gain my life, I've had to lose it," Carol Collopy told us, alluding to her experience with breast cancer, which came at the height of her work as a greatly admired spiritual mentor. For seven years after her mastectomy, she lived an almost hermetic life, seeing only her family and a few close friends, attuning herself to the changes in her body and waiting for cues that would lead her to the next step of her life.

Then, just as she was beginning to emerge from her cocoon, her husband of thirty years had a nearly fatal accident, plummeting two stories from a rooftop to the sidewalk below. For a while it was not clear whether he would live or, should he survive, whether his brain would function normally. He went through a slow and difficult recovery that altered their lives "almost beyond recognition." Carol told us with intensity, "I've had to let the old be cleaved away and give up the things I love the most. I've had to let the threads of the past be pulled out so the pattern of the new can take shape. And it has taken shape. It is taking shape within me. I feel deep within my cells the new being formed through the death of the old."

The experience of descent is primarily a process of learning to trust the neglected or rejected parts of oneself. Women who leave home in this way, therefore, do not need to go anywhere, change jobs, or become involved in new relationships. More often than not, they remain right where they are and go deep within themselves.

Joanna Macy, a teacher of Buddhism and an activist for social and ecological change, left home in this way. In 1978, when she was a graduate student in her forties with a husband and three college-age children, she attended an all-day conference on the biosphere presented by The Cousteau Society.

"My children invited me to that conference," she explained, "and although I learned no new facts, the cumulative effect was devastating. People were talking about the arms race and oil spills and the demolition of the rain forests . . . and it broke through to me somewhere in the middle of the afternoon that this could really be curtains for us all. I saw this fact so clearly that I didn't know how I could stand it.

"For the next year, I lived with despair, although as I soon learned, despair is a social taboo, preferably to be hidden away like a shameful secret. Once I had accepted the real possibility of the earth's destruction, my grief would break through in unexpected onslaughts. Working at home at my desk, I'd suddenly find myself on the floor, curled up in a fetal position and shaking. In company I was more controlled, but even then in those early months, the sight of an egret lighting by the edge of the marsh or the sound of Bach from a nearby piano would unexpectedly pierce my heart, as I wondered how long it would be before that piece of beauty faded forever."

Perhaps one is tempted when hearing a story like Joanna's to feel that anyone who allows herself to succumb to such feelings is not very "spiritually developed," that in fact she is too emotional, too attached to this world. Such criticism is frequently directed toward women who express heartfelt reactions to suffering, and Joanna heard it often, even from those she turned to for support. A psychotherapist who found her attitude perplexing asked, "You have beautiful children, a wonderful husband, a lovely home. Why can't you be happy?" And in the graduate department of religion at Syracuse University where she was working on her doctorate,

Joanna's professors seemed embarrassed when she spoke of this despair. One suggested that there were larger realms of meaning than life on this earth and promptly changed the subject. Another attributed her suffering to personal, psychological maladjustment.

The fact is, however, that almost all of the women we met who left home through a descent process already had profound encounters with reality, encounters which, to use Joanna's phrase, had "an unshakable authority." In many cases, it seems that this connection is what enabled them to experience such depths of feeling. Living through their feelings of despair, rage, jealousy, or helplessness and letting them go, allowing the next layer of feelings to emerge and again letting go, is what enabled the women we spoke with to step beyond the restrictive boundaries of their old homes and enter into new possibilities.

Before this, however, each woman had to come to terms with her own experience in all its particularities. If she judged herself too harshly because her behavior and feeling did not correspond with what others—even those closest to her—seemed to be doing and feeling, she could not cross this threshold and accept the reality of her own life. Each woman had to be emotionally present in her own life and somehow find a way to trust it.

TRUST

Learning to trust the unfolding of one's own life is awkward, painful work that often leaves one feeling exposed and vulnerable. And it does not happen overnight. One woman described this process to us in detail. With a decision that sent shock waves through her community, she gave up her position as retreat director of a large spiritual center on the East Coast to live in relative solitude with her children. At the time of her departure, she was unable to say why she was leaving, but two years later when we interviewed her, she explained, "The old practices weren't working anymore. I found I had absorbed my path, and then there was that moment of having to sever the old, of thinking, 'Oh, my God, I'm on the edge. God is no longer out there somewhere, but in here.' I was swinging back and forth between a very deep cosmic urging and my feeling of terrible limitation. And what it all came down to was: Can I trust myself?

"I remember the moment in a soul-felt prayer when it became very clear to me. I was looking out the window at the landscape, and I sensed something about the meaning of life. What I realized was that I had always remained above it. In that moment I had such a tender and strong feeling in my heart for human beings. I thought of soldiers in battle and artists—people who give everything, squeeze their whole life's energy into living, by sacrifice or by love, putting their juice into life. And I realized I had not been doing that. And at that moment my soul *flew* out and said, 'I want to be with them.' And this is what I chose to do. But now that I'm in the midst of it, I'm starting to freak out.

"I feel like everything is turned inside out for me. The old is certainly not applicable, nor does it work, nor do I feel it's whole enough. On the other hand, this new way is so . . . new. I have no guidelines."

To turn toward the new in such moments can seem foolhardy or even dangerous. We feel frightened, inept, confused. The familiar roles that have let us feel strong and sure of ourselves are gone, and along with them goes the predictability of our lives. To add to our insecurity, anxious friends and family are likely to ask: "Why can't you be satisfied with things as they are?" and "Aren't you afraid you'll regret this?" In fact, that may be exactly what we are afraid of, and we may know almost as little as they about why we're leaving the old ways behind. When we ask ourselves why we want to leave or change, the only response may be a silent yearning or an unrelenting ache in our heart.

"I felt I wasn't very far along," a former student of Tibetan Buddhism told us, as she described leaving the teacher she revered. "I felt I never would get anywhere on my own. But then something arose in me, a trust that something in my life itself was the teacher. And I thought, 'It isn't a tradition that's going to get me where I need to go. And I don't have to become a nun or live in a cloister either. There is a *gnosis*, a direct inner knowing, that is driving me. It's not somebody else's tradition now; it's mine, and I have to follow it.

"In the next year," she continued, "I let my own unfolding occur. And there were many times when I just wept because I was releasing all this *stuff* about what spirituality had to be and what I had to do to experience it. I let it all go. It was as though I had been taken out into the garden and someone said, 'Okay, now you can play!'"

Sage Kimble, a midwife and ceremonialist in the Native American tradition, smiled ruefully as she told us about the first time she decided to leave home. "I made a conscious decision to put my spiritual path first and let the other details fall into place around that—an approach that has a lot of potential for bringing chaos into one's life! But the second time I left, well . . . actually, my beloved left me. I was shocked and I grieved, but, you know, it wasn't like the first time. I knew something was coming, and these losses were making room in my life for a whole new possibility."

"Finally, you see that there is nothing you can trust—nobody, no authority—except the process itself," the spiritual teacher A. H. Almaas observes. "Finally the trust is . . . trusting reality. It is just trust—confidence in the essence itself."[6]

MEINRAD'S STORY

Meinrad Craighead burst into our lives through the publication of her book *The Mother's Songs: Images of God the Mother*. Never had we seen such evocative paintings of the feminine! Frederick Franck, the Dutch artist and writer, calls her images "luminous icons . . . that bring the ancient myth of the Great Mother to life. Breasts, bellies, umbilical cords, menstrual images . . . with nothing coarse, the erotic linked with the sacramental in the manner of worship."[7]

Who was this artist, we wondered, and would she be willing to meet with us? The first question was answered in the preface to her book. Frankly, we were amazed to learn that Meinrad had been a nun in a Benedictine abbey outside London for over a decade before leaving the monastery and moving to New Mexico. The second question—Would she meet with us?—was answered by Meinrad herself. Yes, and we must plan to stay a week, she said, because she had a community of friends who were vitally interested in women's spirituality.

We met at her cottage, which also served as her studio, in Albuquerque. It was March, and the olive trees surrounding her home were already in yellow bloom. The pods on the cottonwood trees bordering the nearby Rio Grande were swelling in the early spring heat. Soon these pods would burst open, Meinrad told us, and release their feathery white puffs to the wind. We heard the echo of this remark a few days later when we learned about Meinrad's departure from the abbey. For it was with just such an explosion of energy that she left the cloistered home in which she had been living and growing for fourteen years.

Meinrad Craighead was born in Little Rock, Arkansas, where she spent the early years of her childhood. Her family moved to Chicago when she was still quite young. It was there that she and her two younger sisters grew up in the middle of a Jewish neighborhood. "I always felt 'other,'" she told us, "because I was Catholic and had a southern accent."

She spent her summers with her grandparents in Little Rock, summers which she described in idyllic terms. "It was just this green-golden pastoral time, a time of enormous freedom," she said. "My grandparents didn't have much money, so it certainly wasn't that we kids were given lots of toys or taken places, but we had the land and we had our ingenuity. It was the only respite I had from Chicago where everything was pavement and even the apartment houses seemed regimented."

When Meinrad was three years old, she began drawing. From the beginning her close relationship with her grandmother was central to her art. "My grandmother was the earliest recipient of my drawings," she told us. "When I was away from her during those long winters in Chicago, it was some solace for me to be able to send them to her as gifts."

By the time she reached adolescence, Meinrad knew that art was the priority of her life. Drawing was an act of thanksgiving for her, she told us, an act that let her express an "overwhelming gratitude just for existence, and it was inextricably linked to prayer. I don't know if praying made me need to draw, or if drawing made me need to pray. I've never been able to identify one without the other." However, she was quick to explain that prayer for her was never limited to religious forms.

"From as early as I can remember, praying was something quite different from praying in church. It was always being alone in nature—under a tree, in a tree, under a bush, digging a hole, walking with my dogs, watching birds, listening to the river." Praying, for Meinrad, has its roots in the natural world of Mother Earth, and from the time of her youth she has relied on it to give direction to her life.

After graduating from the University of Wisconsin with a master's degree in fine arts and teaching for several years in Florence, Meinrad found her prayer life intensifying. "I was praying a lot every day," she told us, "and at one point I began to understand that I was supposed to be in a monastery. 'Oh, my God, that's what comes next,' I thought, and I felt sick at heart."

But Meinrad was also used to following the guidance she received in prayer, and that was what she intended to do this time as well, even when an urbane priest from Rome advised her: "If you go to a monastery, you'll be digging potatoes, peeling potatoes, and eating potatoes for the rest of your life. Do you really feel that God is asking you to give up your very unique gifts for that?"

"Well, it kind of looks that way," Meinrad replied, "because this is what I've been hearing and I've got to do something about it."

Seeing that she was not likely to be dissuaded by anything he might say, the priest offered a suggestion. "I think you should investigate the Benedictines," he said. "They have a tradition of cultural sophistication, and they encourage artists. You might try Stanbrook Abbey in England."

What the priest could not have known was that Meinrad had already contracted with her inner guidance "that whatever the priest recommended, that's where I would go—no matter where it was in the world, no matter what order it was." So when he suggested Stanbrook Abbey, Meinrad knew that if the abbess there accepted her, she would go.

Stanbrook Abbey, on first visit, was "ghastly, absolutely ghastly," she confessed. "But, you know, you do amazing things if you're told from within to do them. What has always been mysterious to me is that I have had the strength to do what was needed, that I've been able to see the options and do what was painful or hard. Even entering the monastery. I knew that was going to be very difficult. But I also knew I had to do it."

When we are on the verge of making a deep promise, it is not uncommon for great resistances and fears to arise. Whatever threatens our reality or present way of life, whatever we know will profoundly change us, often seems more terrifying than inviting. But if we are able to make the commitment, we sometimes experience an unexpected joy.

Meinrad entered the cloister with just such a joy. "I was off the ground. I was levitating," she told us. At first she missed her family, but after a while she adapted to not seeing them. And right from the beginning she was given her own studio where, except for the hours of prayer and other conventual commitments, she was able to spend much of every day drawing and painting. Gradually her reputation as an artist grew, and her paintings were exhibited widely in Europe and the United States. Articles about her appeared in periodicals and books, and she was the subject of several documentary films.

For fourteen years it was a very satisfying life. She loved the rhythms and the repetition of the monastic chants, the rounds of feast days, the tolling of the great bell that called the nuns together for prayer, and the silences. "Nothing disturbed me," she told us.

"We received little formal training in prayer—for which I'm very grateful—so I just got on with my wonderful bad habits."

The year Meinrad celebrated her forty-fourth birthday, she noticed a strong, new theme in her paintings—birds. There were birds nesting on the shoulders of hills, birds flying low over rivers, birds scarcely visible in wet, hidden wildernesses. "Gradually," she told us, "the spirit came sweeping through me, saying, 'Oh baby, you're gonna fly outa' here!'"

She was both exhilarated and terrified. "My God," she thought, "where am I going to go? What am I going to do? I don't know how the modern world works anymore. How do you earn a living?" But some archetype of flight, she said, literally lifted her out of the monastery. "I was so full of wind and flight, it was an insane happiness, a lunacy. And it lasted for months and months, moving my body around, possessing me with its energy." Within a year Meinrad left Stanbrook Abbey without any feelings of pain or guilt.

But why did she need to leave, we wondered? Her life as an artist was flourishing, and, as she later wrote, her bond with the divine continued to flow through her life like a great underground river. Perhaps the answer lay in her expectations. Meinrad had thought monastic life was about freedom of spirit and the risks of an unorthodox life. But "for most of the nuns the enclosed life ensured a continuation of the inherited security of English homes and institutions," she wrote in an article shortly after her departure. It was impossible, disintegrating, she said, "to support a liturgy that exalted a masculine God image and encouraged women to lead limited, subordinated, clerically-defined lives."[8]

Her frustration is apparent, and perhaps it provided a necessary impetus for leaving the monastery. Although we may not like to acknowledge it, when we are in the process of moving away from someone or something that once nourished and sustained us, we often become critical or angry in order to garner enough energy to make the necessary separation.

At the time of our interview with Meinrad six years after she had left the monastery, her perspective was more relaxed. In response to our questions about why she was no longer a nun, she said simply, "I finally outgrew the cloister." And she drew an interesting parallel between life in the cloister and marriage: "When you sign on for life," she said, "you stop listening carefully day by day. Now, maybe marriages and monastic vocations *can* be for life, but that has to be open to the spirit on a day-by-day basis. Otherwise you stop working with the subtleties and liveliness of the relationships. You get less sensitive. You miss the movements of the spirit within you. You miss the feeling of wonder and surprise every time you see the sunrise.

"A lot of people are trapped in monasteries just like a lot of women are trapped in marriages. They stay because they don't know what they'd do financially if they left. That's when the womb becomes a tomb, when you can't find the courage to leave what needs to be left. And, of course, one can justify this decision by saying, 'I've made a vow to God to stay here forever.' Well, it's just opting out of life."

In the cloister, Meinrad told us she had to leave her inner explorations whenever the great monastic bell summoned the nuns to prayers and meals. "Sometimes when that bell would toll, I would hear it in my studio as if it were a million miles away, as if I were swimming up to the surface from really far down." In her natural setting in the Rio Grande Valley where she and her family of hunting dogs make their home, the door between Meinrad's inner and outer life has swung open. Here her life as an artist is in harmony with the rhythms of her environment.

In honor of her fiftieth birthday a couple of years ago, she built an altar in the center of her spacious tree-bordered yard. On top of this square adobe structure with symbols from various spiritual traditions decorating its sides sits a vessel in the shape of a woman's body. Each morning at sunrise Meinrad lights a fire inside it and offers her prayers for the day. And at solstices and equinoxes women friends like to gather at her altar to celebrate.

In her present home, Meinrad has interwoven the aspects of her being in a way that allows for and appreciates differences rather than attempting to blend those differences into a homogeneous whole. For Meinrad, "Mothergod, that force living within me which is more real, more powerful, than the remote Fathergod I was educated to have faith in" is the truer image of divine spirit. But Christianity also has its place. Praying the Psalms, singing the liturgical chants, and especially reading the gospels continue to be important in her spiritual life. "My Catholic heritage and environment have been like a beautiful river flowing over my subterranean foundation in God the Mother," she writes in her introduction to *The Mother's Songs*. "The two movements are not in conflict, they simply water different layers in my soul."[9]

A critical part of home-leaving in a woman's spiritual development is the willingness not to know where she is going. The length of time that is spent in that place of unknowing between the old and the new varies with each person. It depends on many things: her tolerance for uncertainty; her capacity for surrender; her susceptibility and vulnerability to economic, social, and family pressures; and, finally, her own highly individualized timing, which may include but is ultimately beyond all these factors.

When everything familiar has been sheared away—either because we have physically separated ourselves from our "home," or because our inner exploration has taken us beyond our old self—we are presented with a great opportunity for spiritual growth. At such times, we are likely to examine our lives more deeply than we ever have before and be asked to trust far beyond our understanding. T. S. Eliot knew this place very well and expressed it eloquently in his poem, "East Coker":[10]

> I said to my soul, be still, and wait without hope
> For hope would be hope for the wrong thing; wait
>   without love
> For love would be love of the wrong thing; there is
>   yet faith
> But the faith and the love and the hope are all in the
>   waiting.

Leaving home can take us right to the edge of the unknown. But if the timing is not right, or if we are not yet brave enough, we may choose to postpone or avoid going through it. Because the uncertainty and aloneness that arise can be intensely uncomfortable, the wish to escape can be almost overwhelming. Anything that distracts us from looking beneath the surface issues of our lives will tempt us: a new relationship, a different job, moving to a different city or going to the country, taking up the latest form of exercise, attending one more workshop or seminar.

Nor does our culture offer us support for periods of spiritual deepening in our lives. Instead, we are often made to feel neurotic, undirected, or just plain lazy if we are not actively "doing something." In a society whose TV and radio commercials bombard us dozens of times daily with the message that "instant relief" is available for everything from hemorrhoids to headaches, patience and the capacity to trust are not highly valued qualities.

However, the danger of not leaving home is that we can spend the rest of our lives hiding from ourselves. Addicted to love, work, food, alcohol, or drugs, we'll seize whatever we need in order not to hear the silence, clinging to it as if it were a life preserver instead of a straight jacket.

What we have learned from the women whose stories are the basis of this book is that an attitude of allowing, of "not knowing," of opening to the new, can be like rain falling on the hard-packed soil of our lives. If we are willing, it can soften us, so we can feel gratitude and compassion and our own human vulnerability.

This is not to say, however, that home-leaving is without risk. In truth, many of the women we interviewed cycled through periods of anxiety, loneliness, fear, and depression during this transitional time, although in varying degrees of intensity and duration. Several told us that they had contemplated suicide. Marcia Lauck, an author and director of a contemplative community who lives in San Jose, California, described her prolonged struggle between life and death during a home-leaving experience as the "black hole syndrome."

"It was all I could do to get up in the morning, put my clothes on, and move through the routine tasks of everyday living." When we asked why she hadn't sought help from a therapist, she replied, "I didn't feel I had the power to move anything outward at that time. It was all going on inside. And I needed to go through it without psychotherapy or drugs, even though it was very scary. I thought I might be insane. I just didn't know. I found I just had to be willing to wait. And I had to trust what came."

While she waited, Marcia reached out in the only way she was able—she wrote letters. One day, from the "volumes" of letters she had sent to her friends, one came back. Only now it was neatly typed rather than in her own handwriting, and on the top was a note that said, "I thought you should have this back."

"It was such a gift to have that letter returned," she told us. "It was my own clear statement of where I was in my life. It said, 'I feel like all my life every light has been on, that I have always known where I was going and what I was to do. Suddenly, not only have the lights been turned out, but the rooms aren't even the same anymore. So I don't know where I am going. I am just feeling my way along.'"

Marcia sighed, remembering. "I felt for the first time that something stuck inside. It was as if part of me said, 'Okay. At least this is going someplace. You can trust this.'"

If we have learned to trust the inner self when it sings, can we trust it when the singing goes flat or stops altogether? What is it that we trust anyway? By the time we get around to asking that question, all the beautiful and inspiring words we've read or heard or even spoken ourselves seem at best distant echoes of something we once believed. At this point, as one woman put it, "We want to know whether we're going through a 'dark night of the soul' or a depression. If it's a 'dark night,' we'll try to get through it. If not, we want Elavil."

While most of the women we spoke with did experience dark nights of the soul in their home-leaving process, Maria Rifo proved to be an exception. A bright-eyed, trim woman who radiates vitality and competence, Maria had just celebrated her eightieth birthday and been honored by her Northern California community for outstanding volunteer work when we first met her. We had all enrolled in a short course on fathers and daughters, and from the first day of class when Maria told us about her life, we knew that she had a lot to teach us about home-leaving.

Maria was born in a village in Chile. Her mother died when she was only a few years old, and within a short time her father remarried. Although she was fond of her stepmother, Maria felt a special bond with her father, a teacher of Spanish. She could often intuit his needs before he spoke them. "We were strongly connected on the psychic level," she told us.

When Maria was about nine her father made a statement that was to have an enormous impact on the rest of her life: "Men only want women who are rich or beautiful for wives," he told her, "so you must not expect to get married." From that moment on Maria did not regard partnership with a man as a possibility in her life.

Despite her acceptance of her father's pronouncement, however, Maria commented that she felt an inner confidence. "Although I was put down by my father, the beauty of it was that my 'inner' was never dying," she told us. "I always had this feeling inside of being able to open more, to give more."

For the next thirty-three years, Maria lived with her father and stepmother and taught physical education classes at the local school. She was, she told us, a dutiful daughter. When she was fifty-five and had retired from teaching, her father died, and within a year and a half her stepmother also passed away. Maria had not given any thought to what she would do when her parents were no longer alive. "I do things the way they come," she told us. "I take the pieces and build, but I don't say in two years or in twenty years I want to be this or that. I just don't do that."

Alone for the first time in her life and "feeling free," Maria accepted an invitation from a woman friend to travel for a few months. After touring Europe, the two women decided to return home by way of the United States. When they arrived in Washington, D.C., they immediately went to the Chilean embassy. To

Maria's delight, the woman who stepped forward to help them was one of her former high school classmates and neighbors. It turned out to be a fortuitous reunion. The embassy worker was about to leave for a few weeks' vacation, and she offered Maria the use of her home, an offer Maria gladly accepted. By the time the woman returned, Maria had reached an important decision—she wanted to remain in the United States. "I wanted to learn more about your people," she told us. "Not your government, because your government is not liked in Chile, but your *people*."

With the help of her friend at the embassy and because of her fluency in Spanish, Maria qualified for a VISTA assignment with the Hispanic community in Albuquerque, New Mexico. Although she could barely speak English and had almost no money, it was with high spirits that she left for the Southwest. She had a new home and a new job, but, as we shall see, her security was short-lived.

A month or so after her arrival, Maria went to Mexico for the weekend with some VISTA friends. On the return trip, an immigration official discovered that her papers were not in order. Maria had left her passport in Washington, D.C., where she thought it was being processed to extend her U.S. visa. There had been a misunderstanding, however, and as a result, Maria learned she had been living in the U.S. illegally and would not be permitted to reenter.

At that moment Maria became a "woman without a country." Many people face-to-face with such a dilemma would welcome the opportunity to return to the familiar environment of their homeland, an option that Maria chose not to exercise. She had just begun to learn about the American people, she explained, and she wasn't about to give up and go home. Urged by her VISTA supervisor to relocate in either Canada or Mexico while he attempted to arrange for her return to Albuquerque, Maria went to Mexico City to wait.

"I had only enough money for one meal a day so I lost a lot of weight. I got so thin that they couldn't get a fingerprint from me when I applied for my new visa. But I never sat around worrying and feeling helpless. No, no, never. I wanted to make use of the time in a good way. Every day I made the necessary calls to see what could be done, but when I finished with them, I forgot the problems and did something I could enjoy. Any where I could go to learn something, I went.

"Bus fare was very cheap, so I went all over Mexico City and visited many interesting places. On Sundays the museums were free so I would go there and stay all day looking at the beautiful art. On many Sundays I would go to Chapultepec, a huge park, where people taught you for free how to do things like flower-arranging, painting, sewing, math, and English. It was like a big, outdoor school." At the end of three months, Maria received her official immigration papers, as well as the coveted "green card" which allowed her to work in the U.S., and she returned to Albuquerque.

After a year with VISTA, Maria told us that she felt for the first time in her life that she was beginning to open up. She was asking questions about things she didn't understand and confronting people without fear of rejection. Bolstered by her new courage, she attended an event one evening that was to change her life forever. Cesar Chavez was speaking about a new union he was organizing in California for farm workers.

"When Chavez began to speak that evening, it was as if he meditated on each word before he said it. He spoke so slowly and so softly. Each word was linked with the other in such a way that I could feel the truth of what he was saying in my own heart. The very people who were harvesting the food we eat did not have food for their own children." She had witnessed the exploitation of peasants in her own country, and it had disturbed her greatly, but she had felt helpless to do anything about it. "I saw the injustice but I never acted," she lamented. "It never occurred to me that I could do something, that I could organize something myself."

Empowered by her developing self-confidence, Maria went up to Chavez after his talk and said simply, "I want to work with you."

Less than a year later, in 1968, Maria went to California to work full time with the United Farm Workers of America. She was sixty years old—an age when many people are seriously considering retirement. And for the next twelve years, a critical phase in the development of the union, Maria trained in every department. During the early years she served as Chavez's secretary for Spanish correspondence. Later she translated the union's contracts as well as the Hispanic edition of *El Malcriado*, the union newspaper. The workdays were long, often beginning at seven in the morning and continuing until well past midnight, and her responsibilities exacting.

"Working with Cesar," Maria told us, "developed me. He opened my eyes to what I could do."

Although Maria had long been aware of an "inner something" operating in her life, it was not until she left Chile that she was motivated to explore what her relationship to this "inner" might be. "I never tried to develop spiritually in my country," she said. "When I came to the U.S. I felt a little out of everything so I began to go to church. Not so much for the Mass, but to pray. But it was in my work that I actually began to develop spiritually. Cesar had already opened my eyes to things I didn't realize I could do. Everybody has a lot of gifts they don't know about. I was discovering and doing things with no special effort. I was blooming, blooming like a plant without realizing that somebody was putting fertilizer on me.

"Then, too, while I was in Delano I met so many different religious people—not just nuns and priests, but rabbis and Protestant ministers as well. And everyone was so willing to talk to me. They never said, 'You poor old woman, don't you know about this?' "

In 1980, however, Maria left Delano and her work with the union. At the age of seventy-two, she was once again leaving home. "The main thing that had happened to me in those twelve years," she told us, "was that I had come to believe in myself. You have to believe in yourself and then you can be merciful with everybody. I think this is what Jesus said."

Living her philosophy of "doing things the way they come," she accepted an invitation from two nuns for a leisurely drive across the country. In addition to seeing the United States coast-to-coast, they planned to visit friends and volunteers en route who had worked with them in the Farm Workers Union. Except for these scheduled stopovers, Maria had made no plans for the future.

What was it, we wondered, that allowed Maria to navigate so creatively through periods of unknowing and uprootedness that people far younger with more financial security and social support would find harrowing?

When we asked her this question she was quiet for a moment and then replied, "I think the main thing that holds people back is that they are afraid to change and they are attached to material things. I say to people, 'Risk and don't regret what you gave up.' I never think this *now* is forever. Never, never. I say this *now* is now only. I don't know what will come tomorrow, but I have to handle today."

Today, at eighty, Maria makes her home in Santa Rosa. Far from being retired, she works under the auspices of Catholic charities as a liaison for the large Hispanic community in that city, delivering and distributing food to those in need. And, remembering her own childhood frustration at not being able to understand the Mass in Latin, she teaches catechism to the children of Spanish-speaking farm workers in their native language.

"I don't belong to the Mexican group. I don't belong to the farm workers. My work depends on working with many groups, and with the Anglos and the Latinos working together. It's the togetherness that counts. Without that, I am powerless."

Empowerment is Maria's way of helping people. "I never say to people, 'I am going to help you,'" she told us emphatically. "What I tell them is, 'I will work with you.' I want the people who come to me to know they are of value and they can do the same things that I am doing. I want them to discover their own abilities. That way, whether I live or die, they can still believe in themselves."

As if her work and volunteer responsibilities weren't enough to keep her fully occupied, when we talked with Maria she had just enrolled in two courses at the local junior college. Beaming with enthusiasm she described her introductory psychology class and the course she was taking on the New Testament taught by a young rabbi, an ecumenical touch she obviously enjoyed.

"Where do you find the energy for all these activities?" we asked.

"I used to think it had something to do with all the exercise I got in my younger years as a teacher of physical education," she replied. "But now I feel it's more an 'inner energy' that has come since I've developed my relationship with God. There is nothing I want these days. Not money. Not power. Not anything. I'm just doing my thing."

Maria regarded her home-leavings as unique opportunities for learning. But as one woman told us, "The term *opportunity for learning* can be a euphemism for pure hell." And clearly, as we have just seen, each woman leaves home in her own way. However, each of the women whose stories we have told found ways to be faithful to what was coming into form and emerging from within them. Moreover, this faithfulness did not spring from any idealized notion of what she should do or be or believe. It came through risking "encounters at the edgelessness of reality," as Meinrad Craighead puts it, "facing the anxiety of the uncertain and ambiguous" and learning to trust the process unfolding through her own life.

This willingness to trust in the emergent process is, we believe, the great spiritual gift that home-leaving brings to women. As the poet Kabir reminds us, "The miracle of life waiting in the heart of a seed cannot be proved at once." The miracle comes with the waiting. And the waiting takes trust.

Chapter 4
THE TEN THOUSAND GATES

The ten thousand things return to the one.
Where does the one return?

— Zen koan

 We enter our sacred garden through a variety of gates. They open us to that innermost place in ourselves that is at once natural, familiar, and exquisitely intimate. We go through these entry points in different ways and at different times in our spiritual unfolding, searching for them not out of any dreary sense of obligation or duty, but out of a yearning for what is personally real and true. This yearning is essential because it comes from the immediacy of our lives, and that is just what we need to find and live from: the penetrating alertness that lets us connect with what is sacred.

Going through a gate or doorway is a metaphor of immense power, perhaps because it reminds us of how we enter this life. Exiled from the safety of the womb by a hidden timing, sent on a journey through the straits of the birth canal, our passage is fraught with dangers. We can get stuck beneath the pubic bone or strangled by the umbilical cord and never reach the light.

Every child who enters the world through the birth canal believes—at least in part—that there is only one gate and that getting through it is a matter of life and death. Every patriarchal religious tradition, and many shamanic traditions as well, has its own version of this perspective. The message is unequivocal, as these often-quoted lines from *The Sermon on the Mount* illustrate: "Enter by the narrow gate. . . . the gate that leads to life is small and the road narrow, and those who find it are few."[1] There is only one entrance to the sacred, and it is exclusive and exacting.

But from the mother's perspective there are many gates. Unlike the fetus whose crowning achievement is successfully negotiating the birth canal, what is at issue for the birth giver is the willingness to surrender to and be opened by the rhythms of nature flowing through her. To the extent that she pushes with her contractions and regulates her breathing, she acts in cooperation with an already ongoing process.

From the mother's perspective, the gate is as wide as it needs to be. Many arrivals, each one unique and precious, can enter the world through it. And she knows that her gate is only one of many, not only from her experience, but from the intuition that sometimes comes to women during labor and delivery of the unbroken continuity of all those who have given birth from the beginning of time.

Thus two perspectives are potentially available to each one of us: the child's view that the opening to the sacred is singular and narrow, and the mother's perspective that the sacred is manifold and wide. If only one possibility is presented to us, however, we may never recognize and value the other. In particular, if we have been taught only the viewpoint of the child, we may deny the experience of the mother, that there are many, many gates to the sacred and they are as wide as we need them to be.

For this reason, it is important to emphasize that while every woman we interviewed had at least one memory of feeling directly connected with the divine, she did not always recognize it as such at the time. One woman we talked with about gates that had led her into her sacred garden told us, "When I was a girl I would roam through the pastures with my horse, Spotty, and there would be a communion, a great sensuous song of life being sung through us that I have no words for. And later, in lovemaking, I knew that we are called into an ecstatic relationship with life. But there wasn't even a language to call these experiences holy in those days, especially not in the Christian religion I grew up with."

Another woman who is now middle-aged told us about a moment of mystical connection when she was sixteen and attending a religious summer camp. One evening in a prayerful state of gratitude she had gone by herself to a place near the top of a mountain. In that solitude and quiet she had a "split-second revelation of the presence of God," in which she felt she was being asked to acknowledge the gifts she had received by using her abilities to heal others. "I experienced this knowing as illumination," she told us, and in that moment of connection she committed herself to becoming a doctor, a profession she has since followed with great distinction.

In her middle thirties this same woman had another gate experience during the birth of her first child. But "unlike the first, this communion took place in my body, not my mind," she explained. "It permeated and diffused throughout my whole body." However, since she had no context in which to hold this experience of sacred embodiment, she did not speak about it for more than a decade. By then she had grown to understand that the connectedness she felt through her body was simply another entryway into her sacred garden, and one that was every bit as valid and important as the transcendent moment of revelation on the mountaintop.

In the stories that follow we look at some of the many ways in which the women we interviewed went through gateways that led them to a direct relationship with the divine.

BIRTH-GIVING

The doctors cut and groped and stitched and
the blood poured out and the placenta emerged and
this bloody gaping hole just oozed. All the while
"maternity" surrounded the upper part of Karin's

body and suffused her, the baby, and Michael in a
kind of unearthly glow that was in total contrast to
the animality of her bleeding, cut, lower body. I
was shaking by the time I left. . . .

— Judy Chicago
The Birth Project

We forget that our origin is in matter, in the physical body of the
mother as well as in the mystery of what brings life to matter. Perhaps
it is because we rarely witness actual human birth that we forget
who we are and where we come from. Like the shaman, in birth-
giving a woman is poised on the threshold between two worlds. It
is difficult to hold this "two-ness" of birth—our human selves and
the mystery manifesting through us—in our consciousness simultaneously. Traditionally we have dealt with this duality by concep-
tualizing it as paired opposites: matter versus spirit, secular versus
sacred.

But for Jean Bolen, a clinical professor of psychiatry at the
University of California, San Francisco, and author of *Goddesses in
Everywoman*, there were no such facile and divisive categories. Pregnancy and birth were gate experiences that brought her into a
deeper, more instinctual and intimate relationship with the divine
than she had known before.

As a physician, Jean had delivered as many as fifty babies before
becoming pregnant herself. She might have missed the whole experience, she confessed to us later, if she had thought she had a
choice about it. But Jean, who is now in her early fifties, married
at a time when, as she puts it, "it was not a question of *whether* a
woman was going to have a child, but *when*." Except for the pre-
dictable and well-charted physiological changes, she did not antic-
ipate that her pregnancy would have any effects on her practice of
psychotherapy.

But it did. By the end of her first trimester, she found that her
consciousness, usually so reliably focused and at home in her head,
had plummeted to somewhere just above her expanding uterus. A

highly introspective person by nature, Jean was surprised to discover that thoughts and images no longer held any interest for her. "Instead, my sense of 'I' was now located in my body," she said, "and this 'I' was contentedly still, like a rock resting on the bank of a river in the sun."

When she was in her office seeing patients, she could raise her psychic energy to her head and use it to intuit and think. But once they left, she sank back into the center of consciousness in her lower body and "lived there until there was again a need to rouse my mind." Jean, who had always placed a high value on scholarly activities and enjoyed intellectual pursuits, was now face-to-face with the improbable realization "that what was in my uterus was more important and more wonderful than anything in my head."

When it was time for the baby to make its appearance in the world, there was more loss of the self she had come to know as doctor and helper. Labor was an initiation for her. "The 'I' that had accomplished things in the world was absent from the labor and delivery room," she said. "I was any woman anywhere who had ever given birth to a baby. My husband, Jim, was with me through labor and delivery, and this made a tremendous difference. His presence made me feel safe and not at all alone.

"I was in pain while the pain lasted," Jean told us, recalling those final moments when the cresting waves of birth quicken and intensify and a woman may feel she has exceeded her capacity to endure. "And then in the next moment there was no pain at all and my baby, our baby, was born and the experience bonded us all."

Giving birth can be an initiation into adulthood as a woman goes through the trials of pain and fear to know the measure of her own courage and strength. It can be a time of intense bonding with a husband and child. And it can also be a time that brings one into a profound sense of sisterhood. "My sense of species kinship with all women began in that labor room," Jean told us. "I already knew what a male initiation was, having gone through medical school and an internship at Los Angeles County Hospital. But in many ways, having a baby was harder, and it gave me a great appreciation for women everywhere."

For most women, giving birth to a child is a multidimensional experience. But for Jean it was more than that. It was an opening to the sacred in a way she had not known before—through her body. "Embodied revelation," she calls it. "Something I do not have words for happened during that instant of transition," she told us. "The self that was familiar seemed to descend into a warm, dark pool and dissolve, and in that moment there was a knowing of the sacred through my body. I participated in the miracle of creation and it shifted my consciousness. It changed me."

In her book *Listening to Our Bodies*, Stephanie Demetrakopoulos describes this kind of knowing as "a reference point in the consciousness of many women for their whole lives."[2] There is a primal and permanent quality to such knowledge, she says. It is not abstract. When she speaks about her own experience of nursing she describes it as a "total sense of flowing out of self." The intriguing expression she uses is "transcending downward." The psyche renews and discovers itself in this kind of transcendence, she says, not by going beyond the body, but by immersing itself in it.

For Alexandra Kennedy, a psychotherapist who had been meditating for many years before her son Taylor was born, giving birth opened a different kind of gate, one that introduced her to a new form of spiritual practice.

In a personal manuscript, she recalled that at the time of Taylor's birth she "moved into a different dimension marked by timelessness and spaciousness." But as the weeks passed she found that she was being stretched beyond all expectations. Caring for a newborn was far more time-consuming and demanding than she had anticipated, and she no longer had the luxury of uninterrupted hours. "I was forced to put the awareness I had developed through meditation into instant action!" she writes. "Washing the dishes, folding diapers, playing with Taylor—these became my meditation now.

"Being with someone so unprotected, someone who wanted one hundred percent from me, was exceedingly painful," she writes. "It forced me to look at how closed down I had been in all my other relationships. Being a mother is definitely the hardest challenge I have confronted in my life. There is no resting place. No peace to fall back on. Each phase of Taylor's life is followed by another as demanding or more so than the last. And yet watching this robust, incredibly active child grow into a person in his own right is worth the struggle. I am coming into my own innate powers, contacting new reserves from within, because I can no longer hold myself back."

For the women whose stories we have just told, childbirth was clearly a gate to the divine. However, it is only one of many, as a former nun who has given birth to several children reminded us. When we asked if pregnancy and birth had brought her closer to the divine, she replied:

"The whole universe is a miracle. The idea of an infant developing in you being a special mystery . . . well, that's no more wonderful than it would be developing in somebody else, some other woman, or the little kitten in the mama cat. Why can't we become ecstatic over developing life, period? We're constantly participating in it whether we're pregnant or not!"

RECLAIMING PANDORA'S BOX

> The Feminine interprets 'Be ye perfect as your
> heavenly Father is perfect' to mean, 'Be whole and
> complete, in both shadow and light, just as your
> Mother, the Cosmos, is whole.'
>
> — Report of the Committee for the Spirituality
> of the Divine Feminine, Sufi Order of the West
> *Hearts and Wings*

We were sitting in the cozy living room of a small cabin resting high on a bluff overlooking the Pacific Ocean when we began work on this chapter. The cabin had been lent to us for a month by a generous friend, and it was the middle of the winter. A chilling wind was blowing hard off the ocean through the small cracks in the wallboards. Dinner was over, darkness had fallen, and a fire we had made in the wood-burning stove was crackling away, keeping a pot of tea warm. Our plans were to spend the evening writing.

But we were restless. Something about writing this chapter seemed vaguely threatening, and we could not get to work. We began, hesitantly, to talk about our uneasiness. We talked about how often in the course of writing this book we had not wanted to open up locked-away feelings: our anger with each other, personal sorrows and disappointments, the self-deceptions we'd lived with so comfortably for years.

As our discussion gained momentum we had a sense of walking down a dimly lit passageway with a key, on our way to freeing something that had been locked up for a long time. As we allowed ourselves to follow this image, shadows of old stories rose up before us: Pandora unleashing pestilence, sorrow, and mischief in the world by opening the notorious box, Eve eating the forbidden fruit of the Tree of Knowledge, Bluebeard's wife defying her husband and unlocking the door to a forbidden chamber, and centuries of mothers, wives, and daughters burned at the stake because of what they were said to know.

In traditional myths and legends the hero's journey is filled with trials and tests that lead to the achievement of a great purpose. In the case of Parsifal it is the recovery of a sacred object, the Holy Grail. When the young knight finds the lost Grail and heals the Fisher King, a wasteland is transformed into a rich and productive countryside. In many myths about women, however, the reverse is true. When the beautiful and curious Pandora opens the chest that has been given to her by the gods, a once fruitful and peaceful world is turned into a wasteland of war, famine, and disease. For both Parsifal and Pandora the turning point occurs when something that has been lost or concealed is revealed, and in both myths there is an element of magic. But in the case of Parsifal the transformation is for the better; in that of Pandora, it is decidedly for the worse.

Portrayals of women as the holders of keys to locked doors behind which lie demoniacal forces, sin, and death abound in our myths and stories, both sacred and secular. And the message that these stories communicate is that women are innately connected with evil and darkness: when our questioning leads us to oppose male authority and open closed doors, all humankind must forever suffer for our disobedience.

Is this the lesson we'd learned about the consequences of asking questions, we wondered? Is this what we'd stored in our unconscious about what it means to be a woman with a key? We felt shaken, angry, and afraid. Contemplating these old tales, particularly the story of Pandora, had clearly evoked in us deep feelings and fears about the questions we are raising in this book. And it made us think about the underlying ethic in these myths, a simple, straight-forward ethic that still holds today: What you can not control, lock away.

We began to trace the consequences of following this ethic. If we lock away the fearful, painful experiences of our lives—the death of a loved one, a betrayal, or a passion that is not approved by society—we cut them off from their natural cycling. They are not washed by our tears. They are not exposed to the warmth of our heart or the light of our consciousness. And so these old emotions and memories can not break down to become sources of new life. Rather they lie in wait like the Furies in Pandora's box. And that is indeed dangerous. Not because something has been unlocked, as the story claims, but because it has been locked away.

If there is an ethic in the way that women come to spiritual maturity, it is one which places a value on process, on the accep-tance of one's whole experience as the truth. Entering the gate to the sacred marks a beginning, an engagement with the divine that does not seek to exclude darkness from the journey but regards it as a mystery to be solved in its own time. In a sense, it is the story of Pandora redeemed.

.   .   .

Irene Smith first came to our attention through a photograph in the Sunday magazine of the *San Francisco Examiner and Chronicle*. A thin, pretty woman with boyishly cropped hair, she had her hands settled calmly on the forehead of a reclining man. His face was covered with dark purple splotches. There was something compelling about the way she was touching him, as if her hands were an extension of her heart—and she had nothing else in the world to do but be present for this man and hold his head.

The feature article accompanying the photograph told us that Irene was a massage therapist who had started an innovative program in San Francisco for terminally ill patients. Working as a volunteer with Hospice of San Francisco she was assigned to a young man who was very ill with a disease she'd never heard of: AIDS.

"I rubbed his legs," Irene told the reporter, "and it afforded him a tremendous amount of peace and good feeling to balance out his pain. I think it also served as a sign for his friends and family that it was okay to touch him and stay connected. Touching seemed to ease the level of fear and isolation around him."[3]

Fear. In a country consumed with fear of touching and being touched by people with AIDS, Irene was working up to sixteen hours a day, sometimes seven days a week, massaging her patients and encouraging other volunteers to let go of their fear and do the same. "It was an honor to facilitate the work," the article quoted Irene as saying, but not easy. "The level of deterioration . . . is almost beyond what you can cope with visually . . . the long illness, the pain, is very hard for me, because my life becomes extremely connected with theirs. But I feel as if I'm living with purpose now," she concluded. "I'm doing exactly what I want to do and I see that with total clarity."

We mailed Irene a copy of our book proposal along with a letter asking if she would be willing to speak with us in a two-day interview. She telephoned, and in a soft, southern voice said she would like to but that we'd have to schedule several months in advance so there would be enough time. Perplexed, we thought she had misunderstood. Then she explained. It would probably be very difficult to tell us as much about her life as we wanted to know, she said hesitantly, so she would need the additional time to deal with the emotions her memories would call up. "But I'm honored that you've asked me," she said kindly, "and I'm willing to talk to you."

It is hard to know how to begin Irene Smith's story. One looks for clues to explain the chaos that entered her life shortly after high school and carried her on a torturous trip through hell for the next fifteen years. She told us that she was the daughter of a naval officer, that she and her brother grew up in a southern Methodist family. "One of my strongest childhood memories is of Jesus putting his hands on my head when I was a little girl and sick in bed," she said with a sense of awe. "I can still remember feeling those hands touching me."

As an adolescent Irene excelled in school. She demonstrated a gift for acting and was a high-school beauty queen, winning "sweet-heart-this and most-beautiful-that contests," as she put it. Her popularity evoked envy among her girlfriends, and she remembers that their jealousy often made her feel uncomfortable and out of place. A couple of years before she finished high school her parents divorced, and Irene continued to live in the family home with her mother.

Some time after graduation and her eighteenth birthday, the chaos that was to dominate Irene's life until her mid-thirties began. She started to drink heavily and, acting on an impulse, married a man she had known for only two weeks. He turned out to be physically abusive. After only a few months, she had the marriage annulled and moved to Hollywood. Her ambition was to become a movie star.

Irene succeeded in getting a few parts in little theater productions, and there was a promising connection with a well-known Hollywood actress who was willing to open doors for her. But by now she was using LSD and had developed a dependency on speed as well as alcohol. Her career as a budding actress ended at the age of nineteen when, as she explained to us, "I got so stoned I wasn't able to learn my lines."

Looking for work that would keep pace with the relentless beat of her drugged nervous system, Irene took a job as one of the first topless dancers in Southern California. "There would be three to four hundred men in the audience at the club where I worked," she told us, "and I danced in a little box right in the center of them. They'd throw money or come up and drop it in my bikini. It was a wild experience.

"I used LSD and speed daily in order to work. This was before topless dancing became popular, so there were only a few women doing it. But I don't know what other kind of work I could have found because I was so stoned I had to go fast. It became a cycle—I had to use speed to dance and I had to dance in order to get the drugs."

Sometimes Irene worked as a hotel maid during the day and danced at night. When she slept, it was often under the chairs in backstage dressing rooms. She told us, "My condition was very attractive in a way—a beautiful young woman who was very warm, very friendly, and just absolutely gone. I was someone to feel sorry for, someone for the man in the bar, or the boss or owner to take under his arm. It was always, 'Oh you poor dear, let me take you home and look after you.'"

Irene always went. "If I had not been totally naive, innocent really, I would have been killed," she told us. She remembers waking up in strange places with people shooting speed into her. A couple of times she woke up in a garbage can. "But I was never ever afraid," she continued. "I never mistrusted anyone."

"Wasn't there anything that frightened you?" we asked her.

"Only that I'd run out of pills," she replied.

Eventually, Irene arrived in San Francisco where her brother was living. En route there had been dance jobs in Las Vegas, short-lived occupations as a barmaid and cocktail waitress in a southern city, and a number of relationships with men that had not worked out. Now in her early thirties, Irene had become a heroin user.

Needing to support herself, she responded to an ad in a San Francisco newspaper: "Masseuse wanted. No experience necessary. Train you in a minute." Almost immediately she was hired as the receptionist. Several weeks later she met Fred, a charming pimp in his fifties who, she told us, "hung around the massage parlor looking for women who were interested in working for him."

"Let me show you the way to go," Fred would cajole her.

"I couldn't possibly do that," Irene would reply.

But after a while she did. As she explained, "Since I was older and intelligent, Fred thought I could handle whatever might come up, and so he sent me to check out houses of prostitution around California before he sent the other girls there. Some of these owners were unbelievable, really brutal, locking us in our rooms and keeping us going from early in the morning until very late at night."

Don't look. Don't feel. Don't ask questions. Don't say no. Irene just kept going at her accelerated pace, having long ago deadened her senses and feeling with whatever combination of heroin, speed, and alcohol she could put together from day to day. How do you break out of a self-destructive cycle when you're thirty-five and it's the only life you've known for over fifteen years? The streetwise answer is: by hitting rock bottom. But through some act of grace the street wisdom was wrong in Irene's case. Early one morning in San Francisco she got a full dose of honest loathing from someone who loved her, and she stepped off the merry-go-round by herself.

It was barely dawn on a warm day in 1978, and Irene was lounging in a deck chair in the yard of a house she shared with her brother. She had worked all night and now was relaxing with a tall iced-tea glass of straight vodka. Her brother, hurrying down the stairs on his way to work, stopped and stared at her. "Irene," he said, "do you have any idea how disgusting you look?"

Enraged, she sat steaming. As soon as he drove away, Irene leapt out of her chair and raced into the house and straight into the bathroom. She looked hard in the mirror. Then she poured the vodka in the sink and said to the face staring back at her, "I'm never going to have another drink."

"There was no conscious decision," she told us, "but I knew exactly what I had to do. I went into my room and jerked my phone out of the wall and said to myself, I'm not going to leave the house." She got a friend to bring over some pillows, and piling them against two walls, she made a corner for herself in the alcove under the stairs leading to her basement apartment. It was very dark there. "I need to be totally quiet," she told herself. And then she went out and bought a set of earplugs.

"Except for grocery shopping once a day and talking to my brother and my cat, Daddy Doody, I lived in silence for the next fourteen months, wearing earplugs practically the whole time," she told us. "And I didn't go back to work. I made a ritual out of preparing and eating my food and washing my dishes. I totally retrained myself. In the beginning I took lots of Valium and smoked quite a bit, but I never drank. When friends came to visit and wanted to talk about why I wasn't drinking, I just quit talking altogether."

The discrimination and discernment that had been so lacking in her life up till then were suddenly very present. As she explained to us, "Somehow I seemed to know exactly what was needed. I began to eat fresh vegetables, fish and chicken, and I got a couple of books on nutrition and followed them carefully. And I started getting deep-tissue massage. I had my cat as a loving companion, and I knew that I had to get up when the sun got up and go to bed when the sun went down, and in between I just needed to be with me and nobody else."

Besides observing prolonged periods of silence, keeping regular hours, and preparing healthy food for herself, Irene felt she needed to get rid of the toxins that had accumulated in her body from over fifteen years of using drugs and alcohol. In order to do this, she needed to sweat. Since she didn't have a tub, she made a sauna out of her shower by placing a large rock on the floor of the stall and pouring boiling water over it. Then, wrapped up in a plastic suit, she would curl up on the floor and sweat.

One day as she was ending this ritual with a refreshing shower, she was overcome with incredible joy. "Oh, Jesus," she recalls saying aloud as she watched the spray descending over her, "I can't believe this water is so beautiful. It is *so* beautiful." Later when we asked Irene if she had a spiritual practice, she said yes, that it was prayer. "How long has prayer been your practice?" we asked.

"Since that day in the shower," she replied.

Although Irene had made a strong beginning in regaining her sense of self, the next several years brought a series of ordeals and crises on every level—physical, emotional, and spiritual. All the pain that had been stuffed down through long years of acquiescence and drug-induced denial began to surface in full force. Kicking and screaming and beating pillows, Irene began to release a lifetime's accumulation of fear, anger, and grief. During this process of release she acquired the tools that she would later use to help others open up the closed-off parts of themselves. "For, after all, it is our emotions that unfold the lessons we need to learn," she told us.

A year into her recovery process, Irene's fragile world threatened to disintegrate totally. It began one day when she found out that the house she and her brother were renting was being rezoned and she would have to find another place to live. "I was scared to death, of course," she confessed to us. "I had been in a basement apartment for the past fourteen months. A total womb. Now I was going to have to interact and negotiate with landlords, and I had no money at all." Feeling excruciatingly vulnerable and uprooted by her forced exit, Irene received yet another blow: a call from her stepmother telling her that her father had died.

With the help of friends who pooled their resources to pay her first month's rent, Irene pulled herself together enough to move out of the house. For the first time since she had begun her journey to healing, she was alone. "I got up to my new apartment," she told us, "and I didn't have my drugs or alcohol and I didn't have a father. When I looked in the mirror I didn't recognize myself. Suddenly nothing in my whole life felt familiar—not my environment or my habits or the food I was eating—and I really freaked out."

Fear consumed her. She began calling her mother in Dallas several times a day to ask what to eat, afraid certain foods would kill her. Her weight dropped to eighty-eight pounds. "I was starving myself. It was obvious that I was dying," she told us.

In the midst of this devastating downward spiral the phone rang one day, and a woman's voice said, "Hello. My name is Elisabeth Kübler-Ross, and your mother says you need to come to one of my workshops." Irene, who had never heard of Dr. Kübler-Ross's pioneering work in death and dying,[4] said, "Thank you for calling, but I don't know who you are," and hung up. "I don't remember very much about the following days. All I remember is taking money out of the cookie jar and finding myself on the way to Canada where I attended three of Dr. Kübler-Ross's Life/Death Transition workshops in a row.

"Despite the work I had done earlier on my own," Irene continued, "I really didn't go deeply into my pain until I went to Elisabeth's workshops. In those workshops I received real permission to expose the mutilated part of myself. By being truly heard, witnessed, and forgiven I gained the tools I needed to continue living."

At the end of the third workshop, Irene raised her hand to speak. Walking up and down to keep up her courage she announced to the group: "I'm a prostitute and I'm going to become a counselor." Like the promise she had made to herself when she looked in the mirror two years earlier, this was a statement of intention that could only have come from her innermost knowing. Her past, her lack of self-confidence and experience, all argued against the commitment she had just made. "In fact," as she said to us later, "I was practically catatonic whenever I had to speak in front of people because one of the ways I survived in the life I had lived for fifteen years was by keeping my mouth shut. And I was almost always stoned anyway. Talking was simply not a part of my life-style."

But Irene did not allow her past to stand in the way of her future. She simply started to act on her intention. She began by contacting Hospice of San Francisco and volunteering to massage people who were terminally ill. It was 1982 and at that time there were no such massage programs in California.

"It was perfect," she told us. "I had a deep need to do service and surrender myself to Jesus for my own healing and I also needed to prove to others, as well as myself, that I was good and kind. And I had a very deep need for love and affection that was not in any way connected with sex. I could go and sit down with these people who were terribly sick and hold and stroke them. Sometimes I would cry. I was very open and responsive. It's hard for most people to touch and hold those who are dying but I had learned to sit with others in pain during Elisabeth's workshops. I think the personal clearing I went through at that time gave others the permission to expose their pain with me. Being touched in a loving way says 'I care,' and I so much wanted to feel the caring.''

Her work went so well that soon she was volunteering seven evenings a week, after working at the massage parlor all day. But her success brought up a whole new set of fears: "It was terrifying for me to sit in the volunteer meetings," she told us, "especially with women who were nicely dressed. I was constantly afraid of not doing the right things. On top of that I kept thinking they would find out about what I did for a living and not let me continue to be a volunteer. I was paralyzed every time I had to say something in the meetings or training groups.

"What I've come to know, though, is that there are no mistakes. I've really had to look at my life, and I've seen so many things that seemed wrong and out of line, and thought, 'Oh, my God, how horrible. What have I done? What have I created?' But I've also learned a lot of lessons that I couldn't have learned without doing the things I've done.

"I think I'm a witness for hope and acceptance. If my life says anything, it's that there is hope for loving and accepting all pieces of ourselves. The most important thing I've learned is that we're very protected and loved no matter how things seem. No matter how the fabric of our life unfolds, we are here to simply open our hearts and reach out and love and touch and communicate with each other. So however I can do that, that's what I'm doing."

In 1983 Irene contacted San Francisco General Hospital's Unit 5A, the ward set aside for AIDS patients. She talked with the staff about her experience at Hospice and spoke of how deeply deprived AIDS patients were of human touch. As a result, she became the first volunteer to do massage therapy on the unit. "To go in there with 'touch' was an absolute miracle," she told us. Three years later she was funded to train and coordinate massage volunteers of Bay Area hospitals by the San Francisco AIDS Emergency Fund. Today Irene administers Service Through Touch, a non-profit corporation whose volunteers staff fourteen health-care facilities serving people with HIV disease in the San Francisco Bay Area. The organization's audio, visual, and written materials are being used around the world to train massage therapists.[5]

The statement on the back of the Service Through Touch brochure reads: "Touch is a union, a bonding, a making whole." The description goes on to say that Irene's workshops are about healing ourselves through service to others. Perhaps better than anyone we know, Irene's life is an ongoing testament to the truth that "When we are healed, we are not healed alone."[6]

THE HEART OF MATTER

> We are of the earth, made of the same stuff;
> there is no other, no division between us and
> "lower" or "higher" forms of being.
>
> — Estella Lauder
> *Women as Mythmakers*

If there is one thing we know from history, it is that patriarchal models of the spiritual have not been kind to women. Consciously or unconsciously, the constructs that begin with spirit as the highest and descend to matter as the lowest have traditionally relegated women and nature to the bottom of the scale. Based on a cosmology that lies at the root of Western civilization in which the divine has been located outside the material universe, has dominion over it, and is fundamentally transcendent to it, this hierarchical ordering is one that almost all of us carry in our psyches, if not in our hearts.

Philosopher and theologian Elizabeth Dodson Gray calls this hierarchical perspective the "old sacred game" and says its goal is to "get away from the ordinary, the natural, the unsacred—away from women, fleshly bodies, decaying nature, away from all that is rooted in mortality and dying. 'Up, up and away' is the cry of this religious consciousness," she says, "as it seeks to ascend to the elevated realm of pure spirit and utter transcendence where nothing gets soiled or rots or dies."[7]

Yet as many of the women we interviewed are coming to know, the distinction between spirit and matter begins to blur as one honors the sacredness of her feminine nature and her intimate connection with Mother Earth. For Rickie Livingston, the founder and director of a respected institute for personal growth, the willingness to confront directly the old divisions between matter and spirit took her through a gateway to the divine she had never entered before:

"I was studying clowning and mask-making when I discovered my fear of the earth. My teacher had studied with a shaman and was teaching us what he had learned—to explore ourselves by reaching into the six directions: north, east, south, west, down, and up. I was fine until I approached the fifth direction—down.

"We were to repeat silently, 'Five below, below. Five below, below,' while inhaling through our eyes and exhaling out the soles of our feet. The exhale was to go through the feet down into the center of the earth. When we met the energy there, we were to make a mask of its face.

"I closed my eyes and began the breathing apprehensively. Years of spiritual training had taught me to reach up toward the third eye, up to the light, up to higher states of consciousness. By going down I felt I was doing something wrong, perhaps even damaging myself in some way. With every exhale my fear increased. 'The earth is darkness. I don't want to go there,' part of me was saying. 'In the earth there are dark energies, forces that might engulf me. I'm going backwards. I'm losing ground. I'm inviting something terrible into my consciousness.

"Something must have urged me to face this fear and proceed because I decided to stop dancing around the edges of fear and plunged down into the heart of it. Suddenly I was suffocating. I was buried alive. I was choking on blood and soil. The chaos and panic of blind human suffering pressed into me. My flesh was rotting. I was worm-eaten. The blood and agony of birth was in my ears. The smell of fear and death, of destruction and decomposition overwhelmed me. Then I was a skeleton, then dust of bone, then only soil and a long silence.

"From below the silence a strong, sweet feeling began to rise. I was meeting the center of the earth and she was love, a love which supported and embraced everything without exception. A love which drew back from nothing, no matter how horrible. I wept with gratitude as that love enfolded me. I understood with my whole body and being how ridiculous it was for me to strain to hold myself up. All my life I had been completely supported by this love at the center of the earth, but I hadn't noticed because I was always trying to rise above life. I could have surrendered to it. I could have nestled into this mother's arms and lived there safely. I felt compassion and pity for my lifetime of needless, exhausting striving.

"I was shaken, stunned, shocked with gratitude. Weeping, I made a mask with full, soft lips and the most beautiful smile."

When we know through our direct experience that "we are of the earth, made of the same stuff," we can no longer play the old sacred game that separates us from nature and our own bodies. Something inside us shifts. As the poet Rainer Maria Rilke put it, we want our grasp of things to be true and we "don't want to stay folded anymore."[8] Sometimes this means opening up parts of ourselves that have been hidden away for decades, or even for a lifetime. And when this shift occurs, when we are able to reclaim parts of ourselves that have been disowned, reviled, or feared, we may discover that we come to meet the divine more fully too. This is what the following two stories illustrate.

We were sitting around the breakfast table talking with Virginia, who has been a teacher of religion for over four decades. A calm and self-assured woman in her early seventies, she was taken aback when the question of betrayal came up. "Have you ever betrayed your vows to God or to yourself or another person?" we asked.

Virginia paused for several minutes before responding. "I'm at a turning point here," she said. "Can this be anonymous?" We assured her it would be. She began, "All my life I've been aware of being a lesbian, and if I had been born in my daughter's generation, I probably would have had a committed long-term relationship with a woman. But instead when I was young I fell in love with a wonderful man and we married. I have been glad of the choice I made.

"However, when I was in my early sixties, I found myself passionately attracted to a woman. Although I had been attracted to women on several occasions before in my married life, I had never pursued it. But this came at a time when everyone I cared about was very busy with other things, and I didn't feel anyone wanted me. I became aware then of some very unfinished business in my life: I felt I had found myself in other ways, but I had yet to find myself as a woman.

"So I chose to tell the woman how I felt about her and in return I got an absolutely shattering experience of rejection. She could not stand the sight of me from that moment on. Her rejection initiated a period of radical self-examination for me, and also for my husband. Three years later I did have a love affair with a woman for the first time in my life. And I am glad I did. It has developed into a very fine friendship.

"But in answer to your question, I think the most terrible thing for me to deal with throughout all of this was my feeling that I was betraying my marriage vows. I'd been able to keep that promise all those years and then when I was in my mid-sixties I was no longer able to do it.

"It was bad, but in some profound way it was also good. It had to do with integrity. Integrity to myself, to what I had sat on all those years and hadn't expressed in any except sneaky ways so that nobody knew my true feelings. The love affair cleared off all the guilt I had been living with about my sexuality. Even though I had suppressed that part of myself for sixty-three years, the drive to wholeness would not let me be. And though it was a time of anguish for me, my husband, and my friend, we've worked it out. I feel more whole now than ever before in my life."

*   *   *

"To many people I know that I appear to be very liberated, but I have an extremely conventional side to myself," Margaret, a striking dark-haired woman in her middle forties told us as we began our interview with her. "It has always been difficult for me to do things that I know other people may disapprove of."

When we asked Margaret about experiences that were turning points in her spiritual development, she sat pensively for a few moments looking straight ahead. Then taking a deep breath, she told us this story:

"When I was twenty-two, very naive and living in Europe where I was born, I married a man I loved very much. Almost as soon as we married and set up housekeeping in the foreign country where he lived, my husband became impotent. Since he indicated that it was somehow my fault, I did everything I could think of to become the kind of woman he thought I should be. I dressed and did my hair the way he liked and tried to imitate his mother's housekeeping and cooking style. I even learned his native language. But nothing seemed to help.

"After a few years of marriage it became clear to me that all this striving could not be love. Love enlivens you, but I was waking up in the morning with so little life and goodwill that I would even cross to the other side of the street to avoid saying hello to someone. I simply could not summon the energy to smile or ask 'how are you?'

"About this time, to my complete amazement, I fell in love with a woman. It was the most holy and important thing that had ever happened to me because for the first time I felt that I really existed in my own right. I started to come to life! It was as though everything I had tried so hard to do for my husband began to occur spontaneously inside me. My own feminine truths were suddenly mirrored back to me in the experiences of another and this was an incredible revelation.

"Despite its tremendous impact on me, the idea of loving a woman was outside my cosmology at that time—after all, life in

Europe was pretty conservative in the mid-sixties. So I went into Jungian analysis to try and cure myself of feelings that I feared were sinful and perverted. However, when I began having dreams that confirmed that I was being killed psychologically in my marriage I knew something had to be done. After much soul-searching I decided to get a divorce.

"About that time the woman I loved was hospitalized for kidney failure. For several days she lay close to death. I was in great conflict. I had tried everything I could to stop loving her and had failed. In my anguish and anger I concluded that God did not care about me at all. I remember getting down on my knees beside the vacuum cleaner while it was running one day—hoping the neighbors would not hear—and screaming at the top of my voice: 'If you dare kill her you are not a God of love. If you take her you can have me, too. I am obviously not the right kind of woman, so I might as well be dead.'

"And you know what? She lived! I felt that it was the first prayer of mine that He had ever answered. For seven years I had prayed for resolution and healing between myself and my husband. I had prayed to have a child. I had prayed to be made into the 'right kind of woman.' But none of those prayers had been answered. Only this one had been responded to.

"The day I heard that my friend was going to live it was as if a solid brick wall suddenly dissolved in front of me. Behind it appeared a laughing God. 'My, you're a stubborn person,' He said. 'Don't you understand that I want you to love a woman? Now get out of this marriage. I have other work for you to do, with and for women.'

"Falling in love with a woman was my first step to realizing the feminine aspect of the divine. The second was a series of mystical experiences that occurred toward the end of my seminary training. I feel these revelatory experiences were a personal call that led me to the work I am now doing—helping people to connect through what I call the DNA of their personal mythology through myth and spiritual disciplines to the Sophia as well as to the Christ aspect of the divine.

"When I was twenty-five," Margaret told us at the end of our interview, "God was a male in the sky, and sin meant that one was perverted and bad and deserved to be punished. Now, of course, I no longer think that way. I see the divinity as both female and male here on earth and in the unmanifest universe. And sin to me is denying or cutting out a part of who I am. It is any act that is against the natural unfolding of our Divine Self. I believe that each of us needs to discover our own soul story and find the strength to live it. Selling out to someone else's story is a waste of who we are and prevents us from completing the sacred tasks for which we were created."

CONFIRMATION

> May the Lord bless you and keep you;
> May the Lord make His face to shine upon you
>   and be gracious unto you;
> May the Lord lift up His countenance upon you
>   and give you His peace.
>
> — Priestly Blessing
>   *Old Testament*

The stories we have told up to this point have been from the mother's perspective; that is, that the gates which lead one to the divine are many and varied. And yet some of the women we interviewed found their connection to the sacred through the traditional "strait gate" of institutionalized religion. This was true for Marion Woodman. It was the formal rite of confirmation that led her to a new and deeper understanding of herself and her relationship with the divine.

Marion was a schoolteacher in her early forties when she and her husband, Ross, a university professor, decided to spend his sabbatical year studying in England. Freed from her own teaching responsibilities, Marion planned to use this period to attend to her inner life more fully. She began exploring her dreams through Jungian analysis and occasionally she would stop by a church near their lodgings to pray and meditate.

On Thursday night before Easter, Marion entered the church to find that the ornate carpet and tapestries had been removed. As she stood pondering the reason for this, someone turned off the lights and the entire church was plunged into darkness. "What a shocking and powerful experience this was!" she told us. "I remember thinking this is what it would be like to know God. Stark and immediate!"

As it turned out the church was beginning its Maundy Thursday observances. In keeping with the solemnity of the days of Christ's betrayal and death, the altar had been stripped of all ornamentation. During this time the faithful maintained a round-the-clock prayer vigil. What happened next surprised Marion even more. She found that she could not stay away from this vigil. Each day she came to sit in the church, all the while asking herself, "What in the world is pulling me here? I thought I was through with all this stuff."

"All this stuff" evoked Marion's childhood as the daughter of a minister. In her twenties, she told us, she had "viciously turned against institutionalized religion, hating what the church did to ministers and all the phoniness and trappings of ecclesiastical hierarchy." But here she was trekking every day to these Anglican services. Why? "It was the dreams I was having," she explained, "the wonderful, shining dreams of resurrection, of trees and flowers and biblical symbols bursting with light."

After Easter Marion's dreams became more intense. Although torn by doubts and ambivalence, she signed up for a ten-week catechism class. Once the study sessions got underway, however, she realized that there was little room for the reality of her inner world in the dogma of the church. The priest did not know how to respond to her disruptive questions. After all, the purpose of these classes was to instruct people who had a strong desire to *join* the church, not tear it apart. One day after a particularly trying session he announced with finality, "Mrs. Woodman, there's no way you can be confirmed. You're a heretic!"

"Good!" she sputtered. "Fine with me!" And saying to herself,

"I don't want anything to do with the church anyway. I can't stand all those priests parading around in their grand robes and showing off," she left.

Then the dreams changed. No longer were they about flowers and light and resurrection, but "they became haunting and terrible, just terrible," she told us. So Marion returned to the church and met with the priest who had dismissed her. "Father," she said, "I do want to try to bring inner and outer together. I do accept the Christian mystery. Surely, the reality of my inner world won't cut me off from this."

She began a whole new round of classes. From time to time she would tell the priest the dreams she was having. "Mrs. Woodman," he confided, visibly moved after one of these recitations, "if it's all right with you, I won't say anything to the bishop about your unorthodox attitudes about the church."

It was fine with Marion. She was preoccupied with her own difficulties. Why was she going through with this confirmation business anyway? Was there a God or not? If there was no God, were her dreams merely products of her imagination? These questions were consuming her, and soon her inner turmoil was spilling over into her outer life. For one thing, she kept missing her regularly scheduled appointments with Dr. Bennet, her analyst. Convinced that the confusion about the times was his, not hers, she grew increasingly irritated. The day before she was to be confirmed there was an explosive confrontation.

"When I really need a man, he's not there," she told Dr. Bennet in a fury. "You have not been there, just like all the other men in my life who weren't there." And God, she thought to herself. God's just like that too. Trust him and you get betrayed. It's the same old story!"

The analyst pulled out his large green appointment book, saying sharply, "Look here. These are the scheduled hours for the last three weeks. You've missed every one of your appointments. I was here all the time waiting for you. You set up this rejection just like you've done over and over in your life. And now you're doing the same thing with your confirmation."

They talked for the next four hours. After leaving his office Marion wandered all night through the streets of London. She thought about how rejecting she had been of Dr. Bennet, and then she realized how she had also closed herself to God. She could see her great fear that God, in the masculine image, would be like other men in her life. What she had projected onto them she had also projected onto the divine. She felt humbled.

Still uncertain about whether or not she could go through with her confirmation, Marion nevertheless arrived at the church at seven the following morning. The priest was waiting to hear her confession and offer her the sacrament of penance in preparation for becoming an Anglican. This was more than she could take. "Everything in me began to scream in protest," she told us. "I didn't want any priest between me and God. And part of me didn't even want to be an Anglican—too much pomp and circumstance. And I didn't trust the sacrament. I didn't believe that something really happens when you confess your sins and the priest makes the sign of the cross over your head. But all of this protesting was really a way to conceal my deepest fear: that I would not be worthy somehow. That I'd get shafted in the ultimate union."

"Well, I'll be around for a while if you decide to go ahead," the priest told her.

Had she ever been so adrift in confusion and terror in her whole life? What could she trust? Would it be an act of self-betrayal if she let this man serve as an intermediary between herself and God? And what if she decided to go ahead and nothing really happened after all?

From somewhere beneath the frenzied questions came a quiet voice that said, "Yes. I'll do it." So in the depths of Saint Paul's, in the crypt among the monuments to patriarchs and poets, Marion made her confession. And in the moment of confirmation when the bishop put his hands on her head, she felt a shock of energy course through her body. "The light in my head was so brilliant that for an instant I couldn't see anything," she told us. "The only thing I could do was burst into tears. I had been such an arrogant little bitch."

For Marion the gate was narrow and unyielding, so the supplicant had to yield. And in doing so her relationship to the divine took on a new life. However, she told us in our interview that she still does not subscribe to church dogma. "I'm profoundly interested in the mystery of God indwelling, what I would call the feminine face of God, but I have no time whatsoever for the persona of the church," she said. "I wouldn't want you to think my confirmation resulted in my becoming a part of the Christian collective."

Marion has subsequently gone through other gates. These days she enters the unknown through her body in the privacy of her own living room. "I stand with my arms outstretched or dance or lie flat out on the floor and listen with my whole body," she explained. "This is my connection to Sophia, to the Shekhinah."

This gate is wide and it swings open reliably for her. But the first gate among the tombs and foundation stones of Saint Paul's was the legendary strait gate. And at that point in her life it was inestimably important. It allowed the rebellious child to come face-to-face with her fear of being judged unworthy by the divine and to discover that she was wrong.

As the stories in this chapter illustrate, the gates that bring us closer to the mystery are wide and narrow, unorthodox and conventional. Sometimes, as in the cases of Irene Smith and Margaret, they look more like walls than gates. And more often than not, as the stories about women giving birth tell us, our bodies are overlooked as vessels for the divine because they have been so consistently denigrated by patriarchal traditions.

If there is one thing we learned from women about their spiritual development, it is that clinging to ideals about how one ought to be blocks the gateway to mystery, while honoring what is personally true in each moment brings one into relationship with the sacred. Gay Luce, an award-winning science writer and founder of Nine Gates Mystery School, told us: "People use different energetic gates and different spiritual practices, words and philosophies to reach the same unitive consciousness. I try to offer people an experience of many gates so they can know which ones are natural to them. We are not all alike. We may follow different religions, observe different rituals, and have different rules, but we want the same thing: to be opened by the divine."

Chapter 5
INSIDE THE SACRED GARDEN

It was the sweetest, most mysterious-looking place anyone could imagine. . . . Climbing roses had run all over the trees and swung down long tendrils which made light swaying curtains, and here and there they had caught at each other. . . . "How still it is!" she whispered. "How still!'" She was *inside* the wonderful garden, and she could come through the door under the ivy any time, and she felt as if she had found a world all her own.

— Frances Hodgson Burnett
The Secret Garden

 Finally, a woman arrives. She may not know quite where she is or what is growing and what is dead, but she knows she has come through the door of outward searching into . . . well, what? After almost four years of research and thought, we came to an awful halt when we began to write this chapter. What does it mean to come to the end of searching outside oneself for the truth? What does it mean to enter the sacred garden?

We considered a number of possibilities. Maybe, we speculated, to be inside the sacred garden means to know union with the divine beyond the shadow of a doubt. However, while some of the women we interviewed had this clear and enduring experience, most did not. Perhaps, we tried again, being inside the sacred garden refers to a profound sense of interconnectedness with all life. But again, while this was true for some it did not apply to others.

We began to feel like the legendary Procrustes, who offered travelers a pitiless bed. If they were too tall he cut off their feet so that the bed could accommodate them, and if they were too short, he stretched them. No matter how stubbornly we tried to stretch or squeeze the women into convenient categories we could not make them fit. And to make matters worse, there was one question that kept slipping through the already wide cracks of our constructions. It took several forms but basically was this: If you are in despair, are you in the garden?

Eventually, something entirely new began to evolve from asking ourselves these questions. We realized that we had idealized the garden, the inner sacred, as a wonderful place that other people get to. If not quite heaven, we nevertheless were assuming some state of being that would fit nicely with concepts like enlightenment, union with the divine, oneness with all life. Every sense of purpose that calls one to leave the security of home lay beneath our notion of the sacred garden. But what does it mean to come home, to be *inside* the sacred garden?

We believe that there are two parts to being in the sacred garden. One part comes through receptivity, through grace. Going through any of ten thousand gates we have a direct experience of the sacred. We can prepare for this, but how and when it happens is not within our control.

The other part requires choice, an act of conscious intention to embody the sacred in our everyday life. This means that we bring our spiritual insights into every aspect of our lives—when we chop carrots for dinner, drive on the freeway, confer with our colleagues, and play with our children.

Choice lies at the heart of the matter because even if you have not had a direct experience of the divine, once you make a conscious choice to act on what you *do* know, the process of spiritual maturing begins.[1]

"It's not the surface work that's needed now," a Native American teacher told us. "It's the deep work. We need to bring our dreams and visions down to earth and put them into our lives. In my country we can't just stagger around in our visions—the rattlesnake teaches us that. We need to be awake and pay attention to where we place our feet."

When a woman makes the choice to embody spiritual experience in her everyday life, idealizations go out the window. She has to bring in everything—frailties and strengths, doubts and optimism, whatever she longs to conceal and whatever she'd be delighted to flaunt—and live it out.

This takes the utmost humility, because the ego "I" doesn't feel ready or able to live the deepest experience. One woman told us, "I always felt I needed to be more, that there was something that would make me worthy enough to serve God that I hadn't done yet. If only I could clean up something in some dark corner of my soul, then I would be ready.

"Of course, there is no way I could be ready," she continued. "It was only my ego speaking. Only ego hanging on for dear life, telling me I'm not enough. But these days I'm beginning to feel that God's love for me has no conditions. No matter what I've done or how I've done it, no matter how awful things are in the outside world, there is a love which can hold us all. If only we are willing to open our hearts we can do everything we need to do in a much more magnificent way than we ever could have imagined."

Our idealized projections about what it means to be in the sacred garden were the greatest challenge we encountered in writing this book. They fed our self-doubts. When we returned from our interviews, for instance, we weren't sure we had spoken to the right women. "Some of them don't fit," we told each other. Oh, yes, there were a few saintly women who we felt were "in their gardens," but what about everyone else? One or two were depressed, another's life seemed to be in continual chaos, and others had unhappy personal relationships. None were without ordinary human problems.

When we were willing to let go of our idealizations, however, everyone belonged because we realized we were not writing a handbook for saints, but raising questions for wholly human women who are coming to maturity. And this conclusion finally led us back to the garden. What we are describing here is the reality of the adult who knows that there isn't any place to find God but in the here and now of her own life. The adult who decides: *I am going to do my planting and cultivating right where I am. This is my garden.*

The coming to fullness, to readiness, of the sacred in women is
as varied in its forms as a farmers' market at harvest time. There is
no one way to be spiritually mature. Just as a ripe tomato looks
different from an artichoke, and a mature artichoke bears no re-
semblance to a banana or a head of lettuce, each woman evolves
in her own way. What we are talking about in this book is not an
ideal state of being, but an organic process that varies with each
individual.

In the two stories that follow, the women entered their sacred
gardens in very different ways. Jan Kemp made a decision to embody
the moral values she believed in, and direct experience of the sacred
followed. Choqosh Auh-Ho-Ho, on the other hand, was unable to
make a choice until her indecision caused her such anguish that
she determined to overcome the fear that prevented her from living
her truth.

JAN'S STORY

Even before we arrived on the tree-lined University of Georgia
campus in Athens, we had heard about Jan Kemp. In Atlanta they
said her name with such familiarity—"Jankemp," as if it were one
word—that we began to wonder if there was anyone in the state
who didn't know her.

Her story, at the public level at least, is dramatic and satisfying.
Jan Kemp's name was on everyone's lips because one year earlier
she had exposed "the whole little pattern of corruption that glorified
athletes and at the same time exploited them" at the University of
Georgia.

The condensed version of the story is that Jan, a professor of
English at the university, blew the whistle on nine football players
who should have been dismissed for low grades but were given
passing marks. As a result, she was demoted and then fired. She
subsequently sued the University of Georgia for $100,000 in dam-

ages. The trial, held in 1986, turned into a full-scale media event. It exposed the intimate details of what Jan called "a plantation system that uses athletes as raw fodder to produce income for the university, and gives them nothing in return." The six member jury, outraged by what they heard, awarded Jan a staggering $2.5 million.

News of the trial reverberated across the country. *Sports Illustrated* quoted the director of athletics at Notre Dame as saying that some fifty to sixty other schools were doing the same sort of thing with their football players. *Time* called the verdict "a real indictment of the system and not just Georgia['s]. The court is setting an example for other schools and putting them on notice that this abuse can't be tolerated." And Chuck Reece, writing in *Ms.* magazine a year after the trial, concluded: "Nothing... shed so bright a light on the exploitation of college athletes as did Jan Kemp's trial."[2]

But we didn't wend our way through Georgia's green hills in the summer heat solely because of Jan's heroism. A few lines in the *Ms.* article suggested that her courage had been fed in part by Living Faith Fellowship, a church whose members practice laying on of hands and speaking in tongues. We were intrigued: a six-foot two Phi Beta Kappa professor of English in a fundamentalist charismatic church; a refined-looking woman who exposed the tough and dirty underpinnings of big-time college athletics. What a provocative pair of paradoxes, we thought. We must meet her.

Several months later, after a flurry of phone calls and letters, we were sitting with Jan in the living room of her comfortable home outside Athens, listening to her story. It is the story of a woman who made a moral choice that tested her on every level—physical, emotional, and spiritual—before eventually leading her into her sacred garden.

"I had been English coordinator of the remedial learning program at the University of Georgia for three years," she began, "when the director of the program, and an assistant to a vice president of the university, directed me to instruct a professor to raise the grades of several athletes who were failing. I couldn't even fathom doing that and I told him so. Pacing the floor and waving his arms, he demanded, 'Who do you think is more important to this university, anyway—you or . . . ' and he named one of the top basketball players who was failing English. But I refused to change my position."

Within six months there were several more such directives, each of which Jan refused to act on. The conflict came to a head one day when two professors came to her office: "We've got a problem," one of them said. "Between us, we have nine football players who are not going to make it."

"It's not a problem," Jan replied. "Just post their honest grades and let the chips fall where they may. If there's a battle to be fought, I'll fight it."

Something like a distant echo must have sounded then, because those words catapulted Jan into the most challenging five years of her life. "It's during times like these that we call our angels around us," she said later.

Within a few days Jan learned that all nine football players had been given passing marks by her senior administrator. A tenth student with the same failing grades, a woman "who brought no revenue to the university," had been dismissed.

"What do we do now?" the two professors asked.

"I told you I'd fight if it came to that," Jan answered, "but I really don't know yet what steps to take. I've never faced this kind of blatant academic corruption before, but I promise you I'll see it through."

What did "seeing it through" mean, however? "The University had no faculty guidelines for the kind of protest I launched," Jan explained, "because academic crimes like this weren't supposed to happen in the first place." Every night, at first with her parents and then alone, she prayed for guidance. In previous times of crisis she had been impatient and worried until a resolution had been reached. "But the prayer made this situation different," she told us. "For the first time in my life, I felt at peace without a quick resolution. I knew that the answer was coming and that if I acted on my own I would botch it. So I had no choice but to wait."

At the end of six weeks, a letter of protest started forming in her mind. Then one evening as she sat at her desk, it suddenly came together, providing the logic and the language needed to address the university administration. This wait and pray strategy was one of the first times that Jan's inner voice had led her to action, she told us, and she followed it meticulously. The next morning she called a meeting of her departmental colleagues to present the letter of protest. Within two days, however, before the letter could be sent, Jan was demoted.

She began grievance proceedings immediately. A lawyer she consulted told her flatly, "You'll lose without a doubt. There are three vice presidents to represent the university, and no support for you." And lose she did, with the university giving no grounds for her demotion.

Pregnant with her first child and pressured by her husband, Bill, to let the issue drop before she lost her job altogether, it would have been understandable if Jan had decided to accept the legal ruling. Instead she made a courageous decision. Finding two lawyers in Athens who were willing to represent her, she filed suit against the university.

As soon as her suit was made public in the local newspapers, the threats began, first against her friends and colleagues and later against her students. Her colleagues were told not to associate with her if they valued their jobs. "A few—and I do mean a few—stood by me, and every one of them suffered," she told us. "Most were fired." Jan struggled to understand whether she was really doing the right thing.

Although she did not realize it at the time, her suit ignited a powder keg at the university. What made Jan's case dynamite was that the university's athletic program was implicated, specifically the championship football team known fondly as "them Dawgs." Because the Georgia Bulldogs were named in the preferential-treatment accusations, the media were sure to show up in force if the case came to trial. Details of the inside game being played between the university's administration and its athletic association would become national news, not to mention grist for every sports column in the country, and heads were sure to roll at the University of Georgia.

It was not until she learned that her students were being coerced to write slanderous letters about her that Jan began to show signs of breaking. "I wasn't upset when I heard about those letters because the contents were false," she recalled, "but I was sick about the students. Here they were at college and what were they learning? Blackmail. Extortion. Lying. How could anyone *use* students in such a despicable way just to get rid of a troublesome teacher? I couldn't accept it."

She slipped silently into a depression that got deeper and deeper through the summer months as the phone rang daily with male voices speaking obscenites and death threats. No one noticed how benumbed Jan was, only that she seemed to take no interest in preparing for her new baby. Her apathy was accompanied by two other symptoms of a major depression: the conviction that she was evil and the thought of suicide. "I would foolishly pray," she told us, "that if God would let me bring the baby here safely, I would remove myself and heal the university and then no one would have to suffer anymore."

In early August, her son Will was born. Two weeks later Jan attempted suicide and subsequently admitted herself to a psychiatric hospital in Atlanta. Ever the organizer, she tried to persuade the other patients that they were all in the inner circle of Dante's Inferno. "I was an intellectual psychotic," she told us, laughing. "'This is hell,' I'd say to the others. And they'd say, 'No, this is a hospital in Atlanta and we're going to art therapy. Come along.'"

After a month, Jan was released, but within a week she overdosed and returned to the hospital. Then for the first time she spoke openly about the feelings and thoughts she had been keeping to herself, disclosing her unwarranted but very real sense of guilt for the suffering she felt she had caused her students and colleagues. Almost at once the burden that had sapped her energy lightened, and she went home. Although now able to care for her new baby and resume her work, she did not regain her enthusiasm for living.

It was during this time that Jan was persuaded by a woman student who was also a close friend to accompany her one Sunday to Living Faith Fellowship. "I'd never seen a church like it," Jan said later. "It was very, very plain—a gym with metal chairs. No carpets. No choir loft. And the people sang songs of prayer and praise—simple songs unlike the serious hymns I had been brought up with. I couldn't take my eyes off the choir. They raised their hands and showed their fervor by dancing and clapping. I'd never seen people that alive.

"The pastor spoke about the 'blessings of the Lord,' that included ordinary people practicing gifts of healing, speaking in tongues, and prophesying. How glorious it would be to worship like these people do, I thought, but I'm so traditional it doesn't seem possible." A few Sundays later, however, as Jan was sitting in church, she entered a new world. Or, as she put it, a new world entered her. "I *felt* the Holy Spirit come into my body. I mean I felt Him physically. And I didn't even know until then that the Holy Spirit lives within believers."

For the next year, Jan attended Living Faith every week. It was her bulwark in a time of great distress. Preparations for the trial dragged on, she was pregnant again, and her relationship with her husband had become difficult. One Sunday night in April, when she was six months pregnant, something happened that changed her life. She had left church early, slipping out to put Will to bed, and then realizing she had left her sweater on the back of a chair, she returned to get it. The church was dark when she entered, except for a spotlight on the cross. Several people were quietly kneeling at the altar. Jan was about to sit down when the pastor said, "The Holy Spirit is speaking to me. The young woman who is suffering from depression is to come forth for healing."

Jan was startled. "I knew he was speaking to me," she said, "although I had never received a personal call to the altar before." Dazed, she walked down the aisle toward the cross. "Now, if this is real, if I am to be healed tonight, oh, Lord," she prayed silently, "send Bobbi to lay hands on me." Bobbi, a woman whom Jan had seen minister to others and in whom she had much confidence was busy with someone else on the far side of the church. "But as I got closer to the altar, she looked up and started toward me. When we met, I dropped to my knees, and Bobbi placed one hand on my head and the other on my abdomen. 'I know you're concerned about the baby as well as being depressed,' she said.

"The minute she touched me," Jan said, "my vision was kind of veiled. And then I felt a surge of electricity go through my body, starting with my head and going all the way to my toes. When she started praying, I could feel warmth going up my body a little bit at a time, and with it a dark cloud I hadn't even been aware of lifted and was gone. Joy just rushed through me. I thought at first it was a momentary thrill, like a hymn that touches you. But it stayed. The joy has been with me ever since."

Jan's depression lifted completely, and in its place came an aliveness and a sense of confidence that couldn't be shaken. "I knew the baby would be perfect," she said, "and I had a whole new attitude about the litigation. I felt a total commitment to going to trial. I knew with an unshakable certainty that not only would we win, but we would win big." Jan's lawyers were delighted but skeptical about her sudden transformation. "We can't get overconfident," they cautioned. Jan smiled. "I didn't say, 'I think we'll win,'" she told them. "I *know*. I promise you, *we will win*."

By the time the trial date arrived, Jan was ready and so were the media. Reporters from virtually every major newspaper in the country crowded into the Atlanta courtroom, and about a dozen TV cameras were lined up on the courthouse steps. For six days of the four-week trial, Jan took the stand. Each time before testifying, she would say silently her childhood benediction: "Let the words of my mouth and the meditations of my heart be acceptable in thy sight, oh Lord, my strength and my redeemer."

"I knew the lawyer for the university intended to confuse me," Jan said. "He'd ask me questions that I couldn't understand and I wouldn't have any idea where he was headed. I'd open my mouth to ask him to rephrase the question, and eloquent sentences way beyond my capability would pour out, not only answering him but making points that we had neglected to bring out in direct questioning. One of my favorite scriptures explains what I feel happened to me: 'Take no care for what you shall speak. The Holy Spirit within you will provide the words.' And that's what happened. The words just flowed out."

When the six-person jury delivered the verdict, it was clear that Jan's confident expectation was more than fulfilled. "My lawyers never asked for a specific sum for damages," Jan told us. "They simply instructed the jury, 'Send a message to Athens. Speak to them in the only language they understand—money. And make it hurt!'" Newspaper reports describe the "stunned disbelief" in the courtroom that day when the indignant jurors awarded Jan over $2.5 million. In addition, the university was ordered to reinstate her as English coordinator of developmental studies.

When Jan came down the courthouse steps, she was greeted with shouts: "How's it feel to be a millionaire, Jan? How do you feel about your victory?"

The answer she gave was reported on national television that night and by the wire services the next morning: "All the glory goes to God." In the weeks that followed, letters poured in from people who were moved by Jan's public profession of her faith. But some letters were critical. "How can a Christian fight like you did?" the writers asked. "That's not a Christian thing to do."

Recalling this criticism, Jan is still shocked. "A Christian's role isn't merely to endure change," she told us emphatically, "but to cause it. Women in particular are beginning to answer that challenge these days. We've found our voices now and we're starting to use them. We're not passively enduring anymore. We're changing. Silence isn't always golden, you know. Sometimes it's just plain yellow."

Poet and author Tillie Olsen describes times that are "dark with silences," times when she and others remained mute, letting what needed to be expressed die over and over again in themselves. "These are not *natural* silences," she says, not "that necessary time for renewal, lying fallow, gestation, in the natural cycle of creation."

Rather they are dark silences, "the unnatural thwarting of what wants to come into being, but cannot."[3]

Jan Kemp chose to break the dark silence that surrounded her. And in doing so she made a decision that many, many women today are also making: to give voice to what they most care about—to provide the focus of clear speech for what has been hidden or neglected or in need of attention. This truth-speaking is not just small talk or social chitchat. It comes from deeper down, from some urgency to name what is seen, to tell what has been lived through, to put into words—into reality—what would otherwise remain mute.

But even when we know we are being called upon to speak our deepest truth, we cannot always find the courage to do so. Fear can silence us. And sometimes, as Audre Lorde reminds us in a statement she made following the discovery of a tumor in her breast, it takes a great crisis to free us from that fear:

"In becoming forcibly and essentially aware of my mortality, and of what I wished and wanted for my life, however short it might be, priorities and omission became strongly etched in a merciless light, and what I most regretted were my silences. Of what had I ever been afraid? . . . I was going to die, if not sooner then later, whether or not I had ever spoken myself. My silences had not protected me. Your silence will not protect you . . . it is not difference which immobilizes us, but silence. And there are so many silences to be broken."[4]

Choqosh Auh-Ho-Ho, like Audre Lorde, learned that her silence would not protect her. In fact, remaining silent caused her such remorse that she made a decision never to withhold her truth again.

CHOQOSH'S STORY

From the afternoon we arrived at the home of Choqosh Auh-Ho-Ho in Santa Cruz, California, until late the next day when we left, the phone was ringing. Choqosh seemed to be in the eye of several storms, whether it was counseling friends or speaking for a peaceful solution to Navajo and Hopi differences or organizing a campaign to support the claims of California tribal peoples. Speaking out, speaking on behalf of, voicing—all seemed to be essential to her being. "Are you a medicine woman?" we asked her. "If I have to call myself anything," she replied, "I say I'm a woman who speaks with her heart. But that has not always been the case." And with that provocative comment she began her story.

The first thing she told us was that Choꝗosh Auh-Ho-Ho was not her given name. She was born with an "Anglo" name that concealed the fact that her ancestors were Mexican, Spanish, and Indian. It seemed especially important to hide the Indian origins, she said. Her parents had kept this a secret from each other and from their children for a long time. "In me," Choꝗosh told us, "there is a healing and reemergence of the discarded heritage." When she was in her early thirties, her grandfather told her that she was Indian. Several years later she was initiated as a member of the Chumash nation of West Coast native peoples. "For the first time in my life," she said, "I felt like I was home. For the first time, there was a place for me."

Three years later, she was surprised to receive a call from the Chumash medicine man who had initiated her. "We need a representative to go to the International Women's Federation Conference in Iraq. Will you go for us?"

Choꝗosh was flattered but anxious about accepting his invitation. "I was just learning about my Native American heritage," she explained, "and had never done anything in a public way and this was going to be a very large conference—three thousand women would be attending. But the offer was so tempting, I couldn't refuse."

Laden with sage and a sacred medicine bag, Choꝗosh arrived at the Baghdad airport at three-thirty in the morning. Thousands of others were arriving for the conference at the same time, and the airport was teeming with women in colorful native dress from all over the world. Through a cacophony of voices and languages and shouted instructions, the women were led into a lounge where they were given juice and crackers. Then, very cordially, they were asked to place their money, their passports, and all their identification in a basket that was being passed around. No one objected.

Inspectors examined each identification packet. "Anyone who had ever been to Israel or had a Jewish-sounding name was lifted up by the arms and put into a vehicle that was waiting for them," Choqosh recalled. "None of us said anything. I remember hoping and praying that they got put back on a plane that would take them home."

Perhaps others had known before arriving what Choqosh did not discover until the next morning: the Palestine Liberation Organization had organized the event. The PLO organizers led small discussion groups and obligatory bus tours each day. "I began to feel like a prisoner," Choqosh said, "because we were under constant supervision. But even without those watchful eyes, the frustrating, inescapable reality was that the organizers were holding our passports and all our money."

The larger reality was that Iraq was preparing for war with Iran, and the women had arrived at a time of intense surveillance and suspicion throughout the country. Watchful soldiers were standing guard on every corner, tanks were rumbling through the streets, and in Iran itself, Americans were being held hostage.

The atmosphere of the women's meeting was crackling with a kind of agitated excitement. Arrayed in tiers of long tables set in a semicircle and provided with headsets for simultaneous translation, the women looked like delegates to the United Nations. But there was no mention of peace in that conference hall, Choqosh told us: "The air was thick with anger and yelling and accusations. All day long women passed out tracts filled with bitter fury. Many times I wondered whether we had been handpicked to go back to our countries and sow seeds of hatred."

On the next-to-last day of the conference, as the women were returning from one of their daily tours, Choqosh recognized one of the Palestinians pushing her way onto the bus. She paused at the door, looking for someone, and when she saw Choqosh her eyes lit

up. After more determined pushing, the woman squeezed onto the
seat next to Choqosh and nodded hello but remained silent.

"There is something I want to ask you," the woman said softly,
once the bus's roar and voices of the women made it almost impossible for her to be overheard. "But first please listen to my story:
For generations, as long as my family can remember, we lived in a
small village in Palestine. My people are of no politics, no single
religion. We have provided a school where all kinds of children,
many of them refugees, could learn the arts and sciences of the
world. It was a spiritual place but not Islamic.

"When the Israeli soldiers came, they did not understand what
we were doing and so they did not trust us. They took away our
school and home. Many of the children had no families to return
to. With no home of our own and no money, we could not provide
for the children, and they had to leave. I don't know what has
become of them. The school is no more. I went to Canada with
some other people, but my father would not leave his homeland.
He died in Palestine of a broken heart.

"I no longer have any anger about that. What is important now
is a dream I had the night before I boarded the plane to come here."

"Why are you telling me this?" Choqosh asked nervously.

"Because you are Indian, you will be invited to speak. I will not
be permitted to say anything. You must speak for me."

Choqosh asked the woman to continue.

"I dreamed that I got up one morning and took my schoolchil-
dren by the hand. Each child was holding another's hand and our
feet were bare. We began to walk from Iran back to Palestine. Before
us were two great opposing armies. On one side was one army with
their guns and their tanks and their soldiers. On the other side was
the second army standing with their guns and tanks and soldiers.
Between them was a long corridor through which I knew we must
go home.

I began to walk, and I was afraid until I looked up and saw that
all about me and in a great line as far as I could see were women
of all nations and all colors, and Israeli women too. We walked

barefoot carrying our children. We carried our sheep and goats. The soldiers could not shoot us because we were their wives, their sisters, their daughters. These women of the earth joined me and we went back to the Holy Land. That is my dream and I want you to tell it."

"It is your dream," Choqosh answered, "and you must speak it."

"No. I cannot. It would never be allowed," the woman repeated.

Choqosh agreed then to tell the dream. The rest of that day and all through the evening she thought about the dream, preparing a speech in her mind. On the morning of the final day she was dismayed to find herself seated next to the only other Native American at the conference. This woman had made it plain that she disapproved of Choqosh, a "new" Indian, and had refused to speak or even sit next to her throughout the conference. Now, however, the organizers had seated the two Indian women together and asked them to decide which one would address the conference.

Choqosh was in conflict. "I knew if I mentioned anything about peace there would be trouble, so I was afraid to speak. And I thought the other woman had something important to say. She had prepared a paper on the forced sterilization of Indian women in the United States. This was something I hadn't even known about, so I let her speak.

"She added to the hate like so many other speakers we had heard filling the air with stories of massacre and genocide and infanticide. My heart was really heavy and I knew I'd made a mistake. It was about four o'clock in the afternoon, and I decided to go for a walk to get away from the screaming. The harangue seemed as if it would go on forever. As I stepped into the foyer, the beautiful Palestinian woman whose dream I had promised to tell approached me. 'Choqosh,' she said, 'we've been looking for you. We would like you to do the closing prayer.' Although that was all she said, I knew I was getting a second chance."

Choqosh returned to the auditorium where the tirade continued unabated. Pacing back and forth in the rear of the hall, she prepared a prayer that would begin with the dream of peace.

"I was getting scared as the time for closing drew near. I decided to go into the garden for a few minutes. It was almost dark. I knew I was taking a chance because the conference could end momentarily, but it could also go on for a while. There was no telling. Someone was shouting at that point. Everybody was angry.

"All of a sudden the women started coming out. The wonderful Palestinian came running up to me and said, 'Choqosh, where were you? We looked for you. The conference has ended and we had no closing prayer.'"

Choqosh was silent. She looked at us and we looked back helplessly. What was there to say?

"I had an opportunity to share a dream that could have struck at the core of the truth deep inside every one of those women. So many of them had lost a father or husband or son in war. But I was afraid and did not speak. Within two weeks, Iraq attacked Iran and the war was on. The children those women had carried in their wombs and fed and loved were being sent off and killed.

"The moment I heard about the outbreak of the war, I said to myself, Never again. If I am given the opportunity to speak and have a truth within me, never again will I back down. Never again will I be silent. What if I had spoken, I've wondered so many times since. Could it have changed anything?"

Chapter 6

TOOLS FOR THE SACRED GARDEN: PART I

 "Spiritual life is like a moving sidewalk," the Christian contemplative Bernadette Roberts told us one June afternoon in her sister's shady garden. "Whether you go with it or spend your whole life running against it, you're still going to be taken along. Whether you commit yourself utterly or throw in the towel, eventually you'll be swept away."

"You mean commitment isn't necessary?" we asked dubiously.

"Many times in the beginning, I'd say, 'I'm through. Forget the whole thing. I'm just going to go out and have a good time.'" Bernadette laughed as she said this, her pale eyes flashing. "But it didn't work. You know those Zen pictures where the man is searching for his ox, his true nature? Well, in those pictures, *I'm* the ox and the divine's coming in search of *me*. No way to get away. You just cannot escape this."

Bernadette's image of a moving sidewalk stayed with us throughout our research, slipping in slyly as we read authoritative accounts assuring us that spiritual development requires practice and effort.

"Practice is the key to spiritual growth," one respected scholar said. "The key to direct religious experience, direct mystical awareness, is a fiery, engaged practice. You have to pick one practice and do it wholeheartedly," he told an interviewer. "It takes much, much effort."[1]

The moving sidewalk made no comment. It just eased along, and from time to time it picked up momentum. Toni Packer, a former Zen teacher and now resident teacher at the Springwater Center in New York state, spoke about how much meditators want to be "developed." They make great efforts, she said, but their efforts create pressure: "The work of deeply wondering about everything that is going on—wondering who and what one is, and whether there may actually be something beyond the endless struggles of daily life—can never be the result of pressure. A free spirit of inquiry isn't the result of anything. It is there, spontaneously, when we are not dominated by systems of inner and outer control."[2]

We listened to these words and lived with the image of the moving sidewalk, but we didn't trust either. Our own lives had convinced us that spiritual development takes hard work. Nobody cultivates a garden by occasionally sauntering in on a sunny afternoon to pick a few weeds, we told each other firmly.

As we were musing about all of this, Pat awoke one morning about four o'clock and meditated for a while. At some point she felt it was time to go back to sleep, but the meditation had been so marvelous she wanted to prolong it. She tried to force herself to overcome her sleepiness, and then just as she was drifting off she heard her inner voice say, "You always think the way to God involves overpowering the natural. You think it means forcing and suffering. Haven't you learned yet that loving God is as natural and nurturing as sleep? Why do you insist on making it hard?"

Why indeed? We had heard and read so much about spiritual development based on systems formulated by and for men, systems built on successive stages of realization, that we had begun to think of development as some achievement like the development of pectoral muscles or shopping centers. The supposition underlying these systems is, of course, that the entire edifice will collapse, and the spirit-

ual seeker will realize there is nothing to attain in the first place.
Though it is said that this end state cannot be "gotten," that it comes
in its own time or through grace, nevertheless a great deal of effort
and careful training is supposed to be essential before it can occur.

When we began this research we carried so many of these assumptions with us: development is hard work, success comes through
taking a single path and following it resolutely to the end, ideally
a wise teacher shows the way, and so on. Bernadette's moving
sidewalk threw our assumptions into an absurd relief, underscoring
once again how little we knew about women's spiritual development.
We didn't know whether it was easy or hard, whether it was better
to stay with a single path or find one's own way, whether a wise
teacher was a help or hindrance.

By the time we finished our interviews, we had learned at least
two things: We knew it wasn't easy. No one we interviewed had
lived without suffering and loss and great "testing," as some termed
the challenges they faced. And we also knew that the women had
to choose to embody the sacred, not just once or twice, but repeatedly. We realized how often we had projected onto others an
assumption of supernatural ease, but there was no magical change
agent in the lives of the women we interviewed.

"I have to choose every day," one woman wrote to us. "It isn't
easy. So little is left of the old habits that used to cripple me, and
at the same time I have to keep stretching to believe and consistently
trust the light inside. There is something truly empowering about
making these choices, but I have to work at it every day."

Another woman, when asked about the fruits of her long years
of spiritual practice, told us: "There is something that doesn't go
away. An awareness. There may be a temporary clouding over,
getting caught in self-centeredness. But awareness returns." Then
she looked at us sharply. "Is this what you're asking about? Or are
you thinking of some ideal of perfection, of being perfectly aware
and attentive all the time? I don't know anyone like that."

Underneath the question of whether spiritual life is easy or
difficult, far deeper than that question is the truth of how a woman
actually lives her life. The important issue, one woman told us, is

not how to develop spiritually but how to live authentically. "I'm not the least bit interested in spirituality," another said emphatically. "I'm interested in *reality*."

Repeatedly we found that until a woman becomes interested in what is real and true in her own particular life, until she wants personally to "taste and know how good the Lord is," she can pray and practice and perform rituals with great sincerity and discipline without ever coming to the reality beneath the forms. Until this happens, as Joseph Campbell observed, the myth we are respectfully worshipping on Sunday will not be the one that's really working in our heart.[3] But once we are willing to embody the sacred in our lives, our maturing can proceed. We can say in effect, "I already know I'm a child of God. The question is, how can I be an *adult* of God?"[4]

As Marcia Falk, a poet and professor of religious studies, tells us, ". . . we've been stuck in a childhood relationship with a parental God figure, but we can't afford to be there anymore. Far from being arrogant, what this means is taking responsibility, so that we can really, deeply celebrate divinity. Which is a better gift to your parent? To fulfill your own life and to care for the lives around you . . . or to remain in constant dependency? The sick parent will prefer the latter, but that's not my notion of divinity; I don't want a sick parent for God."[5]

It is when we want to become an adult of God that we look for tools to cultivate the sacred garden. Until this point, we have no need for tools because we are eating spiritual convenience food, the products of someone else's cultivation. But now we are ready for a spade, a hoe, a rake, some compost, and perhaps a knowing friend to help us.

Traditionally, the tools available for cultivating direct knowing of the sacred have been highly specialized and difficult to obtain. If one followed a single path and was fortunate enough to find a skillful teacher, he could learn spiritual practices that would help him develop. Rarely were these paths open to women, and even when they were, the tools were narrowly defined. Specific meditational practices, prayers, and rituals were prescribed, while other possibilities for accessing the divine were ignored or forbidden.

In the last decades of the twentieth century, however, this situation has changed in several ways. In North America men and women alike can now choose from an almost limitless number of paths and practices and teachers. Hindu yogis teach next door to South American shamans, and Congregationalist churches share their space with Buddhist and Taoist communities. Jewish men and women become Zen masters and Catholic priests learn Japanese forms of healing and purification.

With so many options and so little background, it is difficult to discern what is really needed. How do we know which tools best fit our needs and which are unreliable or even dangerous? Who can we trust to show us? What are the risks and what are the benefits of these tools, and can a benefit become a risk without our realizing it?

For women in particular, the situation is paradoxically more difficult and more advantageous. It is more difficult because most of these tools, as well as the systems that gave rise to them, have been devised by men and do not adequately meet women's needs. It is more advantageous because women have had to search for new tools. In the words of Saint Teresa of Avila, because "the soul is capable of much more than we can imagine, [it is] very important for any soul that practices prayer . . . not to hold itself back and stay in one corner. Let it walk through [those] dwelling places which are up above, down below, and to the sides, since God has given it such great dignity."[6]

It seems that the women we interviewed, and many others we met and spoke with, have been following Teresa's advice. They are not seeing as a child who is restricted to one corner of a room, but as an adult who lives fully in all the rooms of her house. Women are experimenting with new forms of prayer, meditation, and ritual with a fervor and delight that inspires not only those who are creating these forms but those who share them as well.

In the following pages we describe some of these spiritual practices, a term we use to mean any activity that is engaged in regularly and in depth with the intention of bringing one into a direct experience of the real.

Are practices necessary for women's spiritual development? We do not know the answer to this question. We can say, however, that most of the women we interviewed used some form of spiritual practice in the past and many continue to do so today.

Does this mean then that spiritual development is hard work? That it is not like being a passenger on a "moving sidewalk" leading to the divine? Perhaps we can best answer this question by telling a popular Zen story[7] about an unusual family which was said to be fully awakened to their true selves:

A seeker of truth came to the parents and asked them, "Is it difficult to awaken to our true nature?"

"Very, very difficult," the father replied solemnly. "Like trying to hit the moon with a stick."

But the mother's answer was quite different: "It's the easiest thing in the world," she said. "It's like touching your nose when you wash your face in the morning."

Confounded by their answers, the seeker went to the son and asked him the same question. "It is not difficult or easy," the boy replied. "On the tips of every blade of grass is your answer."

Now thoroughly confused, the man sought out the daughter. "Your father, mother, and brother all gave me different answers," he complained. "Who is right? Is it difficult or easy to awaken to our true nature?"

"If you make it difficult, it is difficult. If you make it easy, it is easy. Do you understand?"

"No," he said.

With that the girl slapped him sharply on the face. Stunned by this, the man's mind became still. "Where are difficult and easy now?" she asked him. He understood. "There's no need to worry about difficult or easy," she said. "Awakening to our true nature is just as it is."

"Easy" and "difficult" are created by our thoughts, so when our minds are still, the opposites disappear. Just now there is nothing to learn. We don't have to accomplish our essential nature, any more than a sunflower seed has to try to become a sunflower. The "hard work" is the human effort that is required to turn consciously toward or align with this essence; to stay with the "moving sidewalk" instead of digging in our heels or turning around and going in the opposite direction.

Just as any plot of soil with seeds and sun and water can become a garden if there is a gardener, so can our lives come to spiritual maturity if we are willing to cultivate them. To cultivate, in its root form, means to inhabit, to dwell within. Learning how to live the dailiness of our own lives while opening continually to the sacred seems to take practice—practice in opening, practice in listening, practice in waiting. Practice also in obeying our inner direction, in speaking out when we are moved to do so, and in accepting responsibility and authority when we are called upon to be bold. And practice also means celebrating and expressing gratitude and "making a joyful song unto the Lord." When we enter such practices wholeheartedly, we bring to life another root meaning of cultivate: to worship.

PRAYER

Sometimes,
when it is all, finally,
too much,
I climb into my car,
roll the windows up,
and somewhere between
backing out the driveway
and rounding the first corner,
I let out a yell
that would topple Manhattan.
How do you pray?

— Margaret L. Mitchell

*   *   *

Praying, the act of communing with the divine, is perhaps the most universal tool we know for cultivating a sacred garden. There is in us, it seems, some deep human need for connecting with truth. And the most direct and accessible way many of us make this connection is through prayer. How we pray, the words we use to name that which we connect with—truth, God, the self, Great Spirit, or nature—do not matter. We sense intuitively when we are "in communion" with our source, and it is then that we feel we are praying.

It is not surprising that prayer lies at the heart of most of the major spiritual traditions in the world. Yet, except for the fixed rituals and formal prayers observed in these traditions, what we learned during our research is that people have a lot of questions and uncertainties regarding prayer. Whom do you pray to and what do you pray for? When and where do you pray? Do you pray alone or with others? Silently or out loud?

Unfortunately, we do not hear very clear answers to these questions from those who have been formally trained to guide us. The reason for this may be more obvious than one would expect. A recent survey conducted among third-year students at one of the oldest and most prestigious divinity schools in North America included the following question: "Have you ever had a deep experience of prayer?" Over 80 percent of the class responded negatively. What is even more confounding is that over two thirds of these students stated they did not pray at all on any regular basis.

Father Basil Pennington, a Catholic priest who discusses prayer in *Finding Grace at the Center*, writes, "Rarely have I found anyone who had been taught in the seminary or the novitiate a simple method for entering into passive meditation or contemplative prayer."[8] Since contemplative prayer has been a cornerstone of the Catholic tradition from the beginning, Father Pennington's findings raise some provocative questions about the priority of prayer in the training of priests today. One Jewish woman we spoke with told us bluntly, "I think the big, awful secret of the church and synagogue today is that many of the religious don't know how to pray. Sexuality is a minor issue next to this."

And, indeed, we seem to be much more comfortable talking about our sex lives than we are sharing information with each other about how we pray. Perhaps this is because praying may be the most personal and intimate thing we do. To pray is to be vulnerable. And in deep, personal prayer we come to know our vulnerabilities in a way that strips us of all our defenses and pretenses. That which is our very essence calls us into communion with mystery, and this joining is a supremely intimate experience.

Although prayer is an act of love in which one can feel profoundly connected to the divine, what we discovered in the course of our research is that it is not always easy—or possible—to pray:

"There are so many faces of God, I don't know which one to pray to."

"I don't know who or what God is, and if I don't know that, I don't know who I am either. I don't know how to pray and I don't know what it means to be myself, to be a woman."

"I don't know who or what to pray to. I think that's what I want most deeply now, to learn to pray."

These are some of the comments we heard during a Feminine Face of God Workshop we gave in Toronto when we were in the early stages of writing this book. They came from an ordained minister, a homemaker, and a nurse. While we were intrigued by the similarity of their remarks, we had no idea at the time why prayer should be such a problem.

Many months later when we were talking with author and artist Meinrad Craighead the issue came up again. Meinrad told us that she had received many letters of thanks from women all over the country who had felt a strong personal response to her book *The Mother's Songs: Images of God the Mother.*

"What kinds of comments do they make?" Pat asked.

"Oh," she said, "they mention various things. But a lot of them say something like: 'It's as if I've been waiting all my life to see the images in your book. I didn't realize how I've been longing for them until I finally saw them. Now I can't imagine being without them. You have taught me about prayer—how to begin to pray, how to begin to be a woman."

We looked at each other. Here was that connection again: Is there a relationship, we wondered, between women saying "I don't know how to pray" and "I don't know what it means to be a woman?"

> As I came to own and accept and celebrate my womanhood as a gift from God, bringing my own new value for the female side of life into prayer, I experienced a kind of inward leaping which was ecstatically physical as well as spiritual; an inward bodily leaping that made me feel God in my nerves and blood and deep down in my bone marrow as well as in my emotions and intellect.
>
> I was not able to approach God with this kind of engagement until I began to open up my prayer life to the feminine aspects of God, and to celebrate my own femaleness in that aspect.
>
> — Rev. Alla Bozarth-Campbell
> "Transfiguration/Full Moon"

We thought about Meinrad's earthy, sacred images of the feminine—women whose breasts are flowing with milk, women of blood and birth—and the profoundly evocative way in which these images spoke to the numbers of women who had seen her book. And we remembered a conversation we had one day with author and Jungian analyst Jean Bolen who said to us, "As long as what is considered sacred is always in the image of men, a whole aspect of what divinity is for women is not accessible to us."

We began to think about the almost exclusive use of male imagery in the major spiritual traditions. Depictions of Jesus, the Buddha, Moses, and Mohammed abound as do countless portrayals of heroic warriors doing battle and claiming glorious, if bloody, victories for God. Variations of the well-known Christian hymn, "Onward Christian Soldiers," echo in both the written and pictorial images of many religions. And while it is true that images of the

Virgin Mary are present in every Catholic church, and that her position is highly venerated, for all that she is beloved, she is never mistaken for God.

We thought about the importance of language, particularly when it is used to teach basic spiritual principles. This is especially true in Judaism and Christianity where there is a great emphasis on the power of logos to lead one to God. "In the beginning was the Word," writes Saint John, "and the Word was with God; and the Word was God."[9] We remembered the formal prayers still spoken by men today in the Jewish and Buddhist traditions, prayers of gratitude for having escaped the fate of being born in a female body. Such liturgies continue to reinforce the centuries-old patriarchal belief that women are simultaneously inferior and dangerous to men on a spiritual path.

Even as we thought about these things, however, we reminded ourselves of the inherent limitation of language to encompass the infinite. What is at issue here is not gender but historical imbalance. And today growing numbers of women feel that patriarchal traditions have alienated them from their deepest and truest understanding of God as Mother. For women who feel this way there is a conscious need to reclaim the holiness of female embodiment and recognize the sacredness of Mother Earth as well. There is a need to remember that not only was "the Word with God" but "the Word was made flesh and dwelt among us."

Meinrad Craighead, who lived many years in a cloistered order, told us, "prayer is the direction and renewal of the whole person, and this involves our bodies. Our bodies are channels to receive and give out divine energy. Real prayer for me has always meant being outside. I know that being by running water facilitates this while being inside a structure does not. I seem to need the possibility of wind blowing through my hair, or I need to feel there's nothing on top of my head. And I very much need to have my feet on the earth. I do believe that energies rise up from the earth into us. There's no doubt in my mind about that. I feel that our connectedness with earth is as physical as the tube which connected us to our mother. We are connected. We don't see tubes, but I think that our feet connect us."

Connectedness with our bodies and the earth as preparation for prayer was echoed by the healer Rosalyn Bruyere, who told us that the reason she keeps so physically fit now is that she never again wants to be in a position "where I can't pray all night in a sweat lodge or hogan or a women's circle or wherever my prayers are needed. I want to be strong enough to do that as long as I live.

"I never pray unless I know where my feet are," she told us. "I put my feet *down* so that the earth rises up in me and I *wait* until it rises up in me. I never pray before the light is here in my body. I pray as well as I can and as beautifully as I can. I sit on my heels, or stand and pray, or walk and pray. Mostly I pray out loud, and now I'm learning to sing my prayers. I've never sung before. I always thought I had a tin ear so I wouldn't sing, but now I'm learning to sing and pray.

"At one point," she continued, "I considered my healing work to be one of endless prayer, so I made a conscious decision not to do my personal prayers for a time. That was a mistake. Now I go out of my way to find opportunities to pray, and I delight in learning how to pray in different ways."

Anthea Francine, a workshop leader and cofounder of Women's Quest, an international network of women exploring and celebrating their sacred journeys, has also become aware of her body as a vehicle for prayer. "There was a time," she told us, "when I thought about joining an ashram so I could be more spiritual. I thought I needed to deny my body more. But what I ended up doing instead was becoming certified as a practitioner of water shiatsu, or *watsu*, as it is called. I do this work outdoors in warm mineral pools fed by natural hot springs. It is exactly the opposite of what I had thought of as prayer or meditation. But it has fed my soul and helped me heal, and now I think of it as a way of praying.

"I'm an embodied person," she added, "and I like bodies. However much I try to transcend and go off in some other realm, God makes me find the holy through my body."

Carol Collopy, a respected spiritual teacher in her sixties, told us a compelling story about the interrelationship between prayer and her body. "After a lifetime of praying and meditating regularly, and counseling many others in these activities, I was told in a meditation one day, 'Do not lift your prayers out of your body. Give up everything that is outside the body.' I found this message very disturbing, but since I have learned to trust my inner voice—it has been the very core of my spiritual life—I felt I must follow it.

"What happened shortly after that radically altered my life. I developed breast cancer followed by surgery, and a very long, slow recovery process. During this whole period of time, nearly seven years, I could not pray, nor did I receive any inner guidance. As you might imagine, I found this extremely distressing. And then one day I felt prayer starting to rise up out of me, and I knew that this prayer was given, not made. Such realness and solidity coming right out of me, right out of my body, it was unlike any prayer I had experienced before and it connected me to the whole of life.

"There is something that happens when you decide not to go out of the body. For the first time I feel a compassion for my own humanness, a willingness to love myself as I've loved God. This is no pleasure trip, however. It feels very risky to go through the personal. I wasn't able to trust this before. I couldn't embrace this kind of love of my own body, of my own self."

For the women whose stories we have just told, there is clearly a connection between prayer and the acceptance of the female body as an aspect of God. But for others the issue of sexuality has never been particularly significant. Perhaps the most certain thing we learned from talking with women about their prayer life is that the ways in which they pray are as various and unique as the women themselves.

And why not, we asked ourselves? Perhaps one reason the word *prayer* either intimidates or alienates so many people these days is that they believe it must be done in a certain way, according to a certain form. And for those who have strong childhood memories of being made to pray as a way to atone for some lesser or greater "sin" they felt or were told they committed, prayer is often viewed as punitive.

But communion with the divine is a deeply personal and mysterious experience, and the women we interviewed described again and again how opening oneself to this mystery can be done in any number of ways. Some pray in solitude; others pray communally. Some pray aloud; others pray in silence. Some do both. Some pray inside, and some outside. Some follow the liturgies and formal prayers of their youth, while others make up new liturgies and rituals. Some chant their prayers and some dance their prayers and some paint or perform or swim their prayers. Despite individual preferences and variations, prayer is an integral part of the lives of most of the women we interviewed. In fact, prayer is a "spiritual practice" for a majority of the women. Meinrad Craighead expressed it this way: "Prayer is about repetition. But then life is about repetition. Rivers are about repetition. Sunrise and sunset are repetition. Breathing is repetition. I mean life itself is repetition. And that prayer should be repetition—how could it be otherwise?"

Just as women pray in a variety of ways, so do their prayers reflect a wide spectrum of beliefs and practices. In addition to the traditional prayers of petition, confession, intercession, praise, and thanksgiving, some women describe prayer as the cultivation and practice of inner attentiveness and receptivity, a special kind of listening or "tuning in." Other women tell us that they no longer feel it is appropriate to ask for anything specific, such as healing, for instance. They believe that to do so suggests that they, rather than the divine, know best what is needed for spiritual growth and well-being. One of these women explained that her prayers often consist of a very simple phrase: "that the best possible divine arrangement be made for whomever I am praying." Prayers of this kind, while clearly petitionary and intercessory in intent, do not follow traditional religious forms.

Often as we talked with women they would recall a special time or situation when the power of prayer became very real. For some it was the first time they had tried to express their feelings in words, and recalling these experiences evoked a sense of wonder and reverence that affected us as well.

"Our family was big on visiting the cemetery regularly, generally about four times a year," Bernadette Roberts began her story as we sat on the patio of her sister's home in Southern California. "Of course we always went on Memorial Day. I loved these pilgrimages. I've always loved cemeteries.

"On one of these visits, when I was about ten or eleven, just as my grandpa and my mother knelt down to say the rosary at my grandma's grave, my father tapped me on the shoulder and motioned me to follow him. We walked a long way, clear back to the entrance of the cemetery, and then continued beyond until we came to a particular area between two gravesites. Pointing down at this space, my father said to me, 'Your little brother's buried under there.'

"'Little brother!' I repeated in disbelief. I never knew I had had a little brother! My mother was a very private person, and she had never told me about him. Standing next to my father that day, I heard for the first time that about two years before I was born my mother had given birth to a 'blue baby,' my little brother. Although the doctors tried everything they could to save him, he was never able to breathe.

"I stood staring down at the unmarked grave as my father was telling me all this. When he finished with his story I looked up and saw that his eyes were brimming with tears, which were slowly starting to roll down his cheeks. The source of his heartbreak, you see, was the thought that he had a child who was not in heaven. Although it is no longer the case, in those days Catholics were taught that if you were not baptized, you could not enter heaven but were consigned to a place called limbo where you remained throughout eternity. And my little brother had died before he could be baptized.

"When my father had finished with his story, he put his arm around me and said, 'Now you know why you're so precious to your mom and me. You're all the more precious because your brother's death was such a tragedy.'

"And then he went on to explain that I, too, had been born a 'blue baby.' 'When you came out,' he said, 'the doctor spanked you but you didn't respond.' You see, he had been in the delivery room with my mother during my birth, and when he saw that I could not breathe, he said everything in him cried out, 'Oh, God, take her. She belongs to you. Don't leave her for me. Take her for yourself.' In other words, please God, let her live long enough to be baptized and then take her to yourself.

"Of course, they were frantically working on me the whole time. And, in fact, the doctor had already baptized me as soon as he saw there was a problem. Then suddenly I began to scream and when my father heard me, he shouted out, 'She belonged to God before she belonged to the world.'

"I thought what a magnificent thing this was that he was telling me and then I saw that he had begun to cry again. It was as if he made a covenant with God, a sacrifice, and God accepted it. A covenant, you know, is very different from a consecration, dedication, or simply praying for another. A covenant requires the willingness to sacrifice what is dearest to our hearts to God. It means putting everything aside—our wills, our desires, our personal self— for God. And, in turn, God accepts and blesses us with special graces.

"In petitionary prayer, when we pray to God on behalf of another, the very willing of good for the other *is* the grace. People can feel and experience this good energy toward them. If all of us would only pray for each other it would be a very different world. As it is, there is a lot of negative energy in the world because we do not pray for one another."

Unlike Bernadette's father's covenant with God during a moment of life and death in a hospital setting, this next story is about a difficult inner struggle of long duration and its resolution within the protective walls of a religious community.

"The most painful period in my life was the first few years following my abortion," Patricia, a lively, attractive woman in her early fifties told us. "I was thirty-four when I made the decision to terminate my pregnancy and recently divorced after a fifteen-year marriage. Although abortion was legal by then, I could not seem to come to terms inside myself with what I had done. Thoughts of innocence and guilt, life and death, pressed in on me like a relentless interrogator demanding right answers to questions for which I could find no answers.

"When my inner turmoil became so obvious that I could no longer hide it, I made an appointment to see a psychiatrist. He listened to my story and diagnosed me as "clinically depressed." Then in a gentle, concerned voice, he asked how I thought he might be able to help me. My response was immediate and unequivocal: 'I've lost my soul,' I blurted out, 'and you must help me find it.'

"In the year of intense therapy that followed—a year that took me deeper psychologically and spiritually than I could ever have predicted—he sincerely tried to do just that. But it was more than a decade later before I really came to terms with my abortion, and what happened still seems like a miracle to me.

"By this time I was forty-eight and had decided to spend the week before Easter at a retreat center in a beautiful, natural setting run by a French order of nuns. I had visited the center before to meditate for several days, and the anticipation of being in this silent, nurturing environment during Holy Week filled me with joy.

"Then a month before I was to go, something unusual started to happen during my regular meditations. Every few days I would hear an inner voice say 'You need to do the spiritual exercises of Saint Ignatius.' Not being Catholic, I was not familiar with these exercises and knew very little about their author except that he had been the founder of the Jesuits. But the message persisted. So the first thing I did when I arrived at the center was to ask Sister Mary W., who was in charge of my stay, if we could somehow incorporate these exercises into my retreat.

"She seemed both pleased and surprised by my request and said that she would like to give the matter some thought. Then, looking me straight in the eye, she asked if there was a particular problem I wanted to work on. The question caught me off-guard. I had certainly not come with any problem in mind. In fact my life had been going along very smoothly, I thought. Yet after only a brief hesitation I heard myself say, 'Yes, there is. You see, I had an abortion twelve years ago, and I have come here to be healed.' And then overcome by a deluge of tears, I was unable to continue our conversation.

"That evening Sister Mary W. brought me a short book by Saint Ignatius containing the spiritual exercises. The next morning she presented me with a plan for adapting them to my retreat. At the beginning of each day she would assign me a story from the New Testament. I was to read it slowly, taking all the time I needed to meditate on its meaning. Then I was to choose someone in the story whom I felt drawn to and let myself become that person, allowing the scenario to develop in whatever direction my imagination led me. Finally, I was to write down everything that happened to me as the story unfolded. At the end of the day we would meet and talk about what I had experienced.

"For three days we followed this procedure. On the fourth day I was assigned the same story in all three synoptic gospels—Matthew, Mark, and Luke. It was the story of the paralyzed man who is carried by faithful friends to Jesus to be healed. When they arrive at the house where Jesus is performing the healings, however, there is such a large crowd that they cannot get in. Being ingenious, the friends carry their companion up to the roof and remove enough of the ceiling tiles to lower him through the opening to the floor below. When Jesus sees the stricken man lying at his feet, he says, 'Take heart, my son; your sins are forgiven. Stand up, take your bed, and go home.' And the man arises and obeys. His healing is complete.

"As I allowed my imagination to carry me into the story, I began to feel that I had a lot in common with the afflicted man. Although

I could move my body, I realized that in some way that was beyond my understanding my psyche had been 'paralyzed' since the time of my abortion and that I had sought out this house in order to be healed.

"As my meditation deepened I actually experienced the sensation of being borne along on a gurney by three very close friends, one on either side of my head and the third at my right foot. Although I knew someone had to be holding up the left end of the gurney, I could not make out who it was. Then raising my head up in order to see better, I made a startling discovery: it was not 'someone' who was holding me up but a delicate gold cord which seemed to be attached to something in the sky. As I followed the cord upward I could see that the end of it was being held in the hands of the tiniest yet most perfectly formed infant I had ever seen. And hovering behind this ethereal cherub, protecting and enfolding it in outstretched wings, was an exquisite angel.

"Suspended in this timeless moment, I was aware of nothing but this luminous vision and a profound silence for what seemed like a very long while. Then I heard a voice speak these words: 'The light of this unborn child is leading you home. This is a deep mystery which you cannot penetrate, but know that you are healed.'

"Later that afternoon as I waited in the dappled sunlight beneath the leafy branches of a graceful oak for Sister Mary W., the truth of those words vibrated through my entire being. I had found my soul. I was well again, whole again, and through this healing I was awakened to the power of prayer and the meaning of grace."

We asked author and poet Maya Angelou about prayer when we spoke with her at her home in Winston-Salem, North Carolina, where she is professor of American studies at Wake Forest University. She was thoughtful for several moments before replying, "My grandmother had two special songs that she used to sing all the time, and they are special to me as well." And in a soft, deep voice she began to sing, "'My Father is rich in houses and land. Holds the wealth of the world in his hands. His coffers are filled with silver and gold, my Father has riches, he has riches untold. I'm a child of the King. . . . '

"If it is true that I am a child of the King," she continued, "I don't believe my Father expects me to beg. I don't see that. It doesn't follow. I'm trying to be a loving child of God, a dutiful and, in the best sense, obedient child. I mean I blow it all the time, but God knows my intention, my willingness, so I don't think it follows that all this energy, all this might, needs me to beg. No, I don't believe that. It just doesn't compute. I believe I am to ask, but not to beg."

And "ask" is just what Maya did when she learned that Guy, her only child, was scheduled to have emergency surgery for complications arising from a broken neck he had sustained in an accident several years earlier. "I went directly to San Francisco to be with Guy. As soon as surgery got underway early the next morning, I drove out to Mission Dolores and I prayed. I had gone there before in a time of trouble—when I was pregnant with Guy and needed help to be allowed to enroll late in a summer school program so that I could finish my high-school education. I had prayed before the statue of Mary then and my prayers were answered. Now I was praying for the life of my son.

"When I got back to the hospital six hours later, Guy's doctor was waiting for me. 'Success,' he said. It was the word I most wanted to hear. I immediately called my sister to tell her the good news. Guy woke up shortly after that. It was late afternoon by then, and everything seemed fine. I stayed around the hospital talking with him and then went back to my hotel.

"At midnight the doctor called me. 'Ms. Angelou,' he said, 'we're losing Guy. We've got him back in surgery and we're losing him. You stay there and we'll call you.'

"Of course, I could not stay in the hotel. I went directly to the hospital, but I didn't go to the surgical floor. Instead, I went to the floor where his room was, and I walked the hall. I walked along past all those half-opened doors, and at times while I was walking I would suddenly feel I was standing on wet sand that was sifting out from under my feet. Then I'd say: 'GRAB YOUR LIFE. HOLD ON TO IT. HOLD ON.' Loud. For three hours I walked and talked. Then I felt solid.

"The doctors came up from surgery. 'Ms. Angelou,' they said, 'we're sorry. He's alive, but he's paralyzed from his neck down.' I whispered, 'I see. I see.' I went down to the intensive care unit and paced in and out waiting for my son to wake up. By seven A.M. he was awake, and I went in and stood looking down at him. Tubes were coming from everywhere. 'Mother,' he said, 'the thing I most feared has happened. I'm paralyzed.'

" 'It would seem so,' I answered.

" 'I'm your only child,' he continued, 'and I know you love me, but I refuse to live as a talking head. If there's no chance for recovery, I want to ask you to do something that no one should ever have to ask a mother.' The tears were just rolling down his face. 'If there's no chance for me to recover, please pull the plug and let me go.'

" 'In that case,' I said, 'TOTAL RECOVERY, I SEE TOTAL RECOVERY. I SEE YOU WALKING, STANDING, PLAYING BASKETBALL, AND SWIMMING. NOW QUIT IT RIGHT NOW. I MEAN IT.' That's what I said. Guy started laughing. He said, 'Mother, please control yourself. There are some very sick people in here.'

"The doctors came to talk with me. They said, 'Ms. Angelou, Guy has had a blood clot sitting on his spinal cord for eight hours. The cord is so delicate that we don't dare breathe on it. He will never be able to move.'

"I said, 'I'm not asking you, I'm *telling* you. My son will walk out of this hospital and I thank God for it—now!'

"One of the doctors started to say, 'We all have to . . .'

"And I said, 'You can't tell me. I'm going somewhere so far, so beyond you, you're not even in it!' And every hour after that I'd say, 'TOTAL RECOVERY. I THANK YOU FOR IT. I'M CLAIMING IT FOR THIS BOY. THANK YOU. TOTAL RECOVERY.'

"The next two days were busy. I called Dolly McPherson, my chosen sister, and she got the whole prayer group at my church together. We had a Jewish sister-friend, and she called people from her synagogue. A Catholic friend called the people she knew in her parish. 'Go everybody, go,' I said. 'Do what you can do.'

"The second night, I was lying on a couch in the ICU waiting room when a nurse came in. She said, 'Ms. Angelou, Guy's moved his toes.' Together we walked to Guy's room. She reached over and pulled the blanket off his feet and Guy moved his toes. I said, 'THANK YOU, GOD. DIDN'T I ASK YOU FOR IT AND DIDN'T YOU GIVE IT TO ME. THANK YOU FOR IT. THANK YOU, GOD.'

"The next morning when I went in to see Guy he said, 'Mama, thank you for your faith. I'll walk out of the hospital.' And that is exactly what he did a few months later. I know that prayer changes things. I *know*. I don't question. I *know*."

INNER GUIDANCE: A HEART SONG

The ancient Hebrew prayer says, "Sh'ma Yisraeil/Hear O one who struggles with God/listen O seeker of the way." Why do we need to listen? Because it is in listening that the inner truth is revealed. Listening as a method of prayer has a long history. Throughout the Middle Ages it was observed by Christian monks in a practice known as *lectio divina*, or divine reading. For the monks this meant reading scripture, or more exactly, listening to it by repeating the words of the sacred text with their lips so that the body itself entered into the process. It was primarily an exercise of listening at different levels: with the bodily ear, with the imagination, with the heart, or with the whole being. Through *lectio divina* the monks sought to cultivate the capacity to listen at ever deeper levels.[10]

Listening to the silence of one's own heart is one of the ways Mother Teresa, renowned spiritual leader and Nobel peace prize recipient, defines prayer. It is also a way in which the women we spoke with receive inner guidance. And virtually every woman we interviewed for this book told us that inner guidance is something she has come to depend on to direct her spiritual path. For one woman there is no question of its importance in her spiritual life. "My only guru is my inner voice," she told us.

However, for Marcia Lauck, a spiritual counselor, inner guidance is not a voice but a "resonance," a sound that tells her when she is on the right track. Irene Smith, the massage therapist and workshop leader, describes it as a "heart voice that speaks to me in words," while Dorothy Maclean, a cofounder of the Findhorn Community, says that for her "there are no actual words, but rather a delicate, pure inner prompting that tells me what I need to know or do." And for Twylah Nitsch, the Seneca elder, inner guidance is "a positive movement in my solar plexus." For many of the other women it is simply an inner knowing or clarity. As one woman put it, "It is like a thought, only you know it didn't come out of your mind."

Most of the women we talked with agreed that learning to listen is a spiritual art form that takes practice. "It's like a spiritual muscle that you exercise. It's a feeling thing," one woman explained. And the second thing they agreed about is that being able to discern between the voice of their personality, or ego, and inner guidance is not an easy thing to do. Developing this discernment, they told us, is a matter of trial and error, as well as trust. And it is an ongoing process. While meditation can be very helpful to some in quieting the mind in order to "hear" more clearly, the ability to "get out of the way and not censor what is trying to come through, no matter how foolish or irrelevant it may seem at the time," was seen as equally important by many women.

Even after the capacity to listen and discern has been relatively well developed, however, there is still the matter of obeying the counsel one has received. And while there is little danger today of being burned at the stake as Joan of Arc was, because she would not acknowledge that the church had more authority than her internal voices, following one's inner guidance can involve risk. This may be particularly true, we learned, if what we are being guided to do seems to threaten our personal relationships or what we have come to regard as our security in the world. As the artist Meinrad Craighead told us, "Being open to the voice within is how your life happens. Again and again, it plunges you into the unknown." What is required, it seems, is a willingness to commit yourself to the whole—known, unknown, and unknowable—and trust the path your indwelling truth is showing you.

While almost every woman we interviewed told us she depends on some form of inner guidance for spiritual direction, no one claimed to be perfect, or even consistent, in being able to follow it. A minister who was honored nationally by her denomination was only one of many who told us she does not always obey "the voice within, even when I hear it. Then when I realize how resistant I'm being, or something backfires, I apologize by saying, 'I heard you and I didn't follow. But please don't stop talking to me, God.'"

Sarah Leah Grafstein, a rabbi in her middle thirties, described her recalcitrance this way: "When I get a very clear message and do just the opposite, I pay the price. At this point in my life, however, I feel as if I'm still apprenticing, and I'm going to blow it a lot in the process." Developing discernment through trial and error is a challenge Sarah Leah is more than willing to take on: "On the one hand I've got a lot to learn," she told us, "but on the other hand, how can God direct our steps if we're not taking any?" It is, we agree, a question well worth considering.

While being able to listen on a deep level and acting on what you hear is certainly a form of prayer, if scrupulous attention is not given to the development of discernment, so-called inner guidance can become just another way to disguise the demands of one's ego. It is very difficult to take issue with anyone who tells us they are acting on inner guidance. In fact, the use or misuse of spiritual teachings to serve the purposes of the ego—"spiritual materialism" as one teacher has termed it[11]—has become all too apparent in the closing decades of this century.

As we were working on this chapter a letter arrived from a friend who has spent her life bringing together people of different spiritual persuasions from all over the world to further peace and understanding on our planet. Although she had no way of knowing we were writing about inner guidance at the time, she expressed some of her own thoughts on the topic in her letter. "There is a lot of work to be done these days," she wrote, "and too many people are waiting around for 'guidance' before they will do anything. This is not an indication of spiritual maturity to me. When you are living in a house with a mess on the floor and dishes in the sink, you don't need 'guidance' to do what needs to be done." As important as inner guidance is to the women we interviewed for this book, we doubt that any of them would disagree.

THE TUESDAY EVENING PRAYER GROUP

As we talked with our friends about what we were hearing from other women about the need to share our experiences of the sacred, someone would invariably ask us, "Why don't you start a prayer group? I could really use that kind of support for my inner life, and I'll bet there are others who feel the same way. I know you're busy right now, but won't you please think about it?"

From time to time we'd "think about it," usually right after one or the other of us had run into someone who wanted to know if we'd started a group yet. But months went by before we did any more than acknowledge that at some point it might be a good thing to do.

Then one morning almost a year after the topic had first come up, we sat down to meditate together on whether or not we were supposed to begin a prayer group for women. The answer was a swift and unequivocal yes. And that is how the Tuesday evening prayer group came into being.

We are seven in number, a mixed group personally, professionally, and spiritually. We are married, divorced, grandmothers, mothers, stepmothers, and childless. Some of us knew each other beforehand, others met for the first time in the group. All of us work—as therapists, as researchers, as writers, as an actress, and as a librarian. We are active and inactive Catholics, Protestants, Jews, and Buddhists. A few of us are "crossbreeds" of two or more of these traditions.

Despite these differences, we share one fundamental belief: that we all participate in a mystery that lies at the heart of our being, and one way we can come closer to that mystery in ourselves and each other is by praying together. Another thing we share is that we are all middle-aged women who have experienced "sitting in silence," whether we do it as a formal meditation practice, or in response to an internal voice that calls upon us to "be still and know that I am God."

We come together for an hour and a half every other Tuesday evening in Sherry's apartment. Despite hectic schedules, no one needs to be reminded about the meeting, and unless a business commitment takes someone out of town, absences are rare. Although we have come to know each other in a precious and intimate way these past four years, we do not see much of each other between sessions. From the beginning, our purpose for coming together has been to share the experience of praying in a small group.

How much this has come to mean to each of us would have been hard to predict, although there were indications from the start. Not one woman we invited to join us said no, and more than one woman's yes was accompanied by eyes filled with tears, which testified far more than her words to the depth of the commitment she was making.

Depth of commitment, however, does not guarantee immunity to those resistances that often emerge after we say we will do something, no matter how much we may want to do it. And resistances did come up for us both individually and as a group. One which almost all of us had to confront in the beginning was a certain self-consciousness about admitting to anyone that we belonged to a prayer group. There seemed to be something embarrassing about acknowledging this. In hindsight, this particular resistance may have been related to the fact that most of us live in Marin County, California, where residents, thanks to national television, are far better known for New Age pastimes and hot tubs than for participating in prayer groups.

Perhaps we feared the term *prayer group* would evoke images of righteous, somber-faced women sitting with folded hands in straight-backed chairs, an impression we did not wish to be identified with or encourage. What is more likely, however, is that our reticence grew out of the feeling that the term describes a group of people who know exactly what they are doing, a claim none of us would feel comfortable making.

So why have we persisted in calling ourselves the Tuesday evening prayer group? The answer is simple. We call ourselves that because we believe that praying together is truly what we do, even though we follow no liturgy or tradition, have no leader, and sometimes find our individual prayers differing from those of the group. Our commitment is to let our hearts lead the way, rather than our traditions or any models of prayer we have been conditioned by in the past.

This is not to say that prayers from our various traditions are unwelcome. Rather, we have made a conscious choice not to be limited by these forms and the familiar and often cherished concepts of the divine they express. One of the things we have discovered during the years we have been together is that, for us, prayer is a continuously evolving process requiring different forms at different times.

What is it then that we do when we come together on alternate Tuesday evenings? The word *silence* is the key to answering this question. The first time we met we agreed that silence would be the container for our prayers as well as a form of prayer in itself. This does not mean, however, that we enter Sherry's apartment under a rule of silence. It is simply that after we have taken a few moments to greet and check in with each other, we quite naturally become quiet.

We sit in a circle on floor cushions with our eyes open or closed, with bodies erect in a lotus position, or with legs folded under or stretched out in front of us, half-reclining. It makes no difference. What matters is that everything that emerges from this silence—a word, an image, a line of scripture or poetry, a probing question—is held by each of us as if it is our collective heart speaking. And it is this heart that we listen to and follow as we pray.

We may pray for a teenager who has recently become addicted to drugs, for an aged parent who is lonely and frightened, for empowerment and encouragement for our families and each other and for the healing of our planet. At some point, each of us also prays in her own way for the other members of the group, a practice many of us follow in our daily prayers as well.

We pray for specific people, but not for specific results. Like some of the women discussed earlier in this chapter, we do not feel we can know what is best for anyone, that such knowledge is beyond our understanding. For this reason, our prayers tend to be simple: that the crisis a person is facing will bring them closer to the deep purpose that guides their life and give them the strength to follow it, that healing may be granted to an individual in a form that will best serve their spiritual growth, that a heart which is closed may open.

From the beginning, we have accepted the fact that while we participate in the mystery, we cannot know it. Yet from this very "not knowing" has come some of our greatest gifts. For in the silence we feel free to voice our doubts and questions when they arise, to just be with them without seeking absolute answers. And as a result we are learning, as Rilke suggested, to "love the questions themselves."[12] Although we do not always know the way to God, our collective heart reminds us again and again as we sit together in the silence that God knows the way to us.

We see ourselves as a process, not as a model. In the years we have been praying together we have cycled in and out of tears and laughter, tragedies and blessings, and felt our souls growing and deepening as we moved through these rhythms of life together. Even those of us who have an aversion to groups feel the powerful bonding that has come to us through prayer, a bonding we all rely on for strength and support. But perhaps the most telling statement of all about our inner process is that no one feels any embarrassment these days about saying out loud, sometimes to a relative stranger, that she belongs to a prayer group.

.   .   .

For all the many ways in which the women we interviewed pray and for all the emphasis on prayer as an integral part of their spiritual maturing, there were times in the life of nearly every woman when she felt she could not pray. A minister who has had many years of experience leading her congregation in prayer described one of these times to us:

"It was after my second husband died and I was faced with bringing up five children alone, one of them a baby. I had almost no financial resources, and it was absolutely necessary that I go out and find a job to support myself and my children. This was a period when I couldn't pray for quite a while, but I know now that I was really praying the greatest prayer. Day after day I just said, 'God, I can't pray. You'll just have to do whatever is right.'"

Another woman who in her thirties had gone through several long bouts of depression and uncertainty about her spiritual path told us, "If you're so far gone and so lost that you can't even begin to pray, just say, 'Please, God, really help me.' And those few words will break through."

In essence, prayer is communion with mystery. And for that reason, there can be no one right way to do it, no prescription for prayer that will minister to everyone's needs. The message implied in the Zen saying, "Don't take other people's medicine," seems equally applicable to the practice of prayer. However, perhaps there is one requisite: that our heart be in it. As Brother David Steindl-Rast reminds us in *Gratefulness, the Heart of Prayer*, "The more we come alive and awake, the more everything we do becomes prayer. Eventually, even our prayer will become prayer."[13]

Chapter 7

TOOLS FOR THE SACRED GARDEN:
PART II

> Qualities like love and compassion are not just
> abstract virtues that are the property of saints and
> adepts. Anyone can develop these qualities in
> themselves by doing spiritual practices. As the
> Buddha said, Come and see. You don't have to be a
> Buddhist; by doing these practices you can see the
> development in yourself.
>
> — Joanna Macy

 What prompts a woman to take on a spiritual practice?
Why would anyone spend hours each day reciting a
mantram or contemplating? What makes someone
light candles and recite prayers to welcome the Sabbath, or trace a medicine wheel to honor the four directions? What
does she want? Why does she bother?

ENTERING THE GARDEN

At first, like anyone entering a hidden garden, we don't know
exactly where we are. Intrigued, we walk about for a while, discovering overgrown paths and alcoves with stone seats and moss-
covered urns. Bending close to the fragrant earth, we kneel down
to find out what might be growing there. We go slowly, feeling like
strangers. Our questions are basic, primordial: Who am I? Why am
I here? If they came when we were children, they were often ac-

companied by delight and fascination, but by the time we reach adulthood, they have become depth charges.

For Choqosh Auh-Ho-Ho, the Chumash activist, these ques-tions exploded in adolescence. "All my life I felt like an out-of-place marble," Choqosh told us as we huddled around her kitchen table, drinking hot coffee and sharing memories. "I was trying to survive in the world with very little education and very little self-confidence. At fifteen, I landed in a convent school where our ward sister whipped herself at night for the sin of being a woman. We girls lay awake in the dark, listening."

She paused, frowning, then hurried on: "But I would have become a Catholic in a minute if they could have answered the questions that were driving me crazy. Is there a God? What is God? How can a man be God? These questions upset everyone, but it wasn't out of disrespect I was asking them. I desperately needed to know what was true. I was sure my survival depended on it."

Searching for the answer to these questions, she read the Bible every night, she told us, going straight from Genesis through to Revelation. She was amazed to discover it was a continuing story instead of short, pithy admonitions. "But in the end it didn't mean a goddamned thing," she said furiously. The night she finished Revelation, she seized the object of her dashed hopes and flung it into the neighborhood swimming pool. The next morning, feeling a little remorseful, she dove down to rescue the sodden scriptures and give them a "proper burial."

There was a book, however, that addressed the questions that were tormenting her. In the middle of our interview she rushed out to rummage through her bedroom. When she returned she was flourishing a tattered copy of Huston Smith's *The Religions of Man*.[1]

"I found this in a book store the year I was fifteen," she said. "I smuggled it back into the convent and it became my survival route. On my knees on that cold, hard marble floor with my back straight as could be, I'd drape my school sweater over my shoulders like a curtain, hiding this little red book. I'd read about Buddhism and Hinduism and especially Taoism."

At this point she opened the book and read: "There is an essence, wonderful, perfect. It existed before heaven and earth. . . ." She continued for some time and ended with a voice so hushed we could scarcely catch her words, "All life comes from this essence, and I rejoice in its power!"

Twenty years later, Choqosh met a Chumash medicine man who initiated her into the tribe of her ancestors and showed her the ancient ways of honoring the earth and the Great Spirit. "The Great Spirit that is in all things," she told us, "is the Tao, the Way, the Great Mystery. I first found it in that cold, long winter of my fifteenth year. But it wasn't till my late thirties that I was given ways to enter it over and over again."

Fasting. Sitting in the fiery heat of sweat lodges. Going on vision quests. "I had been waiting for these a long, long time," she said. "All of a sudden I felt like I was coming home, like the out-of-place marble had finally slipped into its hole. Now there was a fit, and I was being given ways to transmute my fear, to let go of being a victim, to become grateful. To be," she beamed at us, "that essence."

Almost every woman who began her spiritual practice as an adult had questions like the ones Choqosh raised. But rarely were the women able to formulate their questions so clearly.

"I didn't even know what it was that I wanted, but I needed to find out," Toni Packer, who is the resident meditation teacher of the Springwater Center in upstate New York, told us. She recalled a time twenty years earlier: "I was in the passenger seat of the car, holding my baby on my shoulder and looking out at the landscape. My husband was driving—an ordinary, boring Sunday excursion. It suddenly hit me with the most tremendous pain that I was separate from them and from the countryside and everything I could see," she said, "and there was an anguish that lasted long into the night." She thought to herself, I have nothing to do with all of this. But she didn't know what she *did* have to do with, or what she cared about, or what was important in her life. "I didn't know," she said, "and I felt a deep discontent. So I started looking."

Another woman began her spiritual practice, and the depth work of her life, on what seemed to be a whim. "I had heard about a month-long conference for psychotherapists scheduled for January in a warm, scenic spot far from my northern home, and I decided to go. The first week of the conference was to be a Zen retreat, something I did not have the slightest interest in, but it was part of the package, so I took a chance and signed up for that too. Frankly, I was trying to get away from winter because my whole life felt like winter at that point, and I would have gone almost anywhere that promised a whiff of springtime."

She arrived to find the retreat already in progress. Twenty-five figures arrayed in solemn, silent lines sat facing the walls. The silence was to be maintained for seven days, and the sitting periods, alternating with slow walking meditations, were to last fourteen hours a day. The only opportunity to speak was in daily interviews with the Zen master.

The next day, full of trepidation, she walked through the door for her first interview. "Good morning!" the Zen master boomed at her cheerfully. To her astonishment, she burst into great heaving sobs, unable to utter a word. After several minutes, he indicated that she could leave.

"I couldn't figure it out," she told us. "I'd never been a crier. In fact people thought of me, and I certainly thought of myself, as a very stable and reliable person. But day after day, the same thing would happen. He'd say good morning with a big smile, and I'd just bawl."

By the end of the fourth day, something else happened that took her by surprise: silence. "Now it was not only outside but inside me. I couldn't remember ever having known such a silence before," she said. By the end of seven days, there were more silences and other surprises as well. The slapping of waves. Cold wet air. A moth. Not names or categories but actual "suchness." The Zen master called it "just this."

Determined to get more of "just this," she approached him as he was leaving for his home. "I live far away from your center," she said, "but I'd like to do something to be with this... whatever it is. What can I do?"

"Sit," he replied. "And bow one hundred and eight times every day."

She hadn't expected the second part, she told us. The "bows" were full body prostrations that resembled push-ups, and the Zen master and his enthusiastic student teachers had led the retreatants in doing these daily. Her thighs had just stopped aching, and she didn't see why she should subject herself to this peculiar form of torture any longer.

"I hate those bows," she told him flatly. "Give me one good reason why I should do them."

He looked at her intently. "They mean believing in yourself one hundred percent."

Something rose up inside her then, she said, and gave a fierce silent cry: "I don't know what that means, but I want it."

For the next seven years, she sat in meditation and bowed 108 times every morning, not missing more than one or two days a year. On retreats and during certain other periods, she would bow five hundred or one thousand times a day. The bows became not only a spiritual practice, but her way-shower, her teacher. She grew to love them for the ways in which they revealed her own mind.

"In the beginning it was very difficult," she said. "My mind would invent hundreds of reasons why I couldn't bow that morning: it was too cold or too hot or too late or I was too tired or my knees were too sore. When I bowed anyway, my mind would issue constant alarms telling me to stop. And then when I finished, who do you think would skip out to take credit for the whole thing? My mind! 'That wasn't hard at all,' it would say brightly. 'I'm actually getting quite good at this.'

"What an education in fifteen minutes a day!" she continued. "Slowly, by hearing the chatter and going ahead anyway, I began to be able to follow through on promises in a way I never had before. If I told a friend I'd help her, I would show up. No matter what."

She began to trust herself. Once she made a promise, she saw that her whole self would unite behind that promise to keep it. "It's not a matter of willpower," she said. "It's something more natural, a coming into alignment with what's needed in the moment. 'Spring comes, the grass grows by itself,' the Zen saying goes."

With the trust came an intention to be of service in the world. "Before the bows, before the trust emerged," she told us, "I couldn't have made such a lifetime promise. Some inner voice would have mocked me, laughing. 'You?' Now there seems to be a kind of respect, an acknowledgment that such a commitment can be kept."

Some women begin with a hunger for answers, some with discontent, and some on a whim with a hidden yearning. It does not seem to matter.

Dorothy Maclean, one of the three founders of the Findhorn Community in northern Scotland, told us that a strong commitment is invaluable to spiritual development. "We were just three very ordinary people with lots of faults," she said, "but we started that community because we were utterly committed. There's tremendous power in that."

Many of the women we spoke with agreed that a commitment to be of service or a strong intention to awaken and help others is essential to spiritual development. Others named different qualities: sincerity, surrender, love. But it seems to us that nothing is essential except beginning. The woman who did bows for seven years did not have enough trust to make any commitment, so she started right where she was, in a place of no trust, with a practice so simple and concrete that no belief and no understanding were necessary.

The enormous success of Alcoholics Anonymous and other twelve-step programs which are themselves spiritual practices supports our impression that there is no place too hopeless to start from. As Irene Smith told us after her hellish journey through drug and alcohol addiction, "We don't ever have to be stuck. My own life has taught me that. But we do have to live our own experiences—whatever they are."

One artist who has taken great risks in her own life said, "Ultimately, I think you need to follow the intuitive way that unfolds out of you and leads you. The feminine path where you just feel spontaneously, Oh, this is what I want to do. But," she added, leaning forward for emphasis, "you have to give yourself permission to follow that path. If you sit back and think, 'If only I could travel, if only I could have time alone . . .' and never take yourself seriously, nothing will happen. You must do it. Do it! Pack your bag or unpack your closet. Be alone or be with people. Do whatever your inner self is telling you." She leaned back then and sighed. "It's so simple, you know. But you have to honor it."

WANTING TOOLS

"Come and see," the mystical Jewish text called *The Zohar*, the Book of Splendor, invites the reader. "Taste and know how sweet the Lord is," the Bible says. "Be a lamp unto yourself," the Buddha counseled his disciples. Don't just swallow these words, the great teachings of the past urge. Chew them up yourself. Have your own experience. Then you will know for yourself what is real food and what isn't.

When a woman gets to this point, she wants tools, techniques, methods. She wants to cultivate her own sacred garden.

"I started reading *The Three Pillars of Zen*,"[2] Toni Packer told us, "and it captivated me. Instantly. Because, you see, there was a method given. You could do your own sitting meditation from this method. I had read other books and had quite an interest in having a direct experience of insight, but there had been nothing to go on."

Sweet Alice Harris, the community leader from Watts, told us that although she had been praying and singing since she was very young, she didn't know at the time why she did those things. Later, when she attended Bible study classes, she felt real changes taking place in her life. "It was just like I was picking up the tools I needed," she explained.

Joanna Macy, an ecological activist and teacher of Buddhism, was in the Peace Corps in India when she first learned to meditate. It was, she said, a great relief. "I'd been enjoined by religious teachers to be loving or to be still or to be devotional, but never shown how I could develop those qualities until I encountered Buddhism. Here was a tradition that had a respect for method, and you didn't have to believe or have faith. You only had to try it for yourself."

"Better is one's own dharma, though imperfect, than the dharma of another well performed," reads the ancient Hindu text, the *Bhagavad Gita*. It is better to realize the truth through your own immediate experience than to accept without testing the teaching of another.

This insight into the need for actual practice, for "doing it," was eloquently expressed by the Christian contemplative Bernadette Roberts. As a girl she was constantly concerned about whether or not she was really a Christian. Did she honestly believe that Jesus, a man who walked around just like she did, could be God? No, not the One Absolute, she decided.

"My baptism didn't take," she would tell her father. After several years of musing about these questions, she finally asked him, "Suppose somebody could believe some of the doctrine, but not all of it. Would that mean they weren't a Christian?"

"You don't have to understand the mystery of God to be a Christian," he responded immediately. "But you have to practice. If you wait until all the understanding comes before practicing, you'll never understand. It's the practice that gives rise to understanding. So practice, practice, practice!"

"His answer struck me as absolutely spectacular," she told us. "Because you see, if you don't practice, you can say yes, yes to the teachings, but it's totally meaningless. You'll never know the truth of it. So I was content, thinking I will spend my whole life *becoming* a Christian. I didn't know how it would go, or even if it would work. But I had to try—to practice, that is."

DIGGING DOWN DEEP

When tools and instruction manuals and experts become secondary, and the question at the heart of one's life becomes something spare and simple like, "What is growing here?" or "What is this?" we are prepared to fathom what we are. "At a certain point it was time for me to let go of the teachers, stop looking for new tools, and dig down deep inside myself," a young medicine woman told us. A meditation teacher in her sixties echoed the sentiment: "At some point you no longer want comfort or inspiration. You just want the truth."

The stories we have told so far may suggest that a woman searches and finds good tools and then she achieves "spirituality," as if finding a rake and a hoe could grow corn. Of course, it is not that way at all. Time and again women told us about "dedicating my life" or "having a vision" or "finding a teacher or practice." None of these events in themselves changed a single life. At best they encouraged or affirmed the woman's willingness to cultivate the sacred in her life. It is not tools or visions but the repeated conscious use of those tools that lets our seeds bear fruit.

This perseverance is perhaps the hardest part of cultivation to describe, because it is so unique to each life. Sometimes it means using the tools you've been given and working faithfully through dry spells in rock hard soil. Or it may mean throwing the old tools away and making new ones. At other times, as the essayist Ralph Waldo Emerson observed, ". . . teachers, texts, temples fall and all things are made sacred, one as much as another."[3]

In the next two sections we tell the stories of two very different gardeners. The first entered deeply into an orthodox faith, studied with master gardeners, and learned to shape their ancient tools to her own hands. The second also studied with master gardeners and learned a variety of cultivation methods. But then she plummeted down an Alice-in-Wonderland tunnel where she had to find her way alone.

ESSE'S STORY

Esse Chasin, like so many of the women we interviewed, doesn't fit neatly into a single category. Sherry discovered this when she went to interview her on Long Island. "I was a little nervous, I suppose. I knew I was to meet an elderly Orthodox Jewish teacher of Kabbalah, and on the train ride from Manhattan my mind created a vivid picture of a rather severe person dressed in black from head to toe. I wondered if I'd dare ask her the intimate questions we normally raised in our interviews. But when I finally arrived at her front door, a lovely woman with wide, alert eyes greeted me casually. 'Hi, I'm Esse,' she said. 'Come on in and make yourself at home.' I stared. She was wearing a hot pink sweater outfit. So much for my psychic abilities, I thought with relief, as I followed her into the living room.

"The most impressive thing about Esse is her willingness to examine her own decisions and actions," Sherry said later. "Whenever I challenged her, she would look directly at the contradictions in her life and discuss them with an interest remarkably lacking in ego." One of the most open-minded women we interviewed, she is at the same time a traditionalist who trusts systems and believes "there are steps to take, and if you don't take them, you won't get where you need to go."

"My ultimate objective," she told Sherry frankly, "is to transform myself into a spiritual being."

"What does that mean?"

"There is an unmanifest world that holds the design of the universe. I want to awaken my spirituality so I can connect with that reality. I want that connection," she explained.

This is a very traditional spiritual goal, and Esse believes she has to approach it in a systematic manner. "Becoming a spiritual being is a step-by-step process," she said with conviction. "If I want to become spiritual, I have to do the same thing the spiritual men did and in the same traditional way." But, in fact, what she has created is a highly original and evolving form of spiritual practice that does not fit anybody's cookie-cutter version of a "step-by-step process."

The fourth child of devoted Orthodox Jewish parents, Esse grew up in Jamaica, Queens, in New York, during the early part of this century. When she was in her twenties, after many years of Hebrew school and private studies with individual rabbis, she decided to become a teacher herself. At the time, the only school where she could become an accredited teacher of Hebrew was the Jewish Theological Seminary in New York City. The seminary was regarded as "a hotbed of secular Judaism" by her Orthodox family, but with the indomitable certainty of youth, Esse persuaded her parents that she would not be swayed by the radical ideas being taught there.

But she underestimated her susceptibility. One course with Dr. Mordechai Kaplan, who later founded the Reconstructionist movement in Judaism, and her resolve gave way. "Who could have resisted him?" she asked with a wry grin. "He threw himself with passion and brilliance into showing us that Torah, the core of Hebrew scriptures, is a mythology like that of other cultures around the world. I didn't admit it, but I was shocked. I believed, like other Orthodox Jews, that every word of Torah was revealed to Moses directly from God and therefore cannot be altered in any way. Dr. Kaplan opened the door which led me to question that belief."

On the surface Esse's life went along undisturbed. She completed her seminary training in half the usual time, and for the next ten years lived what she called a "kind of crazy life of ordinary chaos," teaching Hebrew in experimental schools and thriving on the adventure of doing things her own way.

When the United States entered World War II and the entire country seemed to be moving and mobilizing, Esse caught the fever and decided to leave New York. She moved to Boston to join a woman friend whose husband had been drafted. She found a job teaching Hebrew and settled in. Then, one Saturday afternoon a few weeks after her arrival, Esse left Orthodox Judaism. It happened

suddenly, without any particular warning, as a quiet stream gathers
twigs and leaves and suddenly, one day, is dammed up.

"I wanted to see a baseball game, of all things," she said. "Even
though it was on the Sabbath, I went anyway. And that was the
first time in my life I had ever used money or traveled or done
anything secular at all on Shabbos. I must have been emotionally
ready for it, however, because I didn't feel any conflict.

"I still loved God," she continued. "That never changed for
me. But I didn't think the rituals of observing the Sabbath or the
dietary laws or the intellectual teachings were connected to God.
Or at least I didn't know how they were connected. Oh, I could
sense a hope for a better society and the possibility for ethical and
moral development, but the teachings and rituals weren't touching
me inside."

Within a few years she returned to New York and married a
man who, although Jewish, was not Orthodox, and began to lead
what her family disparagingly called a "secular life." She stopped
teaching when her first child was born. After giving birth to two
more children, she found herself focusing all her energy on her
family and her "dominating, fiercely independent and remarkably
wonderful" husband.

One day while visiting a friend's home, Esse overheard a phone
conversation the woman was having in an adjoining room. Her
friend was consoling and advising the person on the other end of
the line in ways Esse had never heard before. Provoked by what she
was hearing, Esse queried her friend and learned that she had been
attending "a kind of philosophy class" taught by an elderly woman.
"I'm very interested," Esse told her friend, and a few days later she
was invited to meet the teacher of this mysterious class, a Madame
Popoff. "When I walked into that room," Esse told us, "I felt as
though I'd always been there. I thought, I know this is going to
change my whole life. Now I have found something!"

Madame Popoff taught a spiritual path based on the work of
G. I. Gurdjieff, a spiritual seeker who had traveled through the East
at the turn of the century studying the esoteric teachings of Chris-
tians, Muslims, Indian Hindus, Tibetan Buddhists, and others.

Looking for the core of truth he was convinced lay beneath the outer forms of conventional religions, he synthesized theoretical and practical knowledge that had been virtually unknown in the West and formulated a system for self-transformation specifically adapted to westerners.[4]

Madame Popoff herself had been a student of Gurdjieff's associate P. D. Ouspensky, and her work centered on the Gurdjieff system. "It was a path of self-change based on the objective of elevating yourself from your lowest, most unconscious nature," Esse explained. "By focusing a sharp beam of attention on our thoughts, feelings, and physical body, we were told we could uncover the essence of what we are. Until that time, Madame Popoff told us flatly, we are so much at the mercy of our unconscious habits that we might as well be sleepwalking."

Although no mention was made of God or soul, Esse felt she was being offered tools for discovering an inestimably valuable treasure—her true self. With this hope, and no guarantees, she plunged in. After a year of attending weekly group meetings, Esse's appetite was only whetted. She wanted much more and said so. When Madame Popoff responded by offering to see her on a daily basis, she was delighted.

Esse's experience, however, was far from what she expected spiritual training to be. "We did the most trivial things in the world," she recalled. "Cleaning the house. Shopping. Instead of mailing her check to the electric company, we'd take it directly to the office."

At first Esse felt like an idiot. "What am I doing here?" she wondered anxiously. "She wants her house cleaned and she's using me. It's crazy to do this every day. It's ridiculous." But she felt she had to get to the bottom of the system Madame Popoff was teaching, and most of its methodology was concealed. Madame Popoff herself talked in symbols and metaphors. "Anytime she told me something," Esse said, "I could be sure that wasn't it. I had to be continually alert to figure out what was going on. However, I trusted the tradition, and because of that, I was able to keep going. Eventually it was an inner adventure and a lot of fun. I loved it."

For the next six years the two women worked together in an exquisite rhythm. Their goal was to have Esse observe and then release or change the unconscious habits in her life. Gradually, she learned to be aware of her patterns, stop her automatic reactions, and choose new responses. But Madame Popoff kept exact pace with her. "As soon as I grasped one of the hidden principles, she fed me something else. She knew just what I had overcome—jealousy, petulance, impatience—and she didn't allow me to enjoy my achievement for one minute. She was always pushing for the next thing. So the horizons of my life just opened up, one after another."

At the end of seven years, Madame Popoff felt that Esse had grasped what she needed to get from the system and asked her to leave the group. "I had quite a struggle taking my leave," Esse told us, "even though everything was clearly telling me to go. I remember empowering myself with the Biblical story of the slave who refused his freedom after seven years." If her apprenticeship with Madame Popoff had been successful, Esse would realize the mastery in herself. If not, there was no sense continuing the work.

When Esse entered her sacred garden, she couldn't tell what was dead and what was alive. But she had now taken the equivalent of an intensive gardening course with a demanding master gardener. She had learned how to cut away what was dead and to weed and prune and fertilize what was growing. Now she had to trust that her work would yield a harvest, that what had been hers from the very beginning would bear fruit.

After a few years of sampling various religious traditions including two years with a Sufi order where she was introduced to Kabbalah, the mystical core of Judaism, Esse began to return to her spiritual roots. She was now almost sixty. Not wholly accepting her tradition as she had in childhood, nor flatly rejecting it as she had in her twenties, but from a position of seriousness and skill and deep feeling, she engaged the spiritual teachings of Judaism.

She began with ethics and was astounded to find that the system of commandments and good deeds that had felt like a demanding burden of shoulds and oughts in her youth became a precious resource: "I began to see that the ethical system lets us take personal transformation seriously. We can become alchemists, transmuting the lead of our unconscious selves into gold. And what are our sacred chemicals? The ethics of our tradition.

"Consider the characteristics we're asked to develop: the ability to take insult and blame, compassion, forgiveness, honest speech. It's not a matter of doing this because God commands it, but because the process will bring you to God."

Next, she turned her full attention to the Kabbalistic texts and meditations intended to bring a Jew into communion with the Holy One. In order to do this, she had to return to orthodoxy, to a strict observance of the Sabbath and the ritual dietary laws, among other things. She did this gradually. And in time she was permitted to take classes with the Hasidic rabbis.

"I was overjoyed to be making these inner connections," she told us, "and I soon opened up to the meditations and the Kabbalistic texts we were studying." But she wanted more than that. She wanted to live the reality she was discovering. For several years she continued to take classes and press for ways of bridging the mystical experience into her personal life. One day a friend said, "You know, Esse, you don't need a teacher all the time. Do it yourself for a while."

She decided to follow her friend's advice. For the next two years, she studied alone. Every morning and every evening she would work with the prayer book "on an inner level," sometimes spending two hours a day on the morning prayer. "I wanted to get to my own authentic experience, to feel my own body responding to the prayers," she said.

She spoke the words in Hebrew. Closing her eyes and listening to the sounds, she could feel the words taking shape in her spine and her heart and her hands. She contemplated the meanings of the words. "Love God with all your heart, with all your soul, with all your strength," she would recite, and ask herself, "Do I? How can I love this way? How do I get that feeling inside so I know it in every fiber of my being so I never have to read and remind myself, because it's embedded in my body?"

She personalized the prayers, so every quality of the divine being described was something she brought inside herself. "Compassion. Forgiveness. I want to be like that," she would pray, with great intention. And she would repeat the prayers over and over, because "we need to reinforce the prayers in ourselves. At least I need it every day—I don't know about other people."

Following the tradition of the Hasidic masters, she would become quiet before prayer. "I'd let my thoughts drop away and move into the realization of God. Then I would pray. Then afterwards I would again be quiet." Working with all these forms of prayer, she was "using prayer," she said, to reach God. Prayer for Esse had become a spiritual practice.

And there was one final piece, she told us: ritual. "As a child and young woman, I loved celebrating the religious holidays, but I never really got the meanings. I said finally, 'It's time I really believed there is, in Judaism, the whole thing. It's mine. It's my own tradition. I've got to learn all of it.'"

She looked up at this point with a kind of pain in her eyes and said, "I feel I would never have left Judaism if I could have understood the rituals the way I do today. Now every time I do them, the rituals turn me on inside. It happens physically. Each Friday at sunset when I light the candles for Shabbat, I have an experience of shedding the weekday and opening up to sanctity. Suddenly the room is filled with something else. The indwelling presence, the femaleness of God, the Shekhinah, awakens. There is a simple, deep sense of connectedness—a linking of the indwelling with the transcendent God."

She sat quietly for a long while. "I wish I could have transmitted that to my children," she said.

We believe this is what Esse is doing today: transmitting to her "children"—to women's prayer circles, to returnees to Judaism, and to study groups—ways to live the sacred inner experience in their daily lives. "There's such an intense depth of spirituality available from the wellspring," she says, "that as fast as I learn something, I like to share it." The fullness and beauty of her Orthodox tradition now flows into the whole of her life through the sanctity of ritual, the practicality of ethics, and the mystery of unifying her own particular self with the infinite.

VIJALI'S STORY

"Ah, can you show me the line where matter ends and spirit begins?" These were the words which greeted us on a plaque in Vijali Hamilton's tiny house trailer perched on a shelf high up in the Santa Monica Mountains north of Malibu. We had driven for what seemed like hours over narrow dirt roads filled with axle-mangling potholes to interview Vijali, an artist in her late forties who was living alone in this mountain aerie.

The view itself was worth the trip. Far below us, beyond the gently rolling green valleys to the west, the sun glinted off the Pacific. Above us to the east, massive rock formations threw down late afternoon shadows. "Welcome to my home," Vijali said with an impish grin, seeing how awestruck we were.

We stayed for two days and returned for several more visits. There was something about hiking with this elfin, porcelain-skinned woman among the great stone cities above her home and sleeping beneath the star-bright skies that was probably the closest either of us had ever come to meeting Huck Finn and floating down the Mississippi on that incomparable raft. Then, too, Vijali had a way of inviting us so gently and easily into her spacious awareness, an awareness that seemed to reflect the vastness and quietude of her surroundings, that we, too, felt expansive and peaceful.

However, the most valuable gift we received from Vijali was not the opportunity to live out a childhood fantasy or participate in an expanded state of consciousness. Rather it was the down-to-earth, human perspective of her self-revelations that reminded us again and again to let go of our stubborn tendency to idealize the women we were interviewing. She showed us that right along with an awakened consciousness there can be fears and doubts and longings for intimacy. And that even when one comes to what Vijali calls a "cosmically connected understanding," it can still take years to integrate that understanding into everyday life.

Vijali Hamilton, the youngest person to become a Vedanta nun in North America, studied the teachings of this Hindu tradition under the spiritual guidance of Swami Prabhavananda. Raised by a series of foster parents after her own parents divorced, she was later cared for by her father's parents. When Vijali was nine her father brought her and her grandparents from their home in Dallas to California to live with him. Despite continuous objections from her Christian grandmother, Vijali accompanied her father to the newly organized Vedanta Society in Los Angeles. There she heard lectures on the Hindu teachings and met the first nuns and monks to join the community along with several well-known early followers of Vedanta in this country—Aldous Huxley, Gerald Heard, and Christopher Isherwood.

Although her Christian upbringing and her grandmother's vociferous protestations that this was a "pagan" religion caused her great conflict and fear, she was attracted to the community from the very beginning. "It was the meditation that drew me," she said. "I had been meditating spontaneously since early childhood, and I wanted to learn these techniques which could take me more deeply into what I was already doing naturally." After a year of constant entreaty to her father and to Swami Prabhavananda, Vijali was admitted to the convent of the Vedanta Society. She was fourteen years old.

"For the first four years, it was ecstasy," she told us. "We meditated three times a day. In the evening we had vespers and sang together and played musical instruments and as I had in childhood, I continued to pour my inner feelings into drawing and painting." In the fifth year, at the age of nineteen, Vijali took her Brahmacharya vows to live a celibate monastic life.

For a whole year after this she followed a special practice called *purascharana*. Starting each month on the dark of the moon, she would recite her mantram a thousand times, counting on her rosary. Each night the recitations would be increased incrementally until, by the full moon, she was repeating her mantram fifteen thousand times. "An incredible rapture would come from doing so many repetitions," she told us.

It was wonderful, she said, "until I started growing up." By the time she was twenty, she was filled with dreams and passions that didn't fit at all well with life in the convent. One of these was the sexuality she had vowed to give up.

"I would go on full moon nights when all the other nuns were asleep to the oleander grove with my mind on Krishna, the legendary God-boy who steals the hearts of the milkmaids. I'd put on my white cotton sari without anything under it and dance and sing, letting the breeze play through my long hair that I had to keep pinned up in the day. The night-blooming jasmine would flood my senses and I would call, 'Krishna! Krishna! I want to make love with you.'"

And there were other things too. Vijali wanted to study art. She wanted to go to college. She wanted, she told the Swami, to have the opportunity to make mistakes. "I'm not allowed to make any mistakes here," she said, "and I'm not growing." The Swami did not object. On the morning of her twenty-fifth birthday, with one hundred dollars borrowed from the father of one of her sister nuns, Vijali left the convent.

"I felt I was ready for anything," she told us.

On little more than an impulse, she headed for Canada, the farthest place she could imagine from her convent in Southern California. For the next year Vijali worked days and studied art at the university at night, an intense initiation to the outside world after her protected life in the convent. It was not an easy time. Although now in her late twenties, she was as innocent and gullible as a child. She couldn't discern who to trust and how to protect herself, and for a while she fell in and out of love every few months.

In addition to the pain of broken relationships there were constant financial pressures and a life-threatening health crisis during which she almost died. "It's funny," she told us, "awful things happened to me during that time but I had this tremendous determination that I was going to live. I wasn't going to get caught in some situation that would keep me from living and growing and expanding. I connected to the center of myself that I had known since my early childhood, and to my passion for life, and just kept going."

The urge to express herself through painting, drawing, and sculpture gave purpose to her life during this period, as it would later on as well. It was, she told us, a living stream that connected her to her essence. And her talents were recognized by others, bringing her full scholarships that allowed her to study at Sir George Williams University in Montreal for three years.

At the end of this time, Vijali returned to California, longing for familiar faces and feeling ready to create artwork on her own. She met a fellow artist at the Vedanta Society the week she arrived, and a few weeks later they were married. Dale was fifteen years older than she, with four teenage children. Glad to leave her years of chaotic exploration, Vijali told us that she enthusiastically took on the full-time roles of artist, wife, and stepmother. "I had no outside friends in that time," she added. "Just the family and work."

At the end of seven years, as if an alarm had been set to ring, Vijali was shaken out of her busy domestic life. For two years before this, she had been having sensual dreams that nourished her inner life in ways she had not known before. In the dreams a brown-skinned motherly woman would embrace her lovingly. After a while Vijali began to draw and then to create large sculptural paintings of the "earth mother," as she called her. Then one evening when she and her husband were visiting friends, Vijali walked down a corridor and found herself face-to-face with photographs of "her" earth mother. "That is the remarkable Anandamayi Ma, the Mother of Bliss," she was told. "She is one of the greatest saints of the twentieth century. She lives in India and travels from city to city. Thousands come to be in her presence."

Eager to meet this woman, Vijali quickly raised the money for plane fare by selling several large sculptural pieces. Her friends made arrangements for her and Dale to have a private meeting with Anandamayi Ma. Within a month, the couple was in Benares, sitting in the small room of an ashram where Ma was staying.

"She looked into my eyes for about ten minutes with total openness, without any kind of social barrier. It felt like hours, as if my whole life were bare to her eyes," Vijali told us. Ma repeated this ritual with Dale and then asked if either of them had any questions.

"I was a nun for many years in the Vedanta Society and also have tried other meditation methods since I left the convent," Vijali said. "But what is my real path?"

What Vijali did not say was that she had been doing many spiritual practices in preparation for this trip and secretly imagined that she might stay in India to become a devotee of this great saint, perhaps even becoming a nun again. But Ma's advice was exactly the opposite of what Vijali had anticipated.

"Do what comes spontaneously," Ma replied immediately.

That night, Vijali wrote in her journal: "She has told me to drop all the prescribed rituals and practices, all the spiritual paraphernalia. This is not at all what I expected!"

In the weeks that followed, as Vijali and her husband traveled through India visiting several other ashrams and gurus, she grew increasingly irritated with the trappings of spiritual life. On the day of their departure from New Delhi they learned that Ma had arrived in that city. Quickly packing their bags, they hopped in a cab and drove to where she was staying, hoping to see her before their plane took off.

"As soon as we came upstairs to her room," Vijali told us, "Ma started to laugh a great belly laugh. She was shaking all over, her mouth wide open with this loud, raucous laugh roaring out of her. Her mirth was contagious and we began laughing too, our sides splitting. Tears were streaming from Ma's eyes, her arms flying out from her sides, and I was rolling on the floor with pain in my stomach.

"I had been so serious and tense throughout the trip, but this laugh! Her whole being was flowing out with no restraints and it loosened me up and washed me. People heard our laughter and came running into the room, only to be caught in it themselves. We knew we had to leave or we would miss our plane but we could scarcely stand for the laughter. We backed down the stairs, looking at her, waving and still laughing."

When Vijali returned from India, she didn't know what to do. "I felt," she said, "like I had gone astray from the straight path, and awakened alone in a dark wood. I couldn't follow a spiritual path anymore, at least not in the sense that I had once understood it, because I couldn't bear to make things special—gods and goddesses, swamis and gurus and ashrams, mantrams and practices and rituals. Everything is special, I thought. Mud is special." In her journal she wrote, "I went to India with expectations of being transformed but I have come back the same shy, unillumined person as before."

Vijali spent the next five years of her life in that dark wood. She stopped meditating and began psychotherapy to explore the feelings she had been forbidden and then had forbidden herself. She and Dale divorced in the process, and Vijali moved into a large warehouse by the ocean which she renovated and turned into a home and a studio. There she developed a whole new way of working with synthetic resins that allowed her to make large sculptures. She was rewarded with increased commissions, and soon she was hosting art shows and poetry readings and making new friends. Finally, she told us, she was living a normal life.

"Then one quiet evening," she said, "while I was visiting with friends and listening to music, a slow heat began rising from my heart. It burned its way up through my spine and on out the top of my head, melting everything into a great ocean of light."

This was followed by spontaneous hand gestures and body movements that the Indians call mudras and kriyas. Unable to breathe, sweat pouring from her, Vijali was sure she must be dying. Her friends stood by horrified and helpless. "They actually made it worse," she told us, "because they thought I must be crazy." After nine interminable hours, the energy subsided and the shaken artist returned to her studio, expecting to find comfort in the familiar surroundings. But everything had changed.

"I saw only light patterns," she said, "and there were no boundaries or borders. It was as if my mind had once long ago made up a story about separate objects with boundaries, but the story wasn't true. The true story is that there is a luminous, spacious energy that flows through everything all the time. It's within matter, within things as well as within space, and you can tune in to it at any time, just like changing the frequency on the radio. There is no distance between this essence and ourselves. It is not other-worldly. It is right here, closer than our own flesh."

Change permeated her life over the next year. Her formerly productive work in the studio came to an immediate halt because she could no longer bear to work with the polyester resins and other synthetic materials that had been her media. At the same time, she became aware of a powerful healing energy that radiated through the palms of her hands. Soon friends and friends of friends and then patients referred by doctors were climbing the stairs of the artist-become-healer.

But the healer was unhealed. "I was panicking every day, several times a day," she told us frankly, "wrestling with my own energy and feeling completely bewildered. It had been twelve years since I left the convent. All that instruction, all those different meditation techniques seemed useless in the wake of this blasting energy and consuming light."

After a year she was no longer willing to work as a healer. "It was becoming a profession, and that didn't feel right," she said. "Even though I didn't understand what was happening, I had begun to suspect that the chemical changes going through me were the kundalini transformation that the Indian yogis describe."

Kundalini means "that which is coiled up." It is an energy said to be lying dormant at the base of the spine.[5] Through yoga or other spiritual practices, Vijali had learned, this energy is aroused gradually and slowly awakens each energy center, or chakra, in the body until it ascends through the crown of the head. At that point, the spiritual practitioner is said to perceive the nature of reality that has been hidden beneath the veils of human delusion.

But for Vijali the process wasn't gradual at all. Moreover, she had been doing nothing to arouse it, so far as she could tell. "This is nothing like what I imagined from the Vedanta teachings," she wrote in her journal, "but the chemical change coming through me does seem to be some kind of evolution of consciousness. I want to stay with it. I don't want to get identified with the one phase of this process that lets me do healing."

In a poignant note she added, "The old beliefs and practices seem useless now. I'm desperately struggling to appear functioning and normal. If I start jumping up and doing the crazy movements my body wants to do, I fear people will put me in a hospital."

Intuitively she felt a need to close down her studio and give away her sculptures and paintings to anyone who wanted them. Since her work was well-known, the studio was soon filled with delighted art lovers, clutching their unexpected bounty. The artworks, the books, the big tools for mixing resin, the brushes and oils and canvases—all were given away. "It took about four months," she told us, "to methodically and very carefully close my life. When everything had been disposed of, I tore out the back- and passenger seats of my VW bug and packed in my typewriter, sleeping bag, some clothes and cooking utensils and a few small sculpting tools. Then, with utter relief, I drove south towards the Santa Monica Mountains."

As she told us this part of her story, we were sitting on faded lawn chairs, gazing out at the magnificent, shining Pacific many miles below our mountaintop veranda. The time of her leaving ten years earlier seemed very long ago. "That leave-taking sounds very appealing in some ways," Pat interjected in a back-to-business tone of voice, "but what did you do for money and where did you sleep?"

"There were several thousand dollars in savings from my artwork over the years," Vijali replied, "and I spent very, very little. In addition, many friends opened their homes to me, and I was able to be a houseguest at night while I spent the days outdoors. This seemed to be the perfect solution because all I was sure about was that I had to put my feet on the earth, and I had to find a medium that could express my experience."

Vijali began to spend her days in the sandstone canyons of

Southern California, "stalking great boulders that would let me climb them and put my belly on their rough warm flat places," she told us. "Some days I would hike to the high mountain ridges, pushing my way through the wildflowers and chaparral to get to the very top. When I was out there the energy would come and it would be wonderful. I wouldn't panic. Sometimes I sculpted and sometimes I didn't, but all day long I would be in another state of consciousness. At sunset, I would return to whomever's home I was staying in at the time. I'd say, 'Oh, yes, a good day's work sculpting in the hills,' because I felt I couldn't talk about what was actually going on. This story gave me a framework which allowed me to appear normal."

A framework, however, was not enough. Even in the short time she was with people, the strain of "trying to be normal" was terrible. "I'd sit at the dinner table and the energy would be coming. I'd need to stand, to let my body dance and go into kriyas and mudras. I'd have to hold myself tight just to sit still, and the pain would rack through my body."

She tried to work with the roller coaster energy, but it seemed impossible. "I realized that two things were going on," she said. "One was the original energy in my body and the other was the panic. I knew that fear did not initiate the experience, that it distorted the neutral energy, but I didn't know how to surrender into the energy and release the fear."[6]

For the next two years she tried everything she could think of. She visited meditation teachers and talked with the author of a well-known book on kundalini experiences—all to no avail. At the insistence of her friends she consulted several psychiatrists. One told her she was having anxiety attacks, and another gave her a major tranquilizer that calmed her but disconnected her from her inner life. "I have become one-dimensional and single-leveled," she told the doctor. "I prefer my panics to this."

Eventually she was introduced to a teacher who "lived the energy," a Peruvian medicine man named Don Hildé. Withdrawing a substantial sum from her dwindling savings, she flew to Peru and lived with Don Hildé and his family for several months. "When the energy moved in me there," she told us, "I was totally comfortable. All the panic and pain disappeared, and even when people streamed through the house to be healed by Don Hildé, I was at ease."

But how long can you hide out in the Amazon jungle? After three months Vijali returned to Southern California, hoping that now she would be able to function in her own environment. Within a week, the rush of the freeways and the frenzy of life in Los Angeles sent her scurrying to the safety of a friend's home. Her friend offered her the carriage house adjoining his beach home and gratefully she settled in.

One morning at the end of several weeks of trying to function in Los Angeles, she told us that she had a talk with herself. "Okay," she said. "I've been married and I've been single. Getting the right man isn't it. I've studied with the most evolved spiritual teachers I could find. That isn't it. I've traveled all around the world from ashrams in India to the jungles of Peru. That isn't it either. I've done it all. There's nothing left to do."

But there was one thing Vijali hadn't tried. It was something very simple. She went to the room in which she had been staying and opened her closet door. It was piled full with art supplies and clothing. Methodically, just as she had once closed her life and packed up her little car, she now unpacked the big closet until it was completely empty.

As she was putting her belongings into the garage, she found a gallon of white paint and some brushes. She spent the rest of the day painting the dirty green closet white. By late afternoon the sun filtering through a single window near the ceiling filled the tiny room with light. Her work finished, she showered and changed to fresh clothes, and went back inside the closet. "I put a mat on the floor," she told us, "and I put a stone, a leaf, a bowl of water, and a candle on the mat, and I closed the door. I sat down and said, This is it. There's nowhere else to go."

Before long, a tingling sensation started in her feet and head, and a burning energy began to erupt at the base of her spine, intensifying as it rose up through her navel and exploding into a climax when it reached her heart. "Waves of love flood me radiating outward until my whole being wants to burst with a longing to melt into all souls," she wrote in her journal. "But this passes and my tongue pulls back in my throat. I feel as if I am losing consciousness and gasp for breath. But this time something different happens. I take a deep breath and somehow connect to the convictions of my childhood. I feel a strength in my own center. I know at this moment there is no other help. All is here within me.

"To my amazement, with the movement of my outgoing breath, the ego evaporates and the panic leaves. The rising energy leaps free through the crown of my head, dissolving all boundaries, leaving nothing but light and energy moving freely without restraint."

Her greatest surprise, she told us, was that she knew how to help herself. "All the time I thought that I didn't know what was right for me. But I did know, though it didn't come all at once. I had to work with it. Every day I went into that white closet with the tiny window and sat there teaching myself breathing techniques to move and balance the energy. I learned how to tell when there was too much energy in my head and how to move it down into my belly and womb and into the earth. I cured my chronic bursitis. I sent extra energy out to the world. It was so simple. And from that time on I never again panicked. Never."

Determined to live her life without compromise and feeling the need for solitude, Vijali found what she was looking for—an isolated trailer on Boney Mountain. "When I first came here," she told us, "I couldn't get enough aloneness. I just drank up the silence. It was absolutely necessary at that point to be alone to really integrate the experiences of my life."

By this time the sun had set, and we were resting on cushions inside the trailer, having just finished a dinner of wild greens in a salad, and potatoes, and tea brewed from the fragrant sweet sage we had picked that afternoon. Flickering candles in glasses threw our shadows against the walls. We began to talk about spiritual practices.

"I no longer practice the mantram I was given at thirteen," Vijali said. "It's ingrained in my cells now. Sometimes it dies away but when I need it, there it is, pounding like my heartbeat. And it's the same for other practices too. The Vipassana meditation of following the breath and noticing thoughts and emotions I once did for several years now comes to me spontaneously when I'm off center and I just fall into it.

"You know, all these practices come from someone having time to be alone and experiencing something and then repeating it and playing with what happens. Up here," she continued, sweeping her arms to bring in the dark expanse beyond the trailer, "I like to be playful like that. After sunset, for instance, I get into a gentle flow where everything in my body is connected and the energy is just moving through. My body does a kind of t'ai chi then, but it's not anything I was taught. And I talk to the trees and boulders and little stones and play with them too. You know I've spent years being very rigid about practices. That can be a trap."

"What makes you say that?" we asked.

"Because being rigid cuts you off," she said. "It smothers the subtle messages coming to you from inside yourself. Your goal orientation takes over, and you say to yourself, I'm going to do this practice and it's going to give me this and that. . . ." She shrugged impatiently.

We told her about Toni Packer, the meditation teacher who had renounced traditional Zen practices. "She feels there is no place for formal discipline at all," Pat said. "Even for beginners."

"I wouldn't say that," Vijali replied. "There is a period in the beginning when you are learning a technique or making a connection that is just like learning to play the piano. If you practice once a month, you probably won't learn the technique no matter how inspired you are. The kind of regular practice that makes a groove in your nervous system seems to be necessary at first. Later on there will be a time when the practices are so much a part of you that they come spontaneously, like the joy of life, and you have this loving flow of help that's always available to you, ready to come out when needed."

Sherry broke in. "That sounds good now, but where were the practices when you needed them? When the kundalini energy burned through you every day, not a single thing you had learned in your twenty-some years of doing spiritual practices helped at all. In fact," she pushed on, "do you think those practices may actually have harmed you? After all, when you finally sat down in your little closet and found the peace that had eluded you, it was through the inner connection you had felt since childhood. Maybe doing formal practices and relying on external authorities separated you from that original knowing."

Vijali nodded. These were interesting questions, she allowed. "But quite honestly I feel now that spiritual practices prepared the ground for me to maintain cosmic consciousness and integrate it into my life. It's true that I had to learn to work with the kundalini energy on my own. But how did I know how to do that? To work with my breath, to still my thoughts?

"I needed practices," she continued, responding to our doubts. "It took years for my body to change so it could maintain the transformation. New habits have to be established, or, when the initial force of the experience wears off, the old life patterns take over again. The physical phenomena themselves don't necessarily bring wisdom. They are experiences, flashes. You have to have a way to integrate them.

"So what is it that keeps the doors of consciousness open?" Vijali asked, raising the question to see if she had a conclusion. "I'm sure having a practice helps. And so does an environment like this one that reflects your inner self. And having understanding friends with whom you can be fully yourself. But ultimately, I think you need to have the courage to follow what unfolds from within and leads you. The feminine path. The spontaneous way."

"Sometimes I sit here in the dark for hours and hours," she told us as we were preparing for sleep that first night. "I'll lie back on the cushions and look out the window at the moon coming across the sky and hear the crickets or the owl calling. Something gentle comes around me then, and I feel in total harmony. I feel loved.

Sometimes there is a kind of current from my heart that goes out to the universe, and then it pauses and comes back into me, and goes out again.

"There are streams, matrices, lattices of light that must be some universal pattern. Sometimes you see it and sometimes you don't. But when you relax, it's there like a great web connecting with everything. It feels like it has always been there."

However, even as we were contentedly settling into our sleeping bags looking forward to more visits to this solitudinal sanctuary, Vijali was preparing herself to follow a dream she had had ten years earlier. In the dream she saw herself carving stone and creating rituals in a giant circle that encompassed the earth. A "World Wheel" she called it.[7] Over the next five years, as we were completing our research and writing, Vijali was bringing her World Wheel into form. From the cliffs high above Malibu to the Seneca Indian Reservation in New York State, and on to Spain, Italy, Greece, and Egypt, she has been creating a series of earth sculptures and ritual performance events in a great circle along the 30th latitude. At this writing, she plans to continue the wheel in Israel, the USSR, India, Tibet, China, and Japan. Engaging performers and artists in each place to present the story of their land and their people, she asks three questions: How did you come to be here? What are the problems you face? What will heal you?

"From their responses we create the environmental sculpture and theatre in each country that expresses that place and people," she wrote to us from Italy. "As I do this, I feel I am returning to the origin of art when the shaman painted the walls of caves for the nourishment and direction of the community; when theatre was a spontaneous expression of the hopes and fears of the people; when art was not just a commodity but integral to life because it united the earth, plants, animals, and humans into one interdependent family."

Reading her letter describing her constant travel and interaction with many different people we wondered if she sometimes longed for her aerie on Boney Mountain. "This project is not something I have decided on arbitrarily," she wrote us. "It is a natural evolution and flowering of my solitude on the mountain. I no longer want to sit alone and experience oneness. I want to walk in the world with this oneness. In each country, the people I meet become my family and the land I work on becomes my home. A world family is developing!"

She concluded with a note that could have been written by most of the women we interviewed: "I feel that most people have visions, dreams, and insight as the fruits of their spiritual practices—just as I did fifteen years ago when I dreamt of a giant circle around the world. But we need to *give ourselves permission* to act out those dreams and visions, not look for more sensations, more phenomena, but live out our strongest dreams—even if it takes a lifetime. Too often we wait for the guru, the teacher, the husband or father-figure to approve before we take that step. Or we never take it at all. We have to begin now to give ourselves this permission."

Chapter 8
INTIMATE RELATIONSHIPS

In the beginning everything was in relationship,
and in the end everything will be in relationship
again. In the meantime, we live by hope.

— Jean Lanier
"The Second Coming"

 We live by hope, and our hope for relationship is no
small thing. Relationship is an incontrovertible fact
of life that scientists have been demonstrating repeatedly over the last half century. From the most
advanced scholarship in fields from biophysics to botany, archae-
ology to cell science, sociology to neurophysiology, we are learning
that we belong to one another and are sustained by each other.

Activist and systems theorist Joanna Macy describes this inter-
relatedness by saying that we are dynamic, open, ever-changing
systems which "influence each other so deeply it is hard to decide
where one leaves off and the other begins." Indeed, she says,
whether "we" means cells in a brain or trees in a forest or human
communities and societies, "all boundaries are essentially arbitrary
in this dynamic, flowing web [of life]."[1]

In our personal lives, when we love another or raise a child or
tend a garden or build a business, we experience the enhancement

that comes from this interconnectedness. And when we feel the pain of a beloved friend, or of someone across the planet whose misery flashes across our television screen, we again feel our relatedness.

And yet in our culture, which places such a premium on individuality, we often feel so isolated, so unbonded. "We are in the worst state we could possibly be in to raise human beings—the bottom of the pit," one woman told us. "Families are breaking up, like the clans and tribes of the past have broken up. The mystical teachings of the past are in fragments, lost or forgotten. We wander in states of separation and isolation that are absolutely inhuman."

Women especially feel caught between our fundamental interconnectedness and a sense of isolation. The old ways of being in relationship are layered with rules and stereotypes that hold us rigid and unresponsive to the deeper truths of our lives. Many of us can't or won't return to these old forms, but we are uncertain how to love in a new way.

To quote the ecologist and theologian Thomas Berry,[2] it is as if we are between stories. The old story about who we are and how to live doesn't work anymore, and we don't know what the new story is. Yet we desperately want to find this new story. We want to know how to live in a context of relationship and not betray ourselves. The challenge is to be intimate with another and still remain true to ourselves. When we deny our innermost knowing, silencing our voice in the hope of pleasing others, we avoid this challenge. But we also avoid it when we listen only to ourselves.

To go beyond these self-limiting alternatives, we need to become fully conscious of ourselves and those we love—co-creators in the dynamic, ever-changing systems that Joanna Macy describes. And it is this mutuality that the women we interviewed are exploring in their intimate personal relationships. What they are discovering may very well be the foreword to the "new story" of creating and sustaining intimacy in our lives today.

A GOOD MARRIAGE

"A good marriage shuts out a very great deal," the elderly heroine, Laura, states at the beginning of May Sarton's *A Reckoning*. Toward the end of the novel, she contemplates the question a friend raises, which seems to reinforce her conviction: "Do you suppose growing up always means diluting [our] fierce purpose for the sake of others? [Do you remember] how little we wanted to marry because marriage, we felt, implied surrendering—losing our power to command our own lives?"[3]

The Elders

As we listened to women in their seventies and eighties, we were struck by the extent to which they agreed that a good marriage does, indeed, shut out a great deal. Regardless of whether the women we spoke with were single, married, or had divorced at an early age, they all assumed without question that a woman's work was to fulfill her family responsibilities, and that not until these responsibilities were met should she consider other kinds of work in the world.

Esse Chasin, the teacher of Kabbalah we interviewed on Long Island, spoke about raising her children in the 1950s: "A woman's role was to maintain the home as a model for high values and keep peace and harmony within the family," she told us, "and that is the role I took. My husband was rather dominating in certain things, so everything wasn't always rosy. But I could give up some needs I had in order to cater to him, to let him feel something was his idea when it was actually mine. In fact, I began to find it a great challenge to be the power behind the scenes."

She added later on, "The only thing important enough to argue about was the children. I never argued for myself. If I wanted to do something for my personal growth, I just did it. I didn't engage in what is now called communication, where I'd try to persuade him to see my point of view. I just did what I wanted without discussing it with him. I had confidence in myself."

As we listened to Esse and the other older women, we were impressed by how very difficult it was for them to come forth from a kind of hiddenness within the family. It was as if their relationships acted as gatekeepers to their emergence in the world. Esse, for example, did not start to teach Kabbalah until she was in her sixties. And Twylah Nitsch, a Seneca elder, did not begin to spread the sacred teachings of her people until she entered her seventies.

"After my husband died," Twylah told us, "I knew I had to get down to business and initiate people into the Wolf Clan and spread the teachings of my ancestors. This occupies my whole life now, and I'm having a wonderful time doing it." We asked whether she would like to marry again. "I've already had the best marriage I could ever want," she replied briskly. "I have no desire for anything more."

One spiritual counselor referred to her husband of nearly forty years as "my benevolent jailer." "In most of the time we've been together," she told us, "I've worked at home to ease his constant concern about me. Only recently have I begun to realize how subtly and expertly I've designed my life to stay within the security of his love. This fine tailoring insulated me from a vulnerability to other relationships, and therefore to life, in ways I had not even suspected."

An exception in this age group, a woman whose voice was heard before her children were grown, is now the senior minister of a popular church in Texas. Twice widowed by the time she was in her thirties, she told us, "I was brought up to believe the husband is first, so I never would have put myself forward in those early years. But when my second husband died and I had five children to support, I just had to lose my shyness and go out and knock on doors to find a job."

It was not always a husband who was deferred to, as Maria Rifo, the eighty-year-old community organizer from Chile, explained. "In my country, women were supposed to submit to men and stay at home all the time. If you wanted to move out of your parents' home before you were married, people thought you were going to have a baby. You couldn't just take your own apartment without people thinking bad things." Maria did not marry but stayed with her parents and cared for them until their deaths. At that time, she was fifty-seven years old.

Even though these women have since become sources of inspiration and empowerment in their own communities, most of them are convinced that the work they do would now be difficult, and perhaps impossible, if they had family responsibilities or were in an intimate relationship with a man.

Maria Rifo, for example, said with candor, "I'm not attached to anyone and I'm developing in my own way. I have the freedom to do this because I have no parents and no children. If I had them I might be afraid to change."

Dorothy Maclean, a founder of the Findhorn Community in Scotland who has been divorced since her early thirties told us, "The feeling of being in love is lovely, and it would have been nice to have another close relationship with a man in the years after my marriage. But it hasn't worked out that way." And then she said something we were to hear over and over not only from the older women but from the younger women as well: "I certainly couldn't have done the work I had to do if I'd been a mother and had to look after a family. I've committed myself, unconsciously perhaps, to doing the spiritual life instead."

Dorothy's sense of needing to choose between a spiritual life and an intimate relationship became even more apparent when our discussion turned to marriage vows. Pat opened this part of the interview by confiding, "Right from the beginning I regarded marriage as a sacrament. So when my husband and I ended up getting a divorce, I felt that I had somehow broken my promise to God. With my marriage I had taken a vow, and with my divorce I was breaking it."

Dorothy replied vehemently, "Yeah, but the God within me is far greater than any vows spoken in a man-made ceremony. I only married for the inner reasons, and I stopped for the same ones. So I never even *thought* of feeling guilty about getting a divorce. If you're doing what you're meant to be doing, that comes first over everything." She leaned back in her chair and was quiet for a few moments. Then turning to face us, she said with finality, "I believe that I came into this life with a job to do and I couldn't have done it if I'd been concentrating on a personal relationship."

This is not to say that all of the older women we spoke with separated family life from their spiritual path. Esse Chasin put it this way: "I think that wifehood and motherhood lived consciously can be a very powerful spiritual practice in which we have an opportunity to grow every moment of the day. If a woman moves through her daily life as a wife and mother consciously letting go of her own needs, releasing anger and suffering and resentment, she's building a spirituality in herself that would probably outdistance any sacrifice the men make. But I'm only realizing this today. When I was a housewife and mother I was too bogged down to get it. I think the path of a homemaker is one that needs to be explored and offers enormous opportunities for coming to consciousness. But I never found it for myself."

Our Permeable Boundaries

Women have permeable boundaries. Perhaps it is the experience of our bodies in touch with the bodies of others that makes it hard for us to close down our psyches. Perhaps it is genetic. Or both. Or something else. But our bodies feel the irrevocable connection of the tides with our cycles of monthly bleeding. And in lovemaking we can be penetrated and receive another. And with pregnancy we carry another for nine full moons, more or less. When we separate from that other, we can feed it from our own body. And later the cycles that tie us to the moon and tides stop. And all this is true whether we give birth or not, have sex or not. The possibility is what creates the openness, and this openness is a precious gift.

The distinct flavor of experience which comes with this gift shapes how we perceive reality, how we act, how we create, and what we value. And more than anything else women value relationships. We blend and weave and combine and sustain all kinds of relationships, and this work, this webmaking, not only shapes our lives but makes us profoundly vulnerable to the needs of others.

The older women we interviewed had few doubts about their responsibility: it was to meet those needs, especially if they chose to marry and have children. The middle-aged and younger women were considerably less certain. Almost all of them envisioned the same dreams of enduring love and intimacy that had shaped their elders' relationships. But unlike the elders, the middle-aged and younger women were firmly committed to cultivating and expressing the truth of their innermost experience.

"When I first married, I thought I would never be alone again, physically or emotionally," a businesswoman in her forties told us. "But now I know that the most god-awful loneliness comes when you give up your own inner connection to be continually available to someone else. I'm not at all confident that I can do both, though I still have hopes."

"My marriage is a twenty-four hour a day job," Noelle Poncelet, a psychotherapist and guide in the shamanic tradition, told us. "I work all the time to be true to myself and to be honest with my husband. Not to give in early for the sake of compromise, but to wait, to listen, to find with him the creative solution that comes from putting our two energies together and tolerating the tension of conflict. It isn't easy to sustain our differences rather than watering them down, to let the momentum build until a new solution emerges. But it is exciting, and after thirty years of marriage it's this kind of full-time engagement that lets the spirit of the relationship itself be a teacher for us."

"Have you ever felt you betrayed your vows to God or yourself?" we asked an energetic community activist whose shining eyes and heartfelt enthusiasm inspire people across North America.

"You want to know about betrayal?" she echoed. And suddenly she burst into tears. There was a long pause. When she began to speak again, she chose her words slowly. "By following the only model I knew—the model of marriage—I was perhaps betraying myself. I suppose I could speak of the gratitude I feel for this relationship which has held me so securely for thirty years, but right now my heart hurts. A lot of my life with my husband these days feels like a distraction from what I really care about and want to do. I get so impatient. But truthfully, when I look at this, I think I project onto him some of the limits that I'm actually imposing on myself."

A year later, she gave us an update by telephone. "Things have changed for us . . . again," she said, and now her voice was amused. "I finally went away on a long retreat that I had desperately needed but had been denying myself. It felt so great to be silent and with myself that when I returned, it looked like we were going to break up for sure. But facing that possibility directly, we realized just how much we love each other. We've decided to change a lot about the way we've been living, and we've started a big joint project that is important to each of us and takes our combined energies."

The solution to our permeable boundaries is not to seal them off or barricade our hearts and adopt a "me first" attitude. When we do that, we suffer unbearable isolation. But neither is it to betray the deep sources of wisdom and meaning in our lives. Instead we need to find the unique, and probably unstable, balance that fits us at a particular time, a balance that includes, but is not limited to, the needs of our partners and family.

In Search of a Balance

"What a bottomless pit of darkness I found when I began to explore my own marriage," Susan, a midwesterner, told us. "It started quite unintentionally. I had gone on a two-week spiritual retreat when something inside me opened in a new way. For the first time in my adult life, I felt eager to be alone. I returned home hungry for solitude. During the week I went on long walks in the woods, took time for dream work, and occasionally took other retreats away from home. I seemed to need the quiet to let this inner opening continue.

"Eventually my old accelerated pace slowed way down. Whether

I was alone or with the children, there would be a gentleness flowing through my days, blending with the rhythms of my body and consciousness. It was this gentle steadiness that after a while gave me the courage to look into my relationship with my husband. I'd avoided this for a long time, but finally, like Bluebeard's wife, I couldn't resist.

"What I discovered was that the marriage I'd poured myself into body and soul for the last eight years contained its own dark secret. Without noticing, I'd become so dependent on my husband for my identity that I was willing to do anything at all to avoid his anger or irritation. With laughter and compromise that undermined my self, I'd carefully learned to deflect every possible unpleasantness between us."

Two years after this conversation, Susan told us that she had separated from her husband and was living with her children in her sister's home. "I don't know how to integrate my inner life with my marriage," she said. "I don't know how to find the balance between the separateness I need to nurture my spirit, and being close to my husband. He says he can't bear to continue living separately, that it has to be all or nothing." She hesitated, and then said quietly, "It looks like it will have to be nothing."

All or nothing. The dilemma in Susan's story is an expression of our traditional beliefs about the need to separate the life of the spirit from our everyday relationships. How to actually find a balance between the two was the single most frequent question we were asked in our interviews. "Are you meeting women who are able to be true to their spiritual paths and be in a love relationship with a man?" the women would ask. And before we could answer, they would demand, "How? How are they doing it?"

We began to notice that no one was inquiring whether women could be true to themselves and raise children, or have deep friendships, or even be in a loving relationship with another woman. The questions were explicitly about long-term relationships between men and women. And the real issues that lay beneath these questions seemed to be: In our male-dominated culture, what happens when women no longer need or want to defer to men? What happens when we no longer automatically modulate our personalities or reorder our priorities to accommodate our husband or lover? Does the glue that holds male-female relationships together break down?

The immediate answer, in terms of our research, is yes. Although all but three of the women we interviewed had been married at least once, over seventy percent of the marriages ended in divorce, and less than a third of the women were married or living in committed relationships at the time we spoke with them. Of the latter, several were maintaining separate residences or traveling so extensively that they actually spend less than half the year with their partners.[4]

A more thoughtful and perhaps more accurate answer is that women's expectations about relationships have undergone dramatic changes in the past few decades, and the stories we heard reflect these changes. The middle-aged and younger women we spoke with refused to believe they could not have it all—spiritual path and loving marriage—and almost every one of them had married at least once, expecting to find the balance their elders could not. But very few succeeded.

When we set out to interview women who were sources of inspiration to others, we did not inquire in advance about their intimate relationships. We assumed that we'd find a mix—some single, some married, some living in unmarried but committed relationships. But as we've already indicated, that was not the case. Although almost all of the women had married, not many of those marriages endured.

One woman over fifty told us, "My four children are already grown, and I see no need to repeat something that clearly did not work the first time." She had wanted a marriage that was a way of holiness, she said, like her parents had. "They put God first and foremost in their lives, and that was the essence of their relationship. I thought I knew how this should work—marriage disposing grace. But it didn't work in my case and I have no interest in trying again." Almost every woman we spoke with over fifty was certain she would not marry again. However, almost every one under fifty was ambivalent.

Jan Kemp, a single mother with two young children, is one of the women under fifty who was ambivalent. "I can't believe how happy and independent I am now," she told us. "Since my divorce I make decisions on my own and carry them through just fine. I never expected this overwhelming river of joy flowing through me all the time, especially not a woman living without a man. Who would ever have expected that?

"But I do think about remarrying," she continued, "because I want my children to have a strong male role model. And there is another reason, too. I would love to have what my mother has had for over forty years. She and my father are just like sweethearts, the closest two people I've ever seen, both free to think and feel and work through differences when there is a conflict. That's what I grew up with and that's what I still expect. That's what I thought marriage was supposed to be."

What is a marriage supposed to be? What can it be? Many of the women under fifty are asking themselves these questions. And even those over fifty who do not want to remarry are looking for possibilities of love and mutuality that go beyond the old forms and roles they are no longer willing to accept.

Intricately connected to these considerations is the question of women's sexuality. What does sexuality mean to us as women? Does it relate to our spirituality? And if so, how?

OUR SEXUALITY, OUR SPIRITUALITY

> What do you know about your own sexuality, from the inside?
>
> — Marjory Zoet Bankson
> *Braided Streams*

As we have listened to the ways in which sexuality enters the lives of the women we interviewed, we have been struck by how very difficult it is for a woman to feel her sexuality from the inside. And the reasons for this difficulty, it seems, directly parallel our long silence about what is sacred to us.

Like spirituality, sexuality is an experience of "the most intractable subjectivity."[5] And like spirituality, sexuality has been defined and named by men. "Only male sexual characteristics have been named as real within the patriarchal framework," linguist Dale Spender observes. This naming by men has so affected our collective reality, she argues, that not only men but also women perceive women's sexuality according to men's experience. "The language and thought of our culture . . . afford so little support or substantiation for any possible female meanings that [those meanings] are likely to become unreal and to be abandoned."[6]

"It never occurred to me in adolescence when I was splitting the image of my sexuality from my spiritual body-awareness," Marjory Bankson recalls, "that the aliveness I felt inside would be my own sexuality . . . the words [I knew] did not describe my feelings."[7]

"Now that I am older I think that God is as present in the ecstasy of sexual union as in that of unitive prayer, but when I was younger I could not find that truth so easily," another woman confided.[8]

Just as women's spirituality has been idealized, reviled, dismissed, and otherwise shaped according to men's understanding, so, too, has our experience of sexuality. Now, however, as women poets, visual artists and writers are bringing soundings from these depth levels, we are beginning to hear stories and see images that reflect our own experiences, and to note intriguing resonances between the sacred and the sexual.

"For full enjoyment of sex, for true completeness," the author Maya Angelou told us, "one does the same thing one does with God. One says, 'I am Thine' to that force of energy that has created us. It's only when you can give over the concern about everything else—whether the bills are paid or the phone is ringing—and join that moment, join that other body, that you can have total completeness in sex. So it is the same as the development of true spirituality. You must admit to yourself that you are a part of everything, and then there is total enjoyment. In eating, in sex, in laughter, in crying—complete enjoyment, a complete joining and joy with the other. And why shouldn't we enjoy it? It's all God's gift."

Not all of the women we interviewed feel this way. For some, sex seemed to be a nonissue: normal, but not significant. "None of my mystical experiences had anything to do with sex," one long-time contemplative told us flatly. Another conceded, "Certainly there were times when sexuality had it all for me. Orgasm was divine revelation. Orgasm was nirvana. But now I don't care if I have physical sex or not. What I long for is the union-communion of one heart with another."

A few women told us that they had felt a conflict between their sexual urges and spirituality when they were young, in their teens and twenties and thirties. "Finding the strength not to have sex with a married man, learning not to be such a slave to my body—these have been important steps for me in my spiritual growth," a youthful southerner who had been raised in a strict Christian family told us.

However, enough women raised questions about sexuality and linked it firmly with their spiritual development that we suspect that much of what we have heard about sexual experience is muted by a lack of language. If "sexual" means only intercourse between a woman and a man, and what accompanies that act, if it is under-stood in terms of something done, the exercise of power, the achievement of a goal or climax, then sexuality plays a small role in the lives of most of the women we interviewed.

But if sexuality is defined in terms of women's sensing, knowing, and feeling, if it means, as one woman asserted, "a miracle that is sweet and good and the song of life singing through me," then eros becomes, as the poet Susan Griffin says, "a wild card . . . constantly cracking open the heart." It pulls us beyond our individual selves in a way that undoes the old, sure identities and distinctions and "pulls us off in directions where we lose conscious control."[9]

Rosalyn Bruyere, founder of a large school for healers, told us that as a young healer she was afraid of her sexuality. "When I'm healing," she told us, "I feel this current running through my body that brings life to another. It is very much a sensual experience, and at times people would accuse me of being seductive. But this life-sustaining force that pulses through us to each other isn't seductive. It doesn't want to trap us. We misunderstand it and fear it and starve our bodies of touching and tenderness and sensation in devotion to a deity. However, this is the antithesis of true devotion to deity. We're paying off a false god."

There seems to be little or no language to describe this vital flow that we feel in our bodies, or to distinguish our various experiences of it in making love, in embodied prayer, in healing, in nursing our children, in communicating with a beloved friend or a passing stranger. Do we even want such distinctions, if they could be made? We need them, the mythologist Estella Lauter argues. We need to separate out the way our love feels from the inside, to know when to open and when to close. Such boundaries, she says, are life-supporting for women.[10]

The more we listened, the more we heard how sexuality can extend to and encompass the widest experience of human relatedness. Each of these experiences was uniquely expressive of the individual who described it to us and what she has learned about relationships. Gay Luce, the founder and director of the Nine Gates Mystery School, traced the ways in which her experience of her body and sexuality have changed again and again during her life.

"My mother was a Victorian," she told us. "She considered the body a little repulsive, and there was something vaguely shameful about sexuality. In my early days, I thought my body was a cage to escape from as quickly as possible, and I felt like an imprisoned soul who longed to fly—literally.

"By the time I married at eighteen, however, I seized on sex as a very valuable bridge to intimacy. I didn't know how to come close to another person and neither did my husband. So we used our bodies to find the kind of communion and satisfaction that brought us into deeper contact with each other.

"I divorced in my thirties. I was living in New York City then and I loved exercise and motion and would run for miles with my dog through Riverside Park. My body was a tool for motion and sex; otherwise I didn't notice it unless I was sick. The rest of the time I was a mind sitting at a desk or in front of a TV or talking with people.

"Then in my forties I began working with Tibetan spiritual techniques. As I opened to spiritual energies through a number of different kinds of practices and body therapies, I realized that the body is like an antenna for God. I could tune my body as a huge cosmology of energies, with lattices of light stretching into other lattices of light. Gradually I learned that there isn't anything about our bodies that is not this antenna, this tuning fork for the divine.

"Now my most intimate relationships are not physical but energetic. Sex is no longer what it used to be. Maybe *sex* is not the right word. I feel that what my husband and I were looking for in our twenties, perhaps what most of us are looking for, doesn't have as much to do with physical closeness as it does with a yearning for intimacy. And I think that is a matter of the energy between people. Now I can experience a deep communion just sitting with one of my friends for an afternoon. Or it can come in an instant, driving along and stopping at an intersection, I meet someone's eyes and there is a communion so indelible that for the rest of the day that person's face remains with me. This kind of experience is what sex is really all about to me, and I certainly don't have to be in a marriage or a committed relationship to experience it."

Meinrad Craighead, an artist who lives a celibate life, also describes sexuality in terms of profound and inclusive relatedness. She considers herself a sexual being, she told us, because she is a woman. "Whether we are weaving tissue in the womb or weaving imagery in the soul, our work is sexual: the work of conception, gestation, and birth." She is quite definite that there is a mutuality between the sacred and the sexual, that they enlighten and inform each other: "Our spirituality should center on the affirmation of our sexuality. . . ." she writes. "The Mother has but one law: 'Create; make as I do . . . transform one substance into another . . . transmute blood into milk, clay into vessel, feeling into movement, wind into song, egg into child, fiber into cloth, stone into crystal, memory into image, body into worship.'" And to those who say her art is "too sensual," she retorts that for a Christian, spiritual cannot mean nonmaterial. "Perhaps my work is sensual *because* it is Christian," she says.[11]

A NEW UNDERSTANDING OF LOVE

> With rare exceptions, the drive for men and women to become fully functioning human beings, distinct from one another, is brand new.
>
> — Janet O. Dallett
> *When the Spirits Come Back*

In a process that seems to be one of the least idealized, most robustly down-to-earth we have encountered, some women are tossing their images of perfect marriage and perfect relationship out the window to stretch way beyond the old comfort zones and find their own version of a new story. Others describe something far less intentional, in which "the love you have held closest to your heart falls to pieces, destroying the old certainties, and carrying you to the gateway of something quite unexpected, quite new."

Marion Woodman has an opinion about what is happening in the creation of these new stories: "Real love happens when embodied soul meets embodied soul. Not in spirit, not in that disembodied world where we want to be perfect, but in life." And she adds with a note of exasperation, "It hasn't got anything to do with that neurotic, romantic nonsense that comes from need and passes for love in this culture. This other kind of love is a power that comes through people who are strong enough to contain it, who can accept themselves and each other as imperfect human beings. That's when your heart opens and you come to a whole new understanding of what love is."

Three Marriages

"When I was single it was easy to feel spiritual because whenever I got tired of people, I could just leave," Ann, an exuberant forty-year-old and founder of a large center for creative development, told us. "I had my own well-defined life in a world I could understand and control. But now that I'm married I can see what a limited surrender it was. I had so many rigidities I didn't know about."

She and her husband had been married for about a year when we spoke with her. "This is the hardest thing I've ever done," she told us. "I love my husband, but most of the time I hate being married. I feel so swamped by his energy that I can't find myself at all these days. I'm always aware in the back of my mind of where he is and what he might need or want. When he's away working, my creativity jumps about one hundred and fifty percent.

"And yet," she conceded, "I know this is stretching me far beyond who and what I was when I lived alone and could go off and meditate whenever I felt off balance. Now I have to find my balance, my center, in the midst of this very demanding relationship. From time to time there's a little glimmer of something that makes me feel we'll get through to a real kindness. I won't go back to the old safety, but I don't know how to go forward either. All I can do, I guess, is stay here, tell the truth, and be open to what comes."

"The more total you are, the deeper your relationship can be to any other human being." Elisabeth looked at us through calm gray eyes. "Once you find that inner core of yourself," she continued, "you're free. And that leaves everyone around you free. You're not trying to make them into anything. You're not telling them what's best for them. You *know* you don't know that. What you're doing is receiving them fully as the human beings they are. This is where love begins; it sees the mystery of the other and is just overwhelmed by it."

Then bestowing a radiant smile upon us, she whispered, "It has taken me over half a century of living and twenty years of marriage to even start to come to this new sense of love. And now, of course, the trick is to actually live it."

For the first dozen years of her marriage, Elisabeth told us she was "happy being the woman behind the great man." Editing her professor husband's writings, preparing footnotes to his academic papers, and feeling fulfilled in her own career, she led a busy, contented life. But the idyllic world she was true to on the outside was being undermined from within.

She developed a recurring illness which, along with a series of powerful dreams, focused her attention inward. On two separate occasions she left her husband and her work to spend extended periods of time alone. These respites brought her into states of deep peace and bliss. However, each time she returned home, "there was this overpowering energy that pulled me to my husband, dissolving our boundaries so that we were practically one merged being. There seemed to be no possibility of changing this intense bonding."

Finally, Elisabeth's illness became so severe that she was no longer able to function. "It was then that my inner core began to establish itself," she said, "and I decided that I might as well do exactly what my dreams and intuition were urging me to do. So I arranged to go abroad to a place I'd been dreaming about. I decided to study and travel until I either recovered or died."

"Tell us what happened," we said.

"It was a very gradual and difficult process," she replied, "but also enormously exciting because I was learning how to be very truthful with myself. And of course while I was doing that, I had to recognize my husband as the human being he is and pull back the godlike qualities I had endowed him with. Although all of this took a long time, I remember one sequence of events very well.

"My husband had flown over for a visit, and we were living together in my rather small flat. Lying in my lemon mist bath one morning I was watching his reflection in the steamed up mirror. As he lathered his face, contorting his nose and lips, snorting and sniffing as he guided his razor around them I wondered: How does it feel to live in a male body, to be MAN, partner of woman?

"I kept watching, and suddenly I saw how hard he was working to keep living on this earth and how hard he, too, was searching for the truth of his own life. Seeing his face vanishing in the mist on the mirror, life seemed so fragile, so awesome. I was overwhelmed with love. It wasn't pity. It was admiration and real human love.

"But this love felt different from the idealizing stuff I had projected onto him when I had seen this great god of a man. There was no god in it now. I simply saw a noble human being who was doing the best he could with what he had been given. And the moment I became aware of that, he must have sensed something because he turned around immediately and said, 'I do love you.'

"Later that day, bundled up against the wind, we drove over to the lake at the edge of town. Around and around that lake we walked, talking, questioning, arguing, not knowing what to do about our life together. We didn't want to push or pull or shape each other anymore, and we didn't want to be blended either. What we did want was to find out how to respect and really love each other in our humanness. Not knowing where to begin but determined to make a fundamental change, we pulled off our wedding rings. 'Somehow,' we resolved, 'we are going to work out a whole new relationship.'

Gradually Elisabeth recovered from her illness. Once again she returned to her husband.

"And how are things for the two of you now?" we asked.

"We're not always easy on each other," she responded. "These days my work often requires me to be away from home and he'd like me with him all the time. But the separateness is my commitment to my own soul's journey. I can remember when it would have been inconceivable for us to be apart for more than a week. Sexuality binds you together more when you're young, I think. Now what we have is a deeper, quieter bonding than we have ever had. At times there is just a blinding love that comes in, but we don't have to be together to trust it."

*   *   *

"My husband and I are real partners," Helen, an impeccably groomed woman in her mid-thirties, told us as we sat in her kitchen drinking tea. "We're very good complements to each other in the way we execute the daily living stuff. He works outside and I work inside our home, and that's just perfect for me." Creating an aesthetically pleasing and smoothly functioning home for her husband and two young daughters is an essential part of Helen's love of beauty and order, she explains. "There is something so important to me about being able to do the shopping and cooking and laundering in terms of having a peaceful home. These things bring such harmony to the everyday living which is the very heart of my spirituality."

About seven years after Helen married, however, she began an inward journey that tore away almost all of the certainties and assumptions that had previously guided her. The companionship, comfort, and laughter she had taken for granted in her marriage seemed to disintegrate before her eyes. At first, she struggled to stave off the growing feelings of separation and aloneness, but after several months she gave up trying. It seemed as if she and her husband were living on different planets, she explained. Sometime during this period, she joined a group of fellow seekers and met a man who was experiencing a similar disruption in his life.

"He and I would talk for hours," Helen recalled, "and love blossomed between us very quickly. Soon we were spinning marvelous visions of how we could work together, do groups together, and open a spiritual center. We could see possibilities for partnership far more inspiring and exciting than the ones we were living.

"But I was reluctant to let go of my marriage until I knew it was the 'rightest' thing I could be doing. So I waited. And what a slow process it was! To allow for the changes that our marriage needed, my husband and I had to face the truth that our initial reason for coming together didn't fit anymore. We had to let the old romantic dreams go and then just hang in there waiting, listening within ourselves and to each other, wondering if our relationship had any life left in it. Eventually, we were able to watch it unfold to another stage. Then a few years later when we had children, we had to find each other all over again in an entirely different way. We're finally getting familiar with this continual change. In fact, now we keep our ears open for it."

She paused at this point, her young face looking austere and much older than her years. "You know," she said, "we all have to learn how to chart the inner and outer cycles in our lives. There are initiatory experiences like birth, marriage, lovers parting, jobs lost, everything cracking open. These are times when the old forms are breaking. Whatever has channeled and structured energy in the past breaks open, because a greater awareness and energy has to come in.

"I think we can mistake these times by not labeling them as initiations. We don't have instruction manuals that warn us, 'Something is cracking open to allow the new to enter. This is not about a rocky marriage. It's about a spiritual birth. Use the power that you're feeling to wake up, to bring the next stage of consciousness in.'

"It takes so much energy to establish a new relationship," she sighed. "Sometimes we can save a lot of energy by maintaining what we already have because we can use all that power to go deeper and move through the threshold. But," she cautioned with a rather sharp look, "it doesn't make sense for anyone else to tell you what you need to do. Each of us is so different. We need to wait for our own inner timings, like neurons wait for their firing times. In my own fumbling kind of way, that is what I've always done. Watched the outer cycles and waited for the inner timing to tell me when I need to change and when I need to stay put."

"Watching the outer cycles and waiting for the inner timing." Perhaps it is just this kind of clear-eyed perspective and heartfelt engagement that is required of us if we are to meet the challenge of living in the context of an intimate relationship without betraying our innermost selves. By committing themselves to doing the best they could to stay in touch with their truth, by trusting their relationships enough to speak that truth to their partners, and by being willing to move with the shearing forces of change instead of trying to stave them off or ignore them, the women in these stories found new ways to create and sustain intimacy in their lives.

However, as a spiritual teacher in her late fifties suggested, we may need to look at the breakdown of old forms of intimate relationships and our efforts to redeem them through a much wider lens than we have been using. "I think there is a missing link in our society," she told us. "We don't have enough continuity with the events of our lives because we don't live in extended families or even in nuclear families for very long. So we search for the right relationship or the right partner or the right kind of sex or the right kind of marriage. But the link that is missing doesn't have anything to do with those things. It has to do with a lack of sustained intimacy that gives us our sense of human rootedness. We don't have this base right now, this grounding, but we need somehow to build it."

Chapter 9
THE MAKING OF RELATIVES

> One of the gifts White Buffalo Woman brought
> to the Lakota people was the rite of *hunkapi*, the
> making of relatives. And today, when we really
> care about someone and want to be close to them
> through our whole lives, we adopt them as
> relatives—as sister or brother or grandmother. I
> think this is what we're doing in our world right
> now—becoming relatives. Becoming family with
> each other in a whole new way.
>
> — Brooke Medicine Eagle

 How do we begin to build a base for our relatedness
that provides intimacy and continuity, not just occasionally but over the long term? The women we
interviewed are living out the answers to this question.
Some are involved in new ways of being in intimate relationships,
as we discussed in the preceding chapter. And others, as we explore
in this chapter, are engaged with neighbors, friends, strangers,
ancestors, and even other species in original and creative partner-
ships and communities.

This spectrum of relationships is not surprising, of course. Our
informants are simply doing what women have always done so well:
weaving enduring and often beautiful webs of relationship based on
caring. But what is surprising and may seem paradoxical is the
women's emphasis on solitude as the *sine qua non* for wholehearted
relationship.

Whether married or single, young, middle-aged, or older, virtually every woman we spoke with told us that coming to terms
with and honoring the need for solitude in her life has been essential
to her unfolding process. And most of them added that it has not

been easy. Giving solitude a high priority is difficult, the women told us, not just because expressing a preference for being alone is often disparaged in our extroverted culture, but because it can also pose a threat to personal relationships, especially for women. When women, the traditional nurturers and maintainers of relationships, spend what friends or partners consider too much time alone, they often become targets of criticism and rejection.

Despite this, the women we spoke with place a very high priority on solitude. They regard it as intimately connected with their life purpose, and their commitment to it is reflected in their life-styles. For some this means rising in the early hours of the morning to have time alone, or taking time each day in prayer or meditation. For others the need for solitude is satisfied through gardening or walking or listening to music. Still others set aside several days or even several weeks a year to go on special retreats.

Whatever form it takes, solitude does not have to be structured or even explicitly devotional. "I am here in Vermont, living in a little hut," one woman wrote to a friend. "Like the main cabin, this hut looks out on the lake and mountain, and there are wind chimes, which are very melodious and keep saying, 'Now. Now. Now.' They call me to the present continually. I like that."

Another woman told us, "My psychic energy is like water in a well. Sometimes it gets low, and then what I must do is simply slow everything down and wait for it to rise. It will if I just wait, but not impatiently."

"The longing for solitude is like a toothache with me—sometimes acute, sometimes hardly noticeable, but always there," Mary Morrison, a teacher of gospel studies who is now in her mid-seventies, wrote to us after our visit.[1] "If my husband weren't a person with a strong, natural respect for other people's needs, I don't know what I'd do. As it is, I feel that if I were divided in two, one half of me would be ecstatically living alone, and there would be enough longing for solitude left over to give the other half a few painful moments now and then."

The story of how Mary first became aware of her hunger for solitude is a strong testament to the power of our psyche and our dreams to alert us to what needs attention in our lives if we are to grow spiritually and emotionally.

Mary had just turned forty, and although she had been plagued by fatigue for a number of months, she had not taken it seriously. "After all," she told herself, "feeling tired all the time is just part of being a wife and the mother of three small children." It was not until she was nearly disabled by her chronic low energy that she sought medical help and learned that she was suffering from a serious lung problem. Acting on her doctor's advice, she underwent a lengthy surgery that, happily, corrected the disorder.

In the weeks following her operation, however, Mary did not spring back to health as quickly as she expected. In fact, much to her distress, she felt even less energetic and less interested and able to participate in the activities of her family than before. "It seemed to me that I had returned from that long journey under the anesthetic not at all the same person who had entered it," she wrote in her journal. "And the question kept arising, Who am I now?"

Like a stubborn koan, Who am I? persisted, disturbing her rest at the time when she most needed it. And to make matters worse, as her energy ebbed, she began to be obsessed by snakes. She had waking visions of "snakey head after snakey head," snakes emerging from holes in her front yard, snakes before her eyes as she was falling asleep, and almost every night snakes inhabited her dreams.

"What is happening in my inner country that snakes should begin moving into it?" she asked herself. "Am I supposed to cast them out?" As she struggled with what to do about the serpents, she had a sense of "just a naked 'I'—no arms, no legs, not even much of a brain—standing all by itself." The snakes seemed to her to symbolize the segments of a backbone, of a singular, solitudinal self that she had long suppressed but that now, in her weakened condition, appeared to be popping up everywhere. "One of the things that most bothers me about my new and unfamiliar self," Mary confided to her journal, "is a loss of my former, easy ability to meet the needs of other people or even (dreadful thought) to like them very much or for very long."

Mary began to question everything that was happening to her,

not only the fear and irritability she was feeling in her daily life—
along with the ever-present snakes—but also what all this meant
about her relationship to God. And slowly, uneasily, as she began
to make friends with her "backbone," that part of herself that could
stand alone and make choices, she decided that this part was the
indispensable starting place for her own health and for the healthy
love of her family and neighbors. "And I hadn't known that!" she
scribbled exultantly in her journal. "The importance of this backbone comes with all the force of a revelation!

"You must remember," she hastened to explain, "that this all
happened in the 1940s. Everything I read, everything I heard in
church, was about our excessive pride and the need to humble
ourselves. The last thing I needed—the last thing any woman
needed—was advice about humbling myself! What I actually needed
was to connect with my emotions and accept myself for who I was.
The two years of relative solitude and my snake dreams told me
about the importance of being my own self, when everything and
everyone around was telling me I ought to be some ideal.

"Far from being selfish," she concluded, indignant at all those
years of bad advice, "finding my own self was fundamental because
that's the only part that can relate first-hand to God."

Of all the fears we have heard from women about taking time
and space for themselves, the most common by far was the fear of
being selfish. If there is a mantra that women repeat to themselves
to deny their longing for solitude, it is probably, "Selfish. Selfish.
Am I being selfish?"

For two years following her separation from her husband, Lynette
lived alone in a tiny studio apartment, studying massage therapy,
and asking herself this question. She no longer led the young people's
group at church, or planned and prepared festive parties for her
friends and extended family. She didn't even read the newspaper
much.

"So people call and ask, 'What's happened to you, Lynette? You
used to be so outgoing and giving,'" she told us. "Just yesterday one

of my favorite aunts telephoned and said right out, 'I love you, my dear, but it's clear to me that you're being very selfish pursuing this massage-therapy business. Living in your own apartment with no one to look after but yourself is very selfish and ungrounded!'

"You know," Lynnette told us thoughtfully, "doing something for yourself is like being pregnant. From the outside, being pregnant can look selfish. You take in all this extra food. You sleep more than usual. You are not as interested as you used to be in other people's lives, including the lives of your own family. But inside another life is growing. It needs quiet, nourishment, and rest. At first, no one can see this life, but that has absolutely no bearing on the matter. The inner life is growing and it demands your attention.

"But," she continued, "being pregnant is easier than this other birthing. Because in our material society, we trust the process that gives us something we can see and touch and hear—a live baby. This other birthing—well, who can be sure? So much trust is needed to turn down or tune out the internal critic and focus on what is happening inside you instead of always serving others."

Lynette's reflections and questions about solitude are typical of those expressed by many other women we interviewed once they had decided to honor their need for time alone. But after experiencing the inner renewal and serenity that being alone can bring, their concern about self-centeredness disappeared.

Sara Norwood no longer has any doubts about the need for solitude in her life. For many years, she told us, she was a caretaker, a "giver of chicken soup to all comers," both personally and professionally. Now, as an editor of spiritual books and journals, a full-time partner and part-time stepmother, she is busier than ever.

"I have taken care of dying adults, dying children, incest survivors, and disturbed and handicapped adolescents," she told us, "but all the while I was starving inside myself for love and caring. For the last two years I have focused on myself. I go for walks alone, listen to music, watch the afternoon light slip through the trees. This may look selfish from the outside, but inside I know it isn't. I am nourishing what is real in me."

And here she would agree with Mary Morrison: "True caring

means being able to give from fullness," Sara told us. "And for that I need my solitude. It is the very birthplace of altruism."

"To live is to be related," the Buddhist teacher Vimala Thakar observed.[2] Finding the truth of this in solitudinal moments, the women we spoke with are also translating it into every dimension of their daily lives. Looking to the past, they are claiming their membership in ancient lineages. Turning to the present, they are acknowledging the incalculable value of their friendships. And gazing into the future, they are creating circles, councils, and communities, not just for our own time, but for the generations of children who will follow.

However, realizing this expanded sense of relatedness and connection is not always easy because, as Dale Spender writes in *Man Made Language*, "Where the meanings of women have been discontinuous with the male version of reality they have not been retained. Whereas we have inherited the accumulated meanings of male experience, the meanings of our female ancestors have frequently disappeared."[3] These lines give voice to something many of us have become poignantly aware of in our own search for truth: that each generation of women has had to give birth to its own meanings, largely unaware of what has gone before.

From wicca healers and herbalists to women preachers and mystics to artists and writers and all the others who have wanted to find the inner meanings and express them in outer forms, there has been a sense of being isolated, cut off from those who have stepped into the mystery and could show us the way. It is as if we "emerged from nowhere, as if each of us had lived, thought and worked without any historical past or contextual present," as the poet Adrienne Rich observes. And this disjunction has made not only our work but also our spiritual intuitions and our sense of community with each other seem "sporadic, erratic, orphaned of any tradition of its own."[4]

What do you do in a time when the old ways have fallen into oblivion and the new ways have not yet been discovered, when the lineage that might have served as a link between the two has been fragmented or destroyed? This is the challenging question that Rifke, the monologist in Naomi Newman's play *Snake Talk: Urgent Messages from the Mother* asks.[5] And then, with eminent good sense, she answers, "First you complain, then you fix it."

"Now we are going to make a *new-way* path," Rifke counsels the audience. "So you take a shovel, you take a ground-*haker*, you take a hairpin. If all you got is a hairpin, you take a hairpin and you start digging. And you dig in all directions: up and down, in and out, right and left. Not in a straight line. Nothing natural or interesting goes in a straight line. As a matter of fact, it is the quickest way to the wrong place. And," she warns, "don't pretend you know where you are going. Because if you know where you are going, that means you've been there, and you are going to end up exactly where you came from."

> I am part of a network of events that have
> occurred in the lives of many people, some of
> whom are unknown to me. I know that their deaths
> must have contributed to my life, and that without
> them I would not be who I am. To be aware of this
> is to carry their love within my heart, and to live
> in a spirit of gratitude.
>
> — Jean Lanier
> "The Communion of Saints"

Gratitude, we learned, is one way in which many of the women we interviewed are beginning to gather together the scattered pieces. Brooke Medicine Eagle, a Native American teacher, told us that one of her elders explained the need for gratitude by saying: "Don't you know that the ancient lines of Native women who hold the marriage baskets and sacred bundles have been sending vision through you and feeding you? You have been given energy and love and attention even by those who didn't know you personally, even by those who don't acknowledge you today. Just because someone doesn't recognize you doesn't mean they haven't been praying for you generation after generation."

After pausing for a moment, Brooke continued in a quiet voice, "So I acknowledge the spiritual women and the holders of the sacred medicine bundles as those who feed me. And when I do that, I have deep in my heart the knowledge that I am a strong part of the community. I go ahead and do my work with gratitude to those who have gone before me, even though they may not know or even necessarily like me."

To find our connection to the ancient grandmothers or to elders from another time or culture is sometimes far easier than to appreciate the gifts we have received from our own immediate family: our mothers and aunts and grandmothers.

This was emphatically brought home to us when we attended a lecture in Los Angeles by Twylah Nitsch, known to her Seneca people as Yehwehnode. As an elder of the Wolf Clan she received an enthusiastic welcome, and her audience listened to her speak in respectful silence. Afterward, one admiring young woman said, "It is such a gift to hear your wisdom, Grandmother. How I wish we had others like you! But we have no crones, no elders."

"Yes, you do," Twylah shot back. "You've stuffed them out of sight in old age homes. You can't hear what they have to say. You can't receive what is already in front of you. You don't know how to respect them, to offer gratitude for what they have shared with you."

Taken aback by Twylah's response, the woman asked, "What can we do?"

"Start now," Twylah said. "Start now to acknowledge those who help you and love you. Show your gratitude."

This is what Leah Novick, a rabbi from Oakland, California, is doing. For many years she has been showing her gratitude to Jewish women throughout history who provided spiritual leadership but whose names are almost forgotten, women who were judges and seers and teachers for their people. "Many of them did not have children, others' descendants were killed in the holocaust, so they have no one to say prayers for them," Leah told us. "I want to reclaim their memories and connect to them in the world of prayer." For years she recited memorial prayers for these women in private.

Now, as the leader of a congregation, and in visits to church groups and synagogues across the U.S. she continues to call the names of these women on the High Holy Days and on other days of celebration and recollection. She has chosen to become a daughter to those who had no daughters and in doing this she has adopted a great lineage of female ancestors who might otherwise have been lost.

Sonja Margulies, a Zen teacher, has done something similar. She told a conference of Buddhist women that just as she has for years been chanting the names of her Zen lineage back to the Buddha—all of whom were men—she now repeats the names of her mother and the women she admired as a child in her hometown. "I call the names of these American women," she told her audience, "because they are my lineage as surely as any of the Zen masters who have been my teachers." And then, in the same familiar sonorous tones in which her listeners had heard the names of men chanted for years and even decades, Sonja began to chant the names of the women from her childhood, following each name with the traditional honorific *dai osho*: "Constance Fenne, *dai osho*; Mary Delzer, *dai osho*; Grandma Bringold, *dai osho*. . . ." Three hundred women sat in rapt attention. There was something heartrending about hearing the names of ordinary women like themselves so honored, so recognized.

By acknowledging and thanking those who have gone before us—from the ancient lineage of our female ancestors, from our immediate family, teachers and neighbors, and from the spiritual traditions in which we were raised—we are including ourselves as part of a vast community that extends through time. These acts of inclusiveness help us remember that we are linked by origin and that we do not need to earn our female lineage. It is ours by inheritance.

Expressing gratitude for those who have gone before us is important for a sense of connection and continuity, but it is from those who walk beside us that we can gain the strength and courage to remain true to our purpose. And what many women today are discovering as they "dig a new-way path" is not a teacher or guru or guide, but a "resonator," a friend or sister or companion so true to her own inner reality that she inspires them to be faithful to theirs. Somehow the resonator calls us to our true selves, reminding us and reflecting to us our deepest possibility, asking the difficult questions and encouraging us to take action.

As we began working on this book, one friend complained, "I'm tired of hearing from people who let me know how holy *they* are. Find me women who let me know how holy *we* are!" She was, we think, looking for a resonator. Another woman described the resonator function this way: "I think if I can remain true to my inner sounding, to my tuning fork, I can set up a harmonic in which your tuning fork will begin to vibrate, and you, in turn, will set up a resonance in someone else."

Not all resonators are people we know. Some are strangers, people we may never have an opportunity to meet or thank: "It took everything in me and more to write, produce, and perform my play *Snake Talk*," Naomi Newman told us. "The forces of opposition to my bringing it to the stage were almost overwhelming, and I felt very, very alone. But once I started to perform it, I began receiving letters from women telling me that it was a major event in their lives. One woman—someone I'd never met—wrote a letter so moving and beautiful that it carried me through some of the most difficult months. It gave me the courage to hang in there."

Other resonators may come into our lives briefly, like guardian angels on special assignments: "It was the single, most concentratedly miserable time in my life," Elly Haney, a founder of the Feminist Spiritual Community of Portland, Maine, told us with an ironic smile. "I was teaching theology at a college in Minnesota and asking myself every single day, Why are you teaching what you know you want to change? But it wasn't until I met the philosopher and activist Wilma Scott Heide that my own unspoken questions began to find a voice.

"Wilma was someone who spoke her doubts out loud, directly challenging the assumptions underlying the theology I was teaching.

I listened, fascinated. It was the first time I had met anyone else who was thinking what I was thinking. But unlike me, she was communicating her values. And what was most important, she was living those values—blending compassion and respect for others right along with her anger and challenges. By inspiring as well as demanding change, by calling us to a vision as well as analyzing what was wrong, she demonstrated the spiritual grounding of activism in a way I had never seen before. Meeting her changed everything for me. Eventually I made the decision to walk away from a tenured professorship and start afresh."

Leaving her home and work behind, Elly moved across the continent, searching for colleagues and friends who shared her interest in spiritually motivated activities. And she found them. Within three years, she and enough other resonators had come together to create the Feminist Spiritual Community of Portland, Maine.

One woman we spoke with has been a resonator for many others, as well as having had several women and men serve her in this way. "I think of this in terms of veils," she told us. "In the presence of a person who is real, you take off your veils of illusion. The other person doesn't have to tear them off. You just automatically drop them, either that, or you have to get out of their presence.

"This is what I want from my relationships. I want the freedom to be who I am and I want you to be free to be who you are and I'm not going to try to push you into thinking or feeling the way I do. Then differences about politics, religious dogma, and sexuality can stay on the surface while we're profoundly connected at the soul level. You can recognize this almost instantaneously, and the name for it doesn't matter a bit. It's soul meeting soul. And that's what I'm after: getting closer and closer to that essence, taking away veil after veil."

·   ·   ·

"Sisterhood is the one way black women have survived," author and poet Maya Angelou told us when we asked about her close friendships with women. "We have had to depend on each other. And the weight, the value, we give to our friendship is so large that once it is given, once the hands are taken, it is very hard to lose. You can give up a lover much easier," she said, laughing. "Much easier!"

As we listened to these words, spoken with such intensity, we thought of the women we had interviewed for this book. No matter how many lives they had enriched, how large their work or vision, for some there were persistent feelings of loneliness and isolation. Searching for words to describe what we had sensed from these women, we said, "We've talked with women who are sources of inspiration to others, who open doors and hold them open for others to walk through, but who is there to comfort and hold these women? Who is there to hear them when they express their doubts and questions?"

Maya considered this. "One of the things that I see in traveling around is the number of white women who take friendship lightly and misunderstand what a gift it is, who would give up a dinner with a woman friend to go out with a man. Women so often have been denied respect, true respect. We need to extend this to each other. The conditioning which teaches us to see each other as competitors for men's attention also tells us that relationships between women are not as worthwhile as those between women and men. The ability to respect another human being for what she is offering is the foundation for a friendship. It is not to be taken lightly."

And with that, she got up from the couch and left the room, leaving us to contemplate what she had said. She returned shortly to announce, "I have just called my chosen sister, Dolly McPherson. She's a professor of English here at Wake Forest University, and she's coming over now to meet with us, to talk about sisters. She has her priorities in order, and friendship is right at the top of the list. I think that sex, however one wants it, is always available. But friendship, wheew! That's something to work on and cherish, build, add to constantly."

While we were waiting for Dolly to arrive, we asked how they had come to choose each other as sisters. "A sister is no plaything," Maya responded firmly. "You have to consider. You have to talk about it. After you're friends and you see that you have so much in common and you love each other, you ask, 'Could we be sisters?' If the person says yes, you repeat together, 'You really are my sister.' And then you go about informing both of your families.

"When Dolly and I made sisters in New York, my mother and my son, Guy, came from California to meet her, and I met Dolly's brothers and her one blood sister. Now her brothers are my brothers, and our two families are joined.

"And I have other sisters as well," she continued. "In times of trouble, there are about seven women in the United States I can call at any hour and say, 'Now. Now. I need you now.' And they will come. No questions. No objections. Not . . . Well, I don't feel well . . . I don't know if I can. . . . Nothing, nothing would keep them from me or me from them."

At this point, the doorbell rang, and in a few moments a stately middle-aged woman sailed into the living room. "Sister," Maya said by way of introduction, "I was just about to tell these two ladies how you and I often wonder how people survive without sisters. How we say, 'You'd need a psychiatrist's couch if you didn't have a sister who would straighten you out.'"

Picking up on the thought, Dolly continued, "A sister who will say to you, 'You are wrong. Come here and let me talk to you. Let's sit down together. What is the meaning of this? This is something you have never done before. Why are you acting this way?' I can look back on my life for twenty-five years and see how I have grown through our sisterhood, how I have come to look at things very, very differently. I can see the change in my values and the enrichment of them. And I know Maya sees herself reflected in me. So often we will just be sitting, not saying anything. Then all of a sudden we will both start to say the same thing."

"We do a lot of laughing," Maya added. "And some crying."

"Do you ever get jealous of each other? Competitive?" we asked.

"No. No," they answered in chorus.

"It never happens?" we persisted.

"No," Maya replied. "Just the opposite. If Dolly strives for something, I bring all I have to that. If I'm striving for something, Dolly will give me everything she has. When we put my first novel, *I Know Why the Caged Bird Sings*, together on the floor in my apartment in New York, Dolly said, 'Let's try it this way. Let's take this chapter out and move that one.' So we got out our scissors and cut it up. Then we took tape and taped it back together. We've done this many, many times for each other. Day by day. Doing our life work. Not just talking it or dreaming it, but *doing* it, being present as sisters for each other. That's the best you can hope to be, as I see it."

When Jean Houston, a well-known researcher on the expansion of human potential, met Gay Luce, an award-winning science writer, on a radio program in 1966, there was an immediate recognition that developed into a lasting friendship. "Jean was doing all these far-out things," Gay told us, "and eventually she persuaded me to join her experiments on altered states of consciousness. At first I felt like a guinea pig and found myself resisting all the way. Later, after we got to know each other better, we began teaching together. Jean was so exuberant and outrageous that at times I would find myself moaning under my breath, 'Will she *ever* grow out of this?' What I couldn't know then, of course, was that I would grow into it!

"Our collaboration seemed the most unlikely pairing," she continued, "but gradually I began to find Jean's mind and awareness illuminating and magical. I realized that she was the perfect antidote to the cramped, intellectual atmosphere of Radcliffe and Harvard I had inhabited and was fixated in. Her humor and magnanimity just broke into my conservative world and helped me open up to dimensions of life I had never known before.

"And the friendship! From the very beginning there was a spark of love and trust between us, but as our friendship deepened, I found that this way of being with another woman was entirely new for me. Partly because my childhood relationship with my mother had been so difficult, and partly because the power structure in the world of scientific journalism was mostly male, I hadn't found exciting and confident women to work with. In fact, until my forties most of my friends were men and I had thought I had to have a man on my side to do something worthwhile.

"But here was Jean," she continued, "with such an irrepressible imagination and fearlessness that I was motivated to find my own self-reliance and courage. There was no way I could imitate her powerful dramatics, however—I had to find my own path.

"And now, after twenty-five years and what seems like twenty-five lifetimes later—I find I've absorbed a lot of Jean. I'm no longer relying on scientific data but am teaching and working these days from a realm that is formless, hardly amenable to words. And while I've become far less public, less political and less verbal, Jean has taken the entire world as her classroom, working to expand individual and planetary consciousness in villages from India to Venezuela to the Philippines. It almost seems as if we've changed places with each other in our focus and interest, though both of us are building communities—Jean, around the world, and I in a spiritual family that comes out of the Nine Gates Mystery School I began seven years ago.

"So our paths diverge and meet and diverge again, but that's not what's important. What matters most to me, what I treasure about Jean, is that she has been and continues to be my fellow adventurer, opening up domains of consciousness I hadn't imagined, and sharing with me a depth of abiding love I never expected to find."

THE MAKING OF COMMUNITY

"I see something new in the making," Dorothy Maclean, who has been involved with spiritual communities for over thirty years,[6] told us as we sat talking over tea in the living room of her home in rural Washington. "Communities in the past were generally founded by one magnetic or very wise person, and people would sit at the feet of that person and do what they said. But I see a new type of community emerging, one in which we each tune into our own higher self and no one is higher or better than anyone else, a leaderless community in which we're all leaders."

Almost as soon as Dorothy mentioned this leaderless community, alarms began going off inside our heads. We could see how the very same issue that confronts women in intimate personal relationships can exist, perhaps even more powerfully, in community life. The Jungian analyst Helen Luke has observed that the temptation to betray one's inner truth is at least equally present in the complex relationships of a group. She warns that "submergence in a group," and "well-meant attempts to awaken 'spiritual experiences' through suggestion in groups" and " 'loving' communities in which relationships are lost in an unconscious merging" are appealing but inadequate "substitutes for the lonely way."[7]

Yet if there is one conviction that the women we spoke with expressed with great consistency, it is that the time for individual enlightenment has passed. "We are in a new cycle now," one told us, "and we need each other in order to awaken." "The task is too great, the need too pressing," another said, "for individual messiahs."

We put the conundrum of how to strike a balance between the individual and the collective to Dorothy Maclean. "There's no question that each of us needs to find this balance at various times in our life," she replied. "I think there's a rhythm to our development— a time to be alone, a time to be in community—and I wouldn't put one above the other. Moreover, I don't think you can be a properly functioning member of a group unless you've found your own individuality. Otherwise you're a weak link, you're leaning on the group because you haven't found your own center.

"But once you can stand on your own two feet," she continued, "and if it is time for you to join with others, then something immensely valuable can be created. And it's not at all a matter of needing to submerge your uniqueness. Not at all! If you know who you are, and can be true to your own reality, you won't be threatened by my reality. In fact, you'll affirm my difference because you'll know that's just what I need to activate my deepest talents and gifts."

Affirming individual differences in a collective context is something that the women of the Feminist Spiritual Community of Portland, Maine, have been learning how to do for almost a decade now. Elly Haney, a cofounder of the community, told us how it all began:[8] "It started in the spring of 1980 when I was invited to teach a new course on women and religion at the University of Southern Maine. It was not long before I discovered that most of the women in the class—and what an assortment we were! teenagers, grandmothers, lesbians, heterosexuals, Protestants, Catholics, Quakers, and a Native American—felt alienated from our childhood religions. As it turned out, we also had two other things in common: each of us was searching for a meaningful way to worship, and we all felt a desperate need for the support of women.

"Because my background is in theological ethics and I am an action-oriented person, I gave the class a long-term assignment to 'do' something practical and constructive in the everyday world as part of their course work. My expectation was that they would do studies of peace demonstrations or analyze racial inequality, or maybe research controversial topics like abortion and the right to die.

"But to my astonishment, almost every woman chose to do a ritual! Women who had never performed rituals in their lives began unabashedly leading us in celebrations and meditations. There was singing and drumming and dancing, and along with the singing and drumming and dancing there was anger and deep grief and mystical joy. Tears and feelings we hadn't dreamed were in us suddenly were being expressed. To make a long story short, when the class was over, the women didn't want to stop meeting. Inadvertently, through this depth of sharing we had started to create a community.

"It was about this time that I met Susan Savell, a member of the United Church of Christ's Board for Homeland Ministries. Together we saw an opportunity to do something very innovative: to create a feminist whatever-we-were-calling-it, a feminist spiritual community. So we put together a funding proposal, and with the help and support of many others, it was approved."

But auspicious beginnings are only the first step, and the very heterogeneity that made Elly's class so electrifying soon threatened to blow apart the fledgling community. "In the process of organizing ourselves, questions came up: How much time should we spend in study? In ritual? In meditation? And these questions provoked such different responses in people that the community almost came apart before it got started," Elly told us. "People got *mad* at each other, and I thought to myself, Oh, oh, here we go.

"We debated, argued, listened to each other and anguished throughout that first summer. What we finally came to was commitment to a principle—one of the few principles we have in the community—'In our diversity is our strength.' This commits us to working through conflicts with each other. It means we do not have to follow the dominant American individualistic mode of storming off and setting up a separate community out of frustration with not having our own way. We try to integrate the personal spiritual vision of our members with the community's sense of spiritual purpose."

A commitment to working through conflict is a noble principle, we conceded, but what happens when you actually try to put it into practice? We learned the answer to this question by talking with several long-time members of the community. From the very beginning, each of them told us, Elly and several other mature women created a strong container of loving acceptance. Rather than intervening with advice and opinions, they valued each demand or concern or challenge for the contribution it made.

"I saw my role as being primarily a listener," Elly explained to us. "I guess what I had in mind was that we were going to be pluralistic, that we could include all of us in some way. And I trusted that we could learn how to listen and respect and confront one another, and that this would transform us. I was convinced that through this learning we would come to trust and love and depend on ourselves."

The process of making community is exciting, the women of Portland told us, and at the same time it is a struggle. They are reluctant to limit their size or restrict their membership because they believe in diversity. "But we struggle with how to do this without falling into some kind of least common denominator for the community," Elly explained. "To have community there must be commitment to work through disagreements, to care about each other. When individuals move in and out of the community only to satisfy their needs, without extending themselves to others, they create problems for the community as a whole."

Some of the women spoke about how slow the process can be. Often it seems safer to avoid conflict, they admitted, especially when one does not feel wise enough or "spiritual enough" to speak out and risk being awkward. Others spoke of needing to free themselves from the fear that a bolt of lightning would strike them dead for worshiping the goddess or celebrating the sacred in an untraditional way. They described how tempting it is at times to regard the community as their private refuge, and how this makes them hesitate to include new members who might be challenging or disruptive to their present harmony. What gives them courage, they told us, and helps them to honor the principle of diversity they so value, is sharing their stories with each other. "Hearing the actual stories grounds our principles in the specifics of women's experiences," Elly emphasized. "The stories are our touchstone, the personal truths that make our principles something we want to live."

At the end of our interview with Elly, we asked how she personally had been affected by her six years with the community. "I've become much more willing to share my own spirituality and spiritual development," she replied. "For some reason this has always been more private than anything else in my life. But the reason that I've been willing to share it is the continuing insight that shutting myself up in an ivory tower to find truth just doesn't work!" And then she laughed before adding more seriously, "I believe that truth comes through our gathered body of women sharing stories, music, thoughts, whatever, and the relationships among us. And our community, however fitfully, however tentatively, is the treasure that is bringing us to this grace."

> I believe that we have got to shift our identity
> out of that little prison cage of ego in order to
> survive. We have to find ways to know
> experientially our interconnectedness with all forms
> of life on this planet. Conventional morality that
> tells us we should love our neighbor and ought to
> remember the needy just doesn't work. It's boring
> and we don't feel it inside ourselves. We need
> meditations and games and rituals that will give us
> space to step outside of the human identification
> we've been wearing for so long. And the form I
> love the most is the Council of All Beings.
>
> — Joanna Macy

Of the many forms of community we have encountered, one of the most fascinating is a moveable ritual in which humans have an opportunity to speak for and listen to an unlimited variety of non-human life-forms. The Council of All Beings, as it is called, was developed in Australia in 1980 by Joanna Macy, an American activist and teacher of Buddhism, and John Seed, an Australian ecologist.[9]

"We meet in council because our planet is in trouble," the ritual leaders begin, in settings from the Grand Canyon to a midwestern police armory, from high school gymnasiums to church sanctuaries. "It is fitting now, and it is important that each of us be heard. For there is much that needs to be said and much that needs to be listened to."

And then the participants, who have meditated on and tried to sense into the body of another life-form on this planet, and have made a mask of its face, ask permission to speak on its behalf. One by one, holding up their masks, they begin to speak as the form of life they have chosen to represent.

The voice behind a lichen mask begins: "I turn rock into soil. I've worked as the glaciers retreated, as other life-forms came and went. I thought nothing could stop me . . . until now. Now I am being poisoned by acid rain, and my days are coming to an end because of what you are doing. It is time for you to hear me."

"Your pesticides are in me now," a colorful bird mask laments. "My eggshells are so fragile they break under my weight before my young are ready to hatch."

"I am raccoon," another voice continues. "See my hand? It is like yours. On the soft ground you see its imprint and know I've been there. What marks on this world are you leaving behind?"

"It gets quite formal as people really immerse themselves in the ritual and create," Joanna explained. "The testimony of the beings is often overwhelming. I am continually surprised at the poignancy and eloquence with which they report how rapidly and radically we humans are altering their lives and diminishing their chances for survival."

Periodically, the ritual leader signals that a few of the partici-pants can lay their masks aside and come as human beings into the center of the circle. "When you enter the circle as a human," Joanna told us, "you are not permitted to say a thing. For once, you just listen to what the other beings have to say to you. When most of those present have participated as both humans and nonhumans, there is a kind of turning," she explained, "a recognition of soli-darity. A human may trigger it by saying, 'We hear you. We hear you. We know we're wrecking the world, but we don't know how to turn this around. The system has so much momentum now. What can we do? Can you help us?' "

And then without any rehearsal or prompting, life-forms begin to respond:

"I am deep-diving sea trout. I give you fearlessness of the dark because you have a long, dark way to go."

"I am hawk. I give you my distance vision so you can see far ahead."

"I am caterpiller, and I can sense a great change coming. I offer you humans my willingness to be transformed without knowing what the result will be."

By offering these powers, Joanna suggested, the participants invoke the power within themselves and each other that they want strengthened. "And this naming, this calling upon our common strengths," she says, "is my greatest joy."

When we asked Joanna the same question that we asked Elly Haney—How has this work in community affected you personally?—she laughed delightedly and then surprised us by saying, "For me the deep ecology work is like participating in the universe making love to itself. It's very erotic."

Erotic? What we heard was anguish and pain in the voices she described to us, we told her. Did she mean to say that she found this work fun? Sexual? Revitalizing?

"All of that," she replied, "but a lot more. It's not all light, you know. You rip your belly open too. For us to feel our sorrow and our hope, our pain over what is happening in the world and our interconnectedness to all of life is bittersweet. Because with any great passion, you suffer. As you open yourself to love, you also open to tremendous vulnerability and sorrow. So this work with the Council for All Beings is erotic in the sense of the deep, awesome, tender celebration of life taking form at all.

"This work has taught me that it's in community, in our love for each other, that our interdependence becomes most visible. I feel how much we need these communal forms and how much we have to be faithful to each other, to build ourselves—humans and nonhumans alike—into each others' lives in new ways."

Sometimes being faithful and finding new ways to be part of each other's lives can mean staying right where we are. By choosing to remain in our own community and affirming our love for that community, we claim our right to be there. And this is just what some of the most creative and courageous women we know are doing.

When educator and ecologist Sister Miriam MacGillis was asked whether she was concerned that her provocative lectures might cause the Catholic Church to throw her out, her response was immediate and unequivocal: "If I were pushed against the wall, I wouldn't let anybody throw me out. I am the Church in a new place."[10]

And when an interviewer observed delicately to the innovative Jewish liturgist Marcia Falk, ". . . as you know, you've got detractors within Judaism who would claim that what you're doing is not Jewish," she replied: "Why should I let them define what Judaism is and place myself outside of it? I use Jewish sources, Jewish language, Jewish experience. I call myself a Jew."[11]

The feminist Episcopalian priest Carter Heyward speaks directly about the need for such reaching out and including oneself in. "The church simply cannot go on the way it has," she says. "And we who are priests cannot make the changes alone. We need to have our sisters with us. There need to be the bridges and the networks . . . of support that women find with and through each other." Such matrices, she says, create a "viable and lively ecumenical movement" that is the indispensible key to a woman being able to be in the church and also true to herself.[12]

The making of relatives, it seems, is slow work. It takes not just caring, but the courage to tell the truth to each other and the perseverance to face misunderstandings and emotional struggles— along with whatever else needs to be worked through—in order to grow together over the long term.

Qualities of perseverance and openness don't spring up overnight. They are rooted in long years of yearning for relationship. Adrienne Rich, as we mentioned earlier, describes women as feeling like orphans, cut off from the lineage of all those women who have gone before. Perhaps it is this feeling of isolation that makes us ready now to discover new ways of coming together and joining with each other. Or perhaps this is simply a natural development, precisely what we would be doing at this point in our evolutionary cycle regardless of what has gone before.

However we choose to explain it, the women we interviewed are searching for and finding their connectedness. They are beginning to gather together what has been lost or forgotten or disowned and welcome it into their lives.

There is a Hebrew word that describes this action: *tikkun*. It means to heal, to mend what has been broken, to transform. In the beginning of the world, the legend which is the source of this word goes, the abundant divine light was held in primeval vessels. But somehow—no one knows how—the vessels were shattered, and discord and confusion spread everywhere. The great task for human beings, the story tells us, is to repair the ancient vessels, to gather together the scattered light, to call home all those who have been lost or in exile, to heal the separation and bring peace to our world.

Chapter 10
BEING THE SACRED GARDEN

> At first people refuse to believe that a strange
> new thing can be done, then they begin to hope it
> can't be done, then they see it can be done—then
> it is done and all the world wonders why it was not
> done centuries before.
>
> — Frances Hodgson Burnett
> *The Secret Garden*

 As we start to write this final chapter, an image comes
to mind: the gates of thousands upon thousands of
sacred gardens are flung open from within, accompanied by laughter that cannot be contained. And
with the laughter comes speech, because in our exuberance we are
no longer able to silence ourselves.

We remember how awesome and heavy the words *spiritual responsibility* felt to us as we began to write this book, like a weight,
a duty. We intended of course to meet that responsibility . . . manfully. (Manfully! It just slipped out.) That is how patriarchs would
put it—spirituality as shouldering a responsibility.

But as we write this now, there is another language and another
set of images that come to us. The language, as the women tell
their stories, does not depict a dutiful shouldering of burdens but a
spontaneous and natural letting go, in the same way that apples fall
from a tree when they're ripe and ready for eating. And the images
are not only of women unlocking gates, opening doors, and emerging
from their secret, sacred gardens, but of the new being birthed in

a profusion of forms. Women are dreaming of being initiated by children, and by each other; and they dream of new visions beginning to take shape in developer's fluid and computer tapes with images so new the computers are not yet able to process the information.

The language and images are saying that the process of maturing that fulfills each one of us personally is also what the world most needs from us at this time. A Native American teacher describes this as "an unveiling of what is already inside us." "We are trying to form a new world now," she says, "and what is really new lies in that great womb where all possibilities are. We need to go in and bring it forth."

She speaks particularly to women: "If we who know what it is to bring forth the unknown from our own bodies can't be comfortable with this process, we'll just continue to perpetuate the old ways and we'll all be in trouble. Because, while it's scary for us women, it's far scarier for men who have never had the experience of giving birth and who must be very frightened."

But for all the force of this warning, it is not only stepping into the mystery that brings the fear. The fear comes when we sit down to breakfast. It leans over our shoulder and reads the statistics in the morning paper, numbing us so we don't feel the cold or hunger or terror beneath the abstractions. And often it walks beside us in the evening as we cross a dimly lit street, and whispers to us as we fall asleep at night.

Is it now that we are to open the gates of the sacred garden? Now that our voices are to be heard? Are we to give birth to the new possibilities in times like these? "You could not be born at a better period than the present, when we have lost everything," the French philosopher and mystic Simone Weil[1] wrote in her journal as World War II was gathering. And her words continue to resonate powerfully through us today.

For what we have lost is the certainty that our planet will continue to support life. We now know in a way that humans have never known before that our lives are permeable, fragile, and delicately interwoven with all other life on this planet. Now we know that destruction of rain forests in the Amazon opens the ozone layer in New England, that a nuclear accident in Chernobyl poisons apples in Oregon, that smoke from Michigan turns rain to acid in Quebec. We know in the most down-to-earth ways possible that what we humans do affects not only other humans around the world, but oceans, atmospheres, wildlife, trees, and our children's children's children.

This knowledge, concrete and particular, brings us all to the truth once perceived only by mystics, shamans, and saints: that we are all connected. We know that we, who did not weave the web of life, who are merely a strand in it, can destroy it. We know, as Chief Seattle said over a hundred years ago, that whatever we do to the web, we do to ourselves.[2] This convergence of mystical truth and concrete fact hits us with a double whammy. It is, as one woman told us, "spirituality in the fast lane."

Clearly, it is time to ask ourselves where we are going. And as every woman we interviewed agreed, where we are going, where we must go, is back into daily life. They speak not only of the need to slow down and create an opening for awareness of the sacred in our daily lives, but of the need to embody, to enact, to be a vessel for that awareness so that it flows into all our relationships. Anna Douglas, a Buddhist meditation teacher, said simply: "Our work as women is not to create new spiritual empires, but to bring what we've learned from our practices back home."

Brooke Medicine Eagle told us that a male friend came to visit her one day and spoke for some time about the dangers and crises facing the planet. It is a time, he said, when the deepest kind of spiritual work is needed. Brooke agreed. And then he confided, "Some of us are building pillars of light now to hold up the sky, and you are one of us."

"I think it's quite different than that," Brooke replied. "We don't need to *build* pillars of light! By being willing to receive, we *draw down* the light. It pours through us continually wherever we stand. We need to share it with our community—to talk about it, to live it out and hook it into the earth."

She paused for a moment, reflecting. "That's the challenge for me now," she said. "To be able to stand and hold open a space for spirit to come into all my relationships. My spiritual name is Chalíse, and I feel I need to be what that name says—a chalice, an active, receptive, open space for the Great Mystery. On the other hand, I also need to be a Medicine Eagle who embodies spirit and brings it into daily life. The challenge," she concluded with the smile of a warrior spreading across her face, "is not just to have visions and dreams, but to make them real."

To embody the sacred so deeply that it flows into all our relationships—this, the women say, is where we are going now. It is where we need to go. And, not incidentally, it is where we have come from.

"I am born connected," the artist Meinrad Craighead writes. "I am born remembering rivers flowing from my mother's body into my body."[3] Connected in childhood, we blend with the flow of life. As we mature, the boundaries of self emerge to make their separations between "me" and "you" and "others." This, of course, is essential so that the child can become an individual. But to become an individual is not yet to become mature. Maturing calls for "a stride of soul"[4] in which the experience and discernment of the individual and the connected awareness of the child come together in the responsive, responsible consciousness of the adult who can then take the next developmental step: to be in good relationship with all of life.

The awesome planetary crisis in which we are now living is literally flinging us toward this. And the women we've interviewed are telling us that it is time to take this step, time for the home-leavers to become homemakers, and time for those who have been exiles from the sacred garden to become its gardeners.

We want to emphasize that this new step is not mysticism. Mystical experience—direct knowing of the ineffable mystery—is only knowing. Some might say that this new step is Christianity, the Christianity of the gospels in which Jesus lives the Word, rather than having mystical visions or experiences. Others might say

that it is the realized consciousness of the Maitreya, the Buddha of
the future. Still others will see it as the emergence of the Goddess
in our own time.

And we would not disagree at all. But what seems new to us,
and particularly womanly, is that there is no single savior being
awaited. Rather, the savior is spread out among us, emerging from
each of us as we bring the fruits from our sacred garden into our
daily lives. It is we who must save us.

For every woman we have named, there are a hundred who
speak; for every hundred who speak, there are a thousand who know;
for every thousand who know, there are ten thousand who do not
yet know because their truth lies still deeper than all the ones who
speak and know and can be named.

And every one of us is needed now. To do whatever we can do:
to be named, to speak, to know, to not know. And everyone, the
one who can be named, who can speak, who knows, and who does
not yet know, is within each of us.

Notes

Chapter 1: The Question That Wouldn't Go Away

1. Gerald G. Jampolsky, Patricia Hopkins and William N. Thetford, *Good-bye to Guilt: Releasing Fear through Forgiveness* (New York: Bantam Books, 1985).
2. *A Course in Miracles* (Tiburon, Calif.: Foundation for Inner Peace, 1975).
3. Carol Gilligan, *In a Different Voice: Psychological Theory and Women's Development* (Cambridge, Mass.: Harvard University Press, 1982).
4. Carol Christ, *Diving Deep and Surfacing: Women Writers on Spiritual Quest* (Boston: Beacon Press, 1980), 1.
Epigraph: Janet Kalven, "Respectable Outlaw," cited in Elizabeth Schüssler Fiorenza, *Bread Not Stones* (Boston: Beacon Press, 1984), Dedication.
5. Nelle Morton, *The Journey Is Home* (Boston: Beacon Press, 1985).

6. T. S. Eliot, *Four Quartets*. "Little Gidding," (line 243). (New York: Harcourt Brace Jovanovich, 1943).

7. Irene Claremont de Castillejo, *Knowing Woman: A Feminine Psychology* (New York: Harper & Row, 1974), 87.

Chapter 2: Childhood: Seedbed of the Sacred

Epigraph: William Wordsworth, "Intimations of Immortality," in *English Literature and Its Background* (New York: Dryden Press, 1952), 753.

1. Alice Miller, *For Your Own Good* (New York: Farrar, Straus & Giroux, 1983), xv.

Chapter 3: Leaving Home

Epigraph: Joseph Campbell, *The Hero with a Thousand Faces* (Princeton, N.J.: Princeton University Press, 1972), 58.

1. Gen. 3:23–24, *Tanakh: The Holy Scriptures According to the Traditional Hebrew Text* (Philadelphia: The Jewish Publication Society, 1985).

2. E. A. Burtt, ed., *The Teachings of the Compassionate Buddha* (New York: Signet, 1955), 104.

3. Lawrence Kushner, *Honey from the Rock* (New York: Harper & Row, 1977), 24–25.

4. Meinrad Craighead, *The Mother's Songs: Images of God the Mother* (Mahwah, N.J.: Paulist Press, 1986), Introduction.

5. See Diane Wolkstein and Samuel Noah Kramer, *Inanna: Queen of Heaven and Earth* (New York: Harper & Row, 1983) and Sylvia Brinton Perera, *Descent to the Goddess: A Way of Initiation for Women* (Toronto: Inner City Books, 1981) for two excellent accounts of Inanna's myth. Charlene Spretnak, *Lost Goddesses of Early Greece* (Boston: Beacon Press, 1978) and Jean Shinoda Bolen, *Goddesses in Everywoman* (San Francisco: Harper & Row, 1984) describe the importance of Persephone/Demeter for modern women.

6. A. H. Almaas, *Diamond Heart: Book One* (Berkeley, Calif.: Diamond Books, 1987), 174–75.

7. Frederick Franck, "Spinner of the Red Thread," *Commonweal* 23 May 1986, 313–14.

8. Meinrad Craighead, "Immanent Mother," in *The Feminist Mystic and Other Essays on Women and Spirituality,* ed. Mary E. Giles (New York: Crossroads Press, 1982), 76.

9. Craighead, *Songs,* Intro.

10. Eliot, *Quartets.* "East Coker," (lines 123–126).

Chapter 4: The Ten Thousand Gates

1. Matt. 7:13–14.

Epigraph: Judy Chicago, *The Birth Project* (Garden City, N.Y.: Doubleday & Company, 1985), 28.

2. Stephanie Demetrakopoulos, *Listening to Our Bodies: The Rebirth of Feminine Wisdom* (Boston: Beacon Press, 1983).

Epigraph: This is a paraphrase from the Report of the Committee for the Spirituality of the Divine Feminine, Sufi Order of the West, published in *Hearts and Wings,* Newsletter (Summer, 1989), 4.

3. Dwight Chapin, "The Healing Touch," *San Francisco Chronicle, Image* (Sunday, Feb. 9, 1986), 11–12.

4. Elisabeth Kübler-Ross, *AIDS: The Ultimate Challenge* (New York: Macmillan, 1987).

5. Irene Smith's *Service Through Touch: Guidelines of Massaging People with AIDS* on audio tape is produced by Innerlight Productions, 1465 Hopkins Street, Berkeley, Calif. 94702.

6. *A Course in Miracles, Workbook for Students* (Tiburon, Calif.: Foundation for Inner Peace, 1975), Lesson No. 137.

Epigraph: Estella Lauder, *Women as Mythmakers: Poetry and Visual Art by Twentieth-Century Women* (Bloomington: Indiana University Press, 1984), 216.

7. Elizabeth Dodson Gray, ed., *Sacred Dimensions of Women's Experience* (Wellesley, Mass.: Roundtable Press, 1988), 2.

8. Robert Bly, trans., *Selected Poems of Rainer Maria Rilke* (New York: Harper & Row, 1981), Poem Number 7.

Epigraph: Num. 6:24–26.

Chapter 5: Inside the Sacred Garden

Epigraph: Frances Hodgson Burnett, *The Secret Garden* (London: Michael Joseph Ltd., 1986), 62–63.

1. It seems important to add that someone who can access refined states of consciousness is not necessarily spiritually mature. The feeling of great love that surrounds a guru, the prescience of a psychic, the power of a shaman, the clarity of a Zen master— these spiritual talents or gifts may allow one to help others in coming to the door of the sacred, but the capacity for mystical states of consciousness is not always an indication of spiritual maturity. Spiritual maturity as we define it is the choice to live out of that consciousness in our ordinary moments.

2. Chuck Reece, "Jan Kemp," *Ms.*, Jan. 1987, 46; Ezra Bowen, "Blowing the Whistle on Georgia," *Time*, 24 Feb. 1986, 65; William Nack, "This Case Was One for the Books," *Sports Illustrated*, 24 Feb. 1986, 34–42.

3. Tillie Olsen, *Silences* (New York: Delacorte Press, 1978), 6.

4. Audre Lorde, *Sister Outsider* (Freedom, Calif.: The Crossing Press, 1984).

Chapter 6: Tools for the Sacred Garden: Part I

1. Catherine Ingram, "Ken Wilber: The Pundit of Transpersonal Psychology," *Yoga Journal*, Sept./Oct. 1987, 45.

2. Toni Packer, "On Sitting Meditation," *11 Articles* (Springwater, NY: Genesee Valley Zen Center, 1986).

3. Tom Collins, "Mythic Reflections: An Interview with Joseph Campbell," *In Context* (Winter 1985): 53.

4. This is a paraphrase from Marjory Zoet Bankson, *Braided Streams: Esther and a Woman's Way of Growing* (San Diego: LuraMedia, 1985), 70.

5. Susan Schnur, "Reshaping Prayer: An Interview with Marcia Falk," *Lilith*, 21, (Fall 1988/5749), 12.

6. Teresa of Avila, *The Interior Castle*, trans. Kieran Kavanaugh and Otilio Rodrieguez (New York: Paulist Press, 1979), 42.

7. This is a version of a story Sherry learned from Zen Master Seung Sahn, founder of the Kwan Um Zen School, Cumberland, R.I. Other stories appear in Stephen Mitchell, comp. and ed., *Dropping Ashes on the Buddha* (New York: Grove Press, 1976) and in *Ten Gates* (Cumberland, R.I.: Primary Point Press, 1987).

Epigraph: Margaret L. Mitchell, Untitled. *Ms.*, Dec. 1987, 16(6), 44.

8. Keating et al., eds. *Finding Grace at the Center*, rev. ed. (Still River, Miss.: St. Bede Publications, 1979), 3.

Epigraph: Alla Bozarth-Campbell, "Transfiguration/Full Moon" as cited in Sara Maitland's *A Map of the New Country: Women and Christianity* (London: Routledge & Kegan Paul, 1983), 177.

9. John 1:14.

10. Jacob Needleman, *Lost Christianity* (San Francisco: Harper & Row, 1980), 129.

11. This term was coined by Chögyam Trungpa, Rinpoche, in John Baker and Marvin Casper, eds., *Cutting through Spiritual Materialism* (Boston: Shambhala, 1987), Introduction.

12. Rainer Maria Rilke, *Letters to a Young Poet*, trans. Stephen Mitchell (New York: Random House, 1986), 34.

13. David Steindl-Rast, *Gratefulness, the Heart of Prayer* (New York: Paulist Press, 1984), 48.

Chapter 7: Tools for the Sacred Garden: Part II

1. Huston Smith, *The Religions of Man* (New York: Harper & Row, 1958).

2. Philip Kapleau, *The Three Pillars of Zen* (New York: Harper & Row, 1966).

3. Ralph Waldo Emerson, "Self Reliance" (1841; reprint, *Leading Edge Bulletin*, 20 Dec. 1982), 2.

4. A very accessible exposition of Gurdjieff's teachings is found in Charles T. Tart, *Waking Up* (Boston: Shambhala, 1986).
5. A valuable reference is Swami Sivananda Radha, *Kundalini: Yoga for the West* (Spokane, Wash.: Timeless Books, 1978). See also Richard Maurice Bucke's classic *Cosmic Consciousness*, originally published in 1901 (New York: Dutton, 1969).
6. Dr. Stanislav Grof's research is seminal here, including his early publication *Realms of the Human Unconscious* (New York: Viking, 1975) and more recently *Beyond the Brain* (Albany, N.Y.: State University of New York Press, 1985). Dr. Grof and his wife, Christina Grof, are the founders of the Spiritual Emergence Network (SEN), which offers a referral service for therapists interested in working with those who are having kundalini or other kinds of psychospiritual experiences. SEN also sponsors workshops and offers publications. (Spiritual Emergence Network, Institute of Transpersonal Psychology, 250 Oak Grove Avenue, Menlo Park, CA 94025.)
7. For information about World Wheel write: Earthtrust, 20110 Rockport Way, Malibu, CA 90265.

Chapter 8: Intimate Relationships

Epigraph: Jean Lanier, *The Wisdom of Being Human* "The Second Coming," (Lower Lake, Calif.: Integral Publishing, 1989), 65.
1. Joanna Rogers Macy, *Despair and Personal Power in the Nuclear Age* (Philadelphia: New Society Publishers, 1983), 119, 120.
2. Thomas Berry, *The Dream of the Earth* (San Francisco: Sierra Club Books, 1988).
3. May Sarton, *A Reckoning* (New York: W. W. Norton, 1978), 14, 90–91.
4. Of 38 marriages, 5 ended in widowhood, 27 in divorce (71%); 3 of the women did not marry. Nine of the 30 women we interviewed live in formally committed relationships.
Epigraph: Bankson, *Braided Streams*, 77.
5. Germaine Greer, cited in Dale Spender, *Man Made Language* (London: Routledge & Kegan Paul, 1985), 5.

6. Spender, *Language*, 172.
7. Bankson, *Braided Streams*, 76.
8. Una Kroll, in Spender, *Language*, 102.
9. Susan Griffin, interviewed by Stephan Bodian in "Woman, Nature and Eros," *Yoga Journal* (Jan.–Feb. 1988): 86.
10. Lauter, *Women as Mythmakers*, 203–223.
11. Craighead, in Giles, *Feminist Mystic*, 79.

Epigraph: Janet O. Dallett, *When the Spirits Come Back* (Toronto: Inner City Books, 1988), 27.

Chapter 9: The Making of Relatives

1. Mary Morrison's *Approaching the Gospels Together* is available from the Pendle Hill Bookstore, Pendle Hill, Wallingford, PA 19086. The quotes from Mary's journal are taken from *The Journal and the Journey* (Pendle Hill Pamphlet No. 242, 1982), 16–20.
2. Vimala Thakar, "Interview," *Inquiring Mind* 2 (Winter 1985): p. 1.
3. Spender, *Language*, 53.
4. Adrienne Rich, *On Lies, Secrets, and Silence: Selected Prose 1966–1978* (New York: Norton, 1979), 11.
5. Naomi Newman and Martha Boesing, *Snake Talk: Urgent Messages from the Mother* (produced by A Traveling Jewish Theatre, San Francisco, 1988).

Epigraph: Jean Lanier, *The Wisdom of Being Human*, 99.
6. See Dorothy Maclean, *To Hear the Angels Sing: An Odyssey of Co-creation with the Devic Kingdom* (Elgin, Ill.: Lorian Press, 1980), for a full account of these experiences.
7. Helen Luke, *Woman Earth and Spirit* (New York: Crossroad, 1984), 34.
8. Some of our quotes have been taken from the first chapter of Eleanor Humes Haney's work in progress, *Vision and Power: Shaping a Feminist Theology*. A new version of this is now available as *Vision and Struggle: Meditations on Feminist Spirituality and Politics* (Portland, Maine: Astarte Shell Press, 1989).

9. For more information on the Council of All Beings, see John Seed et al., *Thinking Like a Mountain* (Philadelphia: New Society Publishers, 1988).
10. From a talk by Sister Miriam MacGillis at Community Congregationalist Church, Tiburon, Calif., Mar. 24, 1987.
11. Schnur, "Interview with Marcia Falk," 12.
12. Carter Heyward, quoted in "Return of the Goddess," *Ideas* (produced by Merlin Stone) (Canadian Broadcasting Corporation, January 8, 15, 22, 29, 1986): CBC transcript, p. 30.

Chapter 10: Being the Sacred Garden

Epigraph: Burnett, *The Secret Garden*, 209.
1. Simone Weil, *Gravity and Grace* (London: Routledge & Kegan Paul, 1987), p. 156.
2. Chief Sealth, or Seattle as he is now known, delivered a speech in his native Duwamish to his tribal assembly in the Pacific Northwest in 1854. Notes on the speech were made by an Englishman, and the full text from those notes is given in Seed et al., *Mountain*, 68–73.
3. Craighead, *Songs*, 29.
4. "Stride of soul" comes from Christopher Fry, *A Sleep of Prisoners* (Oxford: Oxford University Press, 1951), p. 47. The full quote is "Thank God our time is now when wrong/Comes up to face us everywhere,/Never to leave us till we take/The longest stride of soul men ever took."

Bibliography

A *Course in Miracles*. Tiburon, CA: Foundation for Inner Peace, 1975.

Allione, Tsultrim. *Women of Wisdom*. London: Routledge & Kegan Paul Ltd., 1984.

Almaas, A. H. *Diamond Heart: Book One*. Berkeley: Diamond Books, 1987.

Bankson, Marjory Zoet. *Braided Streams: Esther and a Woman's Way of Growing*. San Diego: Luramedia, 1985.

Bellah, Robert N.; Madsen, Richard; Sullivan, William M.; Swidler, Ann; and Tipton, Steven M. *Habits of the Heart: Individualism and Commitment in American Life*. Berkeley: University of California Press, 1985.

Berry, Thomas. *The Dream of the Earth*. San Francisco: Sierra Club Books, 1988.

Bolen, Jean Shinoda. *Goddesses in Everywoman: A New Psychology of Women*. San Francisco: Harper & Row, 1984.

————. *Gods in Everyman: A New Psychology of Men's Lives and Loves.* San Francisco: Harper & Row, 1989.

Brantenberg, Gerd. *Egalia's Daughters: A Satire of the Sexes.* Translated by Louis Mackayin in cooperation with Gerd Brantenberg. Seattle: The Seal Press, 1985.

Bucke, Richard Maurice. *Cosmic Consciousness.* New York: Dutton, 1969.

Burnett, Frances Hodgson. *The Secret Garden.* London: Michael Joseph Ltd., 1986.

Burtt, E. A., ed. *The Teachings of the Compassionate Buddha.* New York: Signet, 1955.

Cameron, Anne. *Daughters of Copper Woman.* Vancouver: Press Gang Publishers, 1981.

Campbell, Joseph. *The Hero With a Thousand Faces.* 2nd ed. Bollingen Series 17. Princeton, N.J.: Princeton University Press, 1968.

Chicago, Judy. *The Birth Project.* Garden City, N.Y.: Doubleday and Company, 1985.

Chodorow, Nancy. *The Reproduction of Mothering: Psychoanalysis and the Sociology of Gender.* Berkeley: University of California Press, 1978.

Christ, Carol. *Diving Deep and Surfacing: Women Writers on Spiritual Quest.* Boston: Beacon Press, 1980.

Collins, Tom. "Mythic Reflections: An Interview with Joseph Campbell." *In Context.* Winter 1985.

Craighead, Meinrad. *The Mother's Songs: Images of God the Mother.* Mahwah, N.J.: Paulist Press, 1986.

Dallett, Janet O. *When the Spirits Come Back.* Toronto: Inner City Books, 1988.

de Castillejo, Irene Claremont. *Knowing Woman: A Feminine Psychology.* New York: Harper Colophon Books, 1974.

Demetrakopoulos, Stephanie. *Listening to Our Bodies: The Rebirth of Feminine Wisdom.* Boston: Beacon Press, 1983.

Eisler, Riane. *The Chalice and the Blade: Our History, Our Future.* San Francisco: Harper & Row, 1987.

Fiorenza, Elisabeth Schüssler. *Bread Not Stone: The Challenge of Feminist Biblical Interpretation.* Boston: Beacon Press, 1984.

Fowler, James W., and Vergote, Antoine, eds. *Toward Moral and Religious Maturity*. Morristown, N.J.: Silver Burdett, 1980.

Fowler, James W. *Stages of Faith: The Psychology of Human Development and the Quest for Meaning*. San Francisco: Harper & Row, 1981.

Friedman, Lenore. *Meetings With Remarkable Women: Buddhist Teachers in America*. Boston: Shambhala, 1987.

Galland, China. *Longing for Darkness: Tara and the Black Madonna*. New York: Viking, 1990.

Giles, Mary E. *The Feminist Mystic and Other Essays on Women and Spirituality*. New York: Crossroads Press, 1982.

Gilligan, Carol. *In a Different Voice: Psychological Theory and Women's Development*. Cambridge, Mass.: Harvard University Press, 1982.

Gray, Elizabeth Dodson. *Sacred Dimensions of Women's Experiences*. Wellesley, Mass.: Roundtable Press, 1988.

Griffin, Susan. *Woman and Nature: The Roaring Inside Her*. New York: Harper & Row, 1978.

Griffin, Susan. Interviewed by Stephan Bodian in "Women, Nature and Eros." *Yoga Journal*. Jan.–Feb., 1988.

Grof, Stanislav, *Realms of the Human Unconscious*. New York: Viking, 1975.

Grof, Stanislav, and Grof, Christina. *The Stormy Search for the Self*. Los Angeles: Jeremy P. Tarcher, Inc., 1990.

Haney, Eleanor Humes. *Vision and Struggle: Meditations on Feminist Spirituality and Politics*. Portland, Maine: Astarte Shell Press, 1989.

Hillesum, Etty. *An Interrupted Life: The Diaries of Etty Hillesum 1941–1943*. Translated by Arno Pomerans. New York: Pantheon Books, 1983.

Ingram, Catherine. "Ken Wilber: The Pundit of Transpersonal Psychology." *Yoga Journal*. Sept.–Oct., 1987.

Johnson, Sonia. *Going Out of Our Minds: The Metaphysics of Liberation*. Freedom, Calif.: The Crossing Press, 1987.

Kapleau, Philip. *The Three Pillars of Zen*. New York: Harper & Row, 1966.

Keating, Thomas et al., eds. *Finding Grace at the Center.* Revised edition. Still River, Miss.: St. Bede, 1978.

Kornfield, Jack. "Meditation and Psychotherapy: A Plea for Integration." *Inquiring Mind.* Vol. 5: No. 1, 1988, pp. 10–11.

Kübler-Ross, Elisabeth. *AIDS: The Ultimate Challenge.* New York: Macmillan, 1987.

Kushner, Lawrence. *Honey from the Rock.* New York: Harper & Row, 1977.

Lanier, Jean. *The Wisdom of Being Human.* Lower Lake, Calif.: Integral Publishing, 1989.

Lauck, Marcia S., and Koff-Chapin, Deborah. *At the Pool of Wonder: Dreams and Visions of an Awakening Humanity.* Santa Fe: Bear and Co., 1989.

Lauder, Estella. *Women as Mythmakers: Poetry and Visual Art by Twentieth-Century Women.* Bloomington: Indiana University Press, 1984.

Lenz, E., and Meyerhoff, B. *The Feminization of America: How Women's Lives are Changing our Public and Private Lives.* Los Angeles: Jeremy P. Tarcher, Inc., 1985.

Macy, Joanna Rogers. *Despair and Empowerment in the Nuclear Age.* Philadelphia: New Society Publishers, 1983.

Maitland, Sara. *A Map of the New Country: Women and Christianity.* London: Routledge and Kegan Paul Ltd., 1983.

May, Gerald. *Will and Spirit: A Contemplative Psychology.* San Francisco: Harper & Row, 1982.

Miller, Alice. *For Your Own Good: Hidden Cruelty in Child-Rearing and the Roots of Violence.* Translated by Hildegarde and Hunter Hannum. New York: Farrar, Straus & Giroux, 1983.

Miller, Jean Baker. *Toward a New Psychology of Women.* Boston: Beacon Press, 1976.

Morton, Nelle. *The Journey is Home.* Boston: Beacon Press, 1985.

Needleman, Jacob. *Lost Christianity: A Journey of Rediscovery.* San Francisco: Harper & Row, 1980.

Olsen, Tillie. *Silences.* New York: Delacorte Press, 1978.

Packer, Toni. *The Work of this Moment.* Springwater, N.Y.: Springwater Center, 1988.

Peck, M. Scott. *The Different Drum: Community-Making and Peace.* New York: Simon and Schuster, 1987.

Perera, Sylvia Brinton. *Descent to the Goddess: A Way of Initiation for Women.* Toronto: Inner City Books, 1981.

Popoff, Irmis B. *Gurdjieff Group Work with Wilhelm Nyland.* York Beach, Maine: Samuel Weiser, Inc., 1983.

Radha, Swami Sivananda. *Kundalini: Yoga for the West.* Spokane, Wash.: Timeless Books, 1978.

Rich, Adrienne. *On Lies, Secrets, and Silence: Selected Prose 1966– 1978.* New York: W. W. Norton, 1979.

Rilke, Rainer Maria. *Letters to a Young Poet.* Translated by Stephen Mitchell. New York: Random House Vintage Books, 1986.

Rilke, Rainer Maria. *Selected Poems.* Translation and commentary by Robert Bly. New York: Harper Colophon Books, 1981.

Ruether, Rosemary, and McLaughlin, Eleanor. *Women of Spirit: Female Leadership in the Jewish and Christian Traditions.* New York: Simon and Schuster, 1979.

Satprem. *The Mind of the Cells.* Translated by Francine Mahak and Luc Venet. New York: Institution for Evolutionary Research, 1981.

Schnur, Susan. "Reshaping Prayer: An Interview with Marcia Falk." *Lilith,* No. 21, Fall 1988/5749.

Sinetar, Marsha. *Ordinary People As Monks and Mystics: Lifestyles for Self-Discovery.* New York: Paulist Press, 1986.

Smith, Huston. *The Religions of Man.* New York: Harper & Row, 1958.

Sorokin, Pitirim A. *The Ways and Power of Love.* Boston: Beacon Press, 1954.

Spender, Dale. *Man Made Language.* 2nd edition. London: Routledge and Kegan Paul Ltd., 1985.

Spretnak, Charlene, ed. *The Politics of Women's Spirituality: Essays on the Rise of Spiritual Power within the Feminist Movement.* Garden City, N.Y.: Anchor Press/Doubleday, 1982.

Stanton, Elizabeth Cady. *The Woman's Bible.* New York: Arno Press, 1972. (Reprint edition of 1895 first printing by European Publishing Co., New York.)

Steindl-Rast, David. *Gratefulness, The Heart of Prayer: An Approach to Life in Fullness.* New York: Paulist Press, 1984.

Storr, Anthony. *Solitude: A Return to the Self.* New York: Ballantine Books, 1988.

Tanakh: The Holy Scriptures According to the Traditional Hebrew Text. Philadelphia: The Jewish Publication Society, 1985.

Tart, Charles T. *Waking Up: Overcoming the Obstacles to Human Potential.* Boston: Shambhala, 1987.

Teresa of Avila. *The Interior Castle.* Translated by Kieran Kavanaugh, O.C.D. and Otilio Rodriguez, O.C.D. New York: Paulist Press, 1979.

Thakar, Vimala. *Spirituality and Social Action: A Holistic Approach.* Berkeley, Calif.: Vimala Programs California, 1984.

The Holy Bible, Revised Standard Version (RSV). New York: Nelson, 1953.

The New English Bible. Oxford: Oxford University Press, 1970.

Trungpa, Chögyam. *Cutting Through Spiritual Materialism.* Edited by John Baker and Marvin Casper. Boston: Shambhala, 1987.

Underhill, Evelyn. *Practical Mysticism: A Little Book for Normal People.* New York: E. P. Dutton and Co., 1915.

Walsh, Roger N., and Vaughan, Frances, eds. *Beyond Ego: Transpersonal Dimensions in Psychology.* Los Angeles: Jeremy P. Tarcher, Inc., 1980.

Weil, Simone. *Gravity and Grace.* London: Ark Paperbacks, Routledge and Kegan Paul Ltd., 1987.

Wilber, Ken. *Up From Eden: A Transpersonal View of Human Evolution.* Garden City, N.Y.: Anchor Press/Doubleday, 1981.

Wolkstein, Diane, and Kramer, Samuel Noah. *Inanna: Queen of Heaven and Earth.* New York: Harper & Row, 1983.

Woodman, Marion. *Addiction to Perfection: The Still Unravaged Bride.* Toronto: Inner City Books, 1982.

———. *The Pregnant Virgin: A Process of Psychological Transformation.* Toronto: Inner City Books, 1985.

———. *The Ravaged Bridegroom: Masculinity in Women.* Toronto: Inner City Books, 1990.

Index